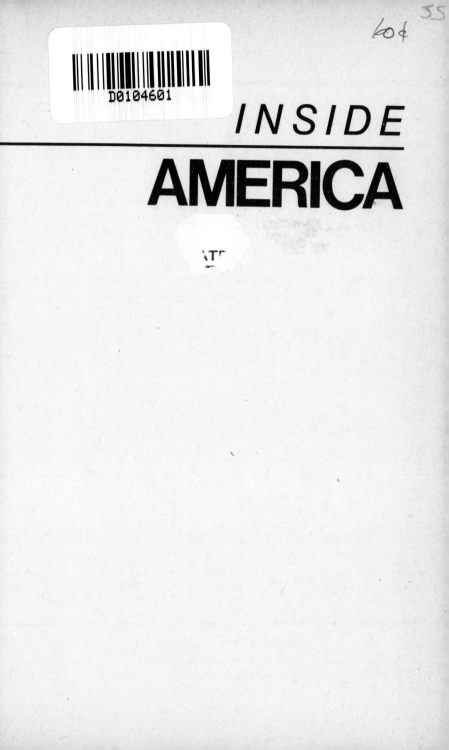

INSIDE

AMERICA

INSIDE
AMERICA

LOUIS HARRIS, 1921-

VINTAGE BOOKS
A DIVISION OF RANDOM HOUSE ■ NEW YORK

Special acknowledgment is made for use of material from the
following polls: *Fears and Fantasies of the American Consumer,* cited on
p. 7, © D'Arcy Masius Benton & Bowles, Inc. 1986; *Newsweek Poll,*
February 5–11, 1986, cited on p. 101, © 1986 by Newsweek, Inc.
All rights reserved. Reprinted by permission; *Survey of Attitudes
Toward Smoking,* cited on p. 111, statistics courtesy of the American
Lung Association—the Christmas Seal People ®; *Newsweek Poll,*
March 6–7, 1985, cited on p. 160, © 1985 by Newsweek, Inc. All
rights reserved. Reprinted by permission; *Newsweek Poll,* November
1986, cited on p. 415, © 1986 by Newsweek, Inc. All rights
reserved. Reprinted by permission; *Newsweek Poll,* July 1986, cited on
p. 417, © 1986 by Newsweek, Inc. All rights reserved. Reprinted by
permission.

Library of Congress Cataloging in Publication Data
Harris, Louis, 1921–
    Inside America.
    1. Public opinion—United States. 2. Public
opinion polls—United States. I. Title.
HN90.P8H37 1987   303.3'8'0973   86-46188
ISBN 0-394-75070-5

Text design by Mary A. Wirth
Manufactured in the United States of America
10 9 8 7 6 5 4 3

63,513

To my colleagues at Louis Harris
and Associates, past and present:
we innovated long enough for traditions
to be made, and then we realized
that we must innovate all over again

CONTENTS

COMMUNITY

THE NATION AND THE WORLD

FOREWORD

The writing of this book has been an enlightening educational experience. I have long felt that my self-appointed assignment as a public opinion analyst was to "cover" the American people—what they feel, what they are disturbed and stressed over, what they hope and aspire to, how they behave in their personal and community lives, and what their prejudices and preferences are. But when Random House president Bob Bernstein challenged me to write this book, I did not really know how much data of real worth about the public and key groups within it existed and were available to provide a sound basis for such a volume. I was happy to discover that there were many superb surveys that I did not know had ever been done. I am richer for them, and I hope the reader will be as well.

With the diligent fourteen-hour-a-day help of Donna Cartelli, my intrepid assistant in this endeavor, the vast majority of published works in the field of public opinion were obtained, reviewed, sifted, and, finally, either rejected or accepted for use. This search was exciting and fully rewarding when such rich quality data as Gallup's report on eating habits, Bruskin's on life-styles, Michigan Survey Research's annual survey of drug usage among high school students, or Roper's admirable update of the Virginia Slims women's status poll were found. I must add to these the splendid work of some of my own colleagues, such as those conducted by Humphrey Taylor and Michael Kagay in the health field.

Along with these exciting windfalls, which reassured me of the ongoing quality of survey research, however, there was also a sense of letdown and even dismay at some of the work in the field that is passed off as adequate polling. Often, research is based on samples far too small to be reliable. Often the questionnaire design is superficial, lacking in structure and depth; sometimes it seems like a quick-and-dirty effort to get a headline.

On a rough approximation, perhaps 10% of all the surveys reviewed were finally used, while about 40% more were adequate but either redundant or not especially significant. But as much as 50% of all the polling material available just did not do credit to the profession. Those polls will not be found in this volume. As one who has felt close to journalists, and indeed, as a practicing reporter and columnist for nearly a quarter of a century, I am saddened by the fact that most media simply do not discriminate between sound and unsound polling results. Having said this, I hasten to add that if a survey research organization's work is not reported here, it should not be concluded that it had little or no merit. Much work of real worth was eliminated only because of the constraints of space.

It must be emphasized that *Inside America* does not systematically cover *every* important aspect of life in the country, nor every key strand of public opinion. It does cover many of the major facets of family life, personal and social problems, reactions to emerging crises and trends, the latest in political developments, and perspectives on war and peace, the economy, and values. My intention has been to report in the aggregate and in detail just what the life in America is during the mid-1980s and where it appears to be heading. In many ways this is a study of the collective character, foibles, and aspirations of a people. It is not reported with the intent

of proving any particular preconceived assumptions or conclusions, nor does it draw any sweeping judgments about how
good or how flawed the American people might be at this
juncture of their history. Instead, I trust it tells it the way it
is—no more and no less. When we are greedy and predatory
as a people, as we are in our material quests these days, then
that is reported fully. Or when we are dedicated to the greater
good in overwhelming numbers, as is the case in environmental matters, so too is that reported in depth.

What finally was included were those subject matters that
I saw as indispensable and critical to report, on the basis of
what sound research was available. The selection was undoubtedly influenced by my own judgment of what was and
was not important.

Although this is my sixth book dealing with public opinion,
I felt from the outset that it had to be different from the
others. The mandate of Bob Bernstein was that it would be
a paperback written in a popular style, albeit sound and
documented in all aspects, that would be an authoritative but
thoroughly readable account of who the American people are,
what they think, how they behave, what they worry about and
aspire to.

Thus, in the end, sixty-five chapters were written, each
covering a different subject, and grouped in three separate
sections. The first part deals with the personal lives of people,
the second with many of the outside world problems that
impact on people's lives and thinking these days, and the
third with the mainstream political and economic life of the
country. Thanks to a major suggestion by Becky Saletan, my
editor, an essay has been placed at the end of each section
that attempts to put the substance of the section into a broader
perspective and framework. At the end of each chapter there
is an "Observation" section—mercifully short, I hope—
which puts forth my own comments about the foregoing text.
This is an old Harris research procedure, since I have long

been wedded to the controversial notion that research should not be reported unless those who generate it understand its meaning and then fulfill the obligation to tell the reader just what it really means. There are many in my field who part company with me on this view, arguing that researchers should just accumulate facts and not ponder their meaning.

The reader will wonder why so much of the research of the Harris firm has been included in this book, since the intent has been to draw upon *all* of the available published material in the field. While I am not so arrogant as to maintain that the bulk of worthwhile work in the field emanates from Louis Harris and Associates, I am proud to say that the caliber of work turned out by our organization is uniformly among the best in the field. Undoubtedly, the immediate accessibility of our own research influenced my judgment to include more rather than less of it here. I hope the reader will forgive me for that indulgence.

I must acknowledge help from many quarters. In addition to the yeoman work done by Donna Cartelli, Barbara Winokur, head of information services at the Harris firm, was at all times a remarkable and solid resource. Humphrey Taylor, president of the firm, and David Krane, head of operations, were both encouraging and all too willing to tell me whatever was wrong with what I was writing. Author Joseph Lash, my old friend and mentor, went through the chapters and offered sage advice and wisdom, as did Edward Block, another dear friend and longtime client, who was recently retired as a top executive of AT&T. The process of writing this book has helped make me a personal computer freak—thanks to Cynthia Johnson; I now possess three personal computers and take one with me wherever I roam for any period of time.

My constant companion in this venture was my beloved wife, Florence Yard. She read the entire text, gave balanced criticism to every chapter and essay, and pointed out inconsistencies, long-winded passages, and even subjects that lacked focus. Florence is basically a reader of fiction, one who is not inclined to pore over my technical writings, and served in many ways as the acid test for this book. If she thought the subject matter was appealing, I was convinced it would also interest sizable numbers of others. She has been indispensable to this project because, aside from allowing me to wreck our social life for the better part of a year, she not only put up with all the ruminations I am prone to express out loud about a work in progress but read every word I wrote for this book.

—Louis Harris

New York
January 1987

PART ONE

HOME AND FAMILY

MIRROR, MIRROR ON THE WALL: WORRY OVER PERSONAL APPEARANCE

■ HOW OFTEN DO PEOPLE THINK ABOUT HOW THEY LOOK?

Two out of every three adults in the United States say they fidget, fuss, take furtive glances in windows and mirrors, and study other people's reactions to the way they look. It is not overstating it to report that a solid majority of the American people are close to being obsessed with their physical appearance.

The biggest difference, of course, is between men and women. While 54% of men say they often think of their physical appearance, a much higher 75% of women say the same. And 40% say they spend a lot of time on how they look. Many years ago, sociologist David Riesman invented the phrase "other-directed," meaning that most Americans were more concerned with what others thought of them than what they thought of themselves. The segments of the population who spend the most time tinkering with themselves to look better are young people, those in the highest income brackets, big city residents, residents of the Northeast, the best-educated, blacks, singles, and, of course, women.

But perhaps the depth of Americans' obsession with and insecurity over their looks emerged when people were asked if they would like to change something about their personal appearance. A nearly unanimous 96% said they would, 94% of all men and 99% of all women.

PERSONAL APPEARANCE: WHAT PEOPLE WOULD CHANGE

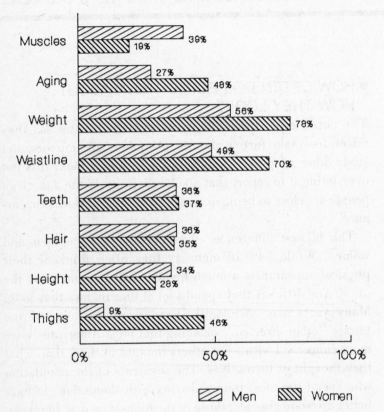

	Men	Women
Muscles	39%	19%
Aging	27%	48%
Weight	56%	78%
Waistline	49%	70%
Teeth	36%	37%
Hair	36%	35%
Height	34%	28%
Thighs	9%	46%

Here is what men want changed about their physical appearance:

□ 56% volunteer that they would like to change their weight, a sign that a majority of men have the vanity about fitness normally associated with women.

□ 49% would like to trim their waistline.

□ 39% would like to develop their muscles, a sign of the macho residue in American life.

□ 36% want to change their teeth.

□ 36% would change their hair if they could. Baldness in particular worries men, despite the myth that bald men are more virile.

□ 34% would like to change their height, most to be taller. To be short is ignominy among American men.

□ 27% would like to find a way not to show the evidence of aging. This is an area of sly attentiveness for men; many use hair dye, for example, without telling anyone about it.

□ 21% want to change their overall physique. Men as well as women worry about their shape.

□ 20% would like to change their complexion.

□ 19% would change their nose if they could.

Women have a longer and more substantial list of changes they would like to make in their physical appearance:

□ 78% would change their weight. Fully 35% would like to lose 25 pounds or more, another 16% from 16 to 25 pounds, and 14% between 11 and 15 pounds. Obviously, American women are close to being obsessed with weight and, as a later chapter reveals, are not doing a very effective job of fulfilling their desire.

□ 70% are worried about their waistline, tied closely to their weight problem, and would like nothing more than to trim it.

□ 48% would like to make changes to cover up tell-tale signs of aging.

☐ 46% would like to change their thighs if they could find a way.

☐ 38% would like to do something about their buttocks, again a slimming problem.

☐ 37% want to change their teeth.

☐ 35% would like to change their hair (presumably something they can do).

☐ 34% would like to change their legs, a formidable task.

☐ 33% are really concerned about their wrinkles.

☐ 32% would like to change their bust.

☐ 29% would like to overhaul their entire physique.

☐ 28% wish they could change their height, often to become taller.

☐ 26% would like to have a different complexion.

☐ 21% would like to change their nose.

☐ 21% would like to change their hands.

☐ 19% would like to change their muscles, meaning to have less of them.

☐ 18% would change their feet, mostly to make them smaller.

☐ 16% would change the entire shape of their face.

☐ 9% would change their ears.

OBSERVATION

These rampant obsessions of both men and women about their looks have produced an obvious boon for the cosmetics industry, plastic surgery, diet doctors, fitness and shape advisers, fat farms, and a host of other enterprises.

To some extent, these attitudes suggest the positive and healthy attribute of really caring about one's person. But they are also just as indicative of a compulsion to be better looking and hence more acceptable at any cost. The insecurity of being rejected for not looking right physically is partly the artifact of advertising designed to capitalize on these fears and apprehensions.

There was a time a little while ago when people wanted to go back to a natural look, as was evidenced by women forgoing makeup and hair dyeing. Now the dominant desire is to *be acceptable,* whatever that might mean. To have others admire one's looks now ranks high on the lists of both men and women, especially the young, even if those looks are only superficial and wildly deceiving. The race to make one's physical appearance stunning in order to be admired is on in full force in America in the late 1980s.

America in the Eighties, conducted by R. H. Bruskin Associates, November 1985, among a national cross section of 1,900 adults.

Fears and Fantasies of the American Consumer, conducted by D'Arcy Masius Benton & Bowles Consumer Panel, January and March 1985, among a national cross section of 1,550 adults, released March 1986.

STRESS: A SINGULAR MARK OF MODERN LIFE

■ WHO FEELS STRESS

A substantial 89% of all adult Americans (158 million people) report experiencing high stress. Fully 59% say they feel "great stress" at least once or twice a week, while more than one in four (30%) report living with high stress nearly every day.

Stress is obviously part of the price paid for being affluent and successful. Close to twice as many high-income as low-income people report suffering from such tensions. By the same token, the more educated people are, the more likely they are to experience great stress. Whites feel more stressed than blacks. Professional and executive types suffer more heavily from stress than do those in other occupations.

■ SYMPTOMS OF STRESS

Stress manifests itself through a seizure of nervousness, anxiety, and tension, say 26%. Almost as many (24%) report that stress comes on in the form of headaches. However, another one in five (19%) say stress shows in their anger and irritability with others. Stress also takes its toll in fatigue, another 12% report. Finally, one in nine (11%) say that stress is accompanied by a sense of depression. Other symptoms of stress include muscle aches and tensions, stomachaches and tensions, an overall feeling of upset, an increased heartbeat, insomnia and loss of sleep, a rise in blood pressure, a feeling of frustration, crying, sweating, yelling and screaming, compulsive eating, and loss of appetite.

■ TAKING STEPS TO CONTROL STRESS

Although over six in every ten people who suffer from stress take steps to control it, a significantly high three in ten do nothing. Younger people, those with lower income and less education, and blue-collar types are likely to do less to control their stress.

The three main steps people take to relieve their suffering are to prepare themselves mentally for it (50%), to do something physically to relieve it (43%), or to alter their social behavior to avoid stressful situations (15%).

Steps people take to prepare themselves mentally for stress are to fortify their determination not to let certain things bother them, to pursue a hobby that takes their minds off stress, to read, to think about the causes of stress, to engage in meditation or prayer, and to play or listen to music.

Physical activities undertaken to relieve stress include exercise, concentrated relaxation, breathing exercises, and slowing down the pace of physical movement.

Socially, stress sufferers learn to avoid stressful social situations, to create pleasant social occasions with friends and relatives, or to seek out therapy or other forms of counseling.

■ STRESS-PRONE TYPES

The people who tend to suffer most from stress are those who pay attention to every detail in their work and in their personal lives (44%), those who are perfectionist about everything they do (42%), those who never have enough time in the day to finish the work they are supposed to do (37%), those who feel there might be something chronically wrong with their health (14%), and those who feel they have little control over their future health (38%).

OBSERVATION

Stress is a serious and painful affliction that besets the most successful and most affluent people in this postindustrial modern society. The more successful and more affluent people are, the more they suffer from stress. Close to 64 million Americans suffer regularly from a great deal of stress and do absolutely nothing about it. Another 114 million take some steps to alleviate their stress, girding themselves mentally for its onslaught, seeking refuge in meditation, or plunging into exercise and social situations which can somehow minimize the brooding and discombobulating moments when stress strikes.

It is not overstating the case to conclude that in 1986 the U.S. is a stressful society, with many people having seizures of nervousness, anxiety, headaches, stomachaches, anger, fatigue, and depression on an everyday basis. Most poignant of all, is the fact that those who get the most work done in this society are precisely those most likely to suffer the pain and anguish of stress.

Prevention in America III: Steps People Take—or Fail to Take—for Better Health, conducted by Louis Harris and Associates for *Prevention Magazine*, November 15–26, 1985, among a national cross section of 1,256 adults, released November 1986.

Prevention in America IV: Steps People Take—or Fail to Take—for Better Health, conducted by Louis Harris and Associates for *Prevention Magazine*, November 14–30, 1986, among a national cross section of 1,250 adults, released May 1987.

WEIGHT: A NATION OUT OF SHAPE

■ WAISTLINE WOES

When each person in a cross section of the adult population is asked simple questions about his or her height, weight, and body structure, it is possible to get a reasonably accurate estimate of just how many are overweight, underweight, and about right.

The news is hardly heartening to a nation that is supposedly on a big health kick:

☐ Only a relatively small 23% of all adults are within range of what health authorities view as acceptable weights.
☐ An even smaller 18% are underweight and need to beef up.
☐ But by far the most sizable group, 59% of all adults (105 million) are overweight. They are above the weight range according to the Metropolitan Life Insurance Company tables, and their health is presumably at considerable risk. Most of the overweight are residents of the Midwest (61%), those who live in small towns and rural settings (67%), those with incomes $15,000 or below (58%), blacks (64%), people 50 years of age and over (70%), men (66%), blue-collar types (62%), those who don't try hard to maintain good nutrition (64%), and those who get little or no exercise (65%).

■ HALF A TRY TO EAT PROPER FOODS

When asked about eleven key nutrition practices that are commonly agreed upon, an even 50% of the adult public say they really "try a lot" to live up to the rule book. However, the other 50% report that even though they know better, they don't follow the ground rules for a sound diet. Sound nutrition is found most often among those who live in the West, women, blacks, older people, and those who are in excellent health.

Here are the number of people who say they try hard to live within the eleven basic rules of good nutrition:

☐ 63% say they are getting enough vitamins and minerals in foods or in supplements, while 37% say they are not.

☐ 65% report making a real effort to eat vegetables in the cabbage family, such as Brussels sprouts and cauliflower, while 35% do not.

☐ 59% say they try hard to eat enough fiber from whole grains, cereals, fruits, and vegetables, while 40% do not.

☐ 57% report great efforts to get enough calcium in foods or in supplements, while 41% admit they do not. However, the difference between men and women on calcium is dramatic. While only 48% of men make an effort to eat enough calcium, a much higher 66% of women say they do. Of course, calcium deficiencies are a more serious problem among women than men. The message that women should eat more calcium obviously is striking home.

☐ 56% say they try hard to avoid eating too much fat, but 44% don't even really try.

☐ 57% report making a real effort to avoid eating too much salt or sodium, but 42% say they do not.

☐ 49% claim they try to avoid eating too much sugar and sweet food, but the other 50% have largely given up.

☐ Only 46% say they avoid eating too many high-cholesterol foods, such as eggs, dairy products, and fatty meats, but a much higher 54% do not make much of an effort to do this.

☐ 34% report trying hard to avoid beverages containing caffeine, such as coffee, tea, and certain soft drinks, but a much higher 65% do not take part in that effort.

☐ 31% say they try to eat fish twice a week, but 69% do not.
☐ 36% report trying hard to avoid foods that contain additives, such as preservatives, colorings, and artificial flavorings, but 62% do not.

■ EXERCISE: A SOMETIMES ACTIVITY

While 76% claim to get regular exercise, in fact only 33% take strenuous exercise three or more days a week. A majority of 53% of all adults are basically sedentary, performing token exercises at best. It is little wonder that 65% of this group is overweight.

OBSERVATION

The basic facts sadly do not bear out all the press notices of a nation off on a big health, nutrition, and exercise kick. If anything, the latest results indicate that exercise may be falling off, overweight going up. If 20 minutes a day could be taken away from the table and spent doing rigorous exercise, between-meals nibbling abandoned, sweets and fats avoided, the results would dramatically turn around. People are gaining knowledge, but up to now have almost totally lacked the will to do what they know very well they ought to do. In a word, in 1986 America was a nation sorely in need of weight and conditioning discipline.

Prevention in America III: Steps People Take—or Fail to Take—for Better Health, conducted by Louis Harris and Associates for *Prevention Magazine,* November 15–26, 1985, among a national cross section of 1,256 adults.

Prevention in America IV: Steps People Take—or Fail to Take—for Better Health, conducted by Louis Harris and Associates, November 14–30, 1986, among a national cross section of 1,250 adults, released May 1987.

PETS: HALF A NATION OF ANIMAL LOVERS

■ HOW MANY OWN WHAT KIND OF PETS

Just over one in every two households own a pet (57%). All told, there are approximately 100 million pets in the U.S. today. Dogs and cats dominate, with only 5% owning a bird, 2% fish, and another 2% a hamster, guinea pig, gerbil, or mouse or rat.

A sizable 37% own a dog. The 32 million households with dogs are more likely to be found in the Midwest and West than in the East or South. As one moves out from the cities to the suburbs and to open spaces, the number of dogs increases, with 43% of rural folk having a dog. But the wealthier the family, too, the more likely it is that they will own a dog. Many more whites than blacks or Hispanics own dogs. By age, baby boomers are more likely to own one. More women than men own all kinds of pets. Blue-collar people are far more likely to own dogs than are white-collar types.

A smaller 23% own a cat, and cat owners are most likely to be found in the West, in small towns and rural places, and among whites, those with no higher than a high school education, baby boomers, and professional and executive families.

One in every eight homes (12%) have both a dog and a cat, and they report that the pair get along as two dogs or two cats might. Pluralism appears to produce peaceful coexistence in the pet world.

■ CARE AND FEEDING OF DOGS AND CATS

The median interval that a dog owner takes his pet to the vet is every 5.2 months; only 13% wait over a year for such a visit, and 4% never take their dogs at all. A visit to the vet is most often taken to get shots (66%), a yearly physical (34%), or because of illness or accident (15%). Another 6% go to the vet for surgery and 4% to board their dogs while they are away from home.

Cats don't receive nearly as frequent attention from their owners. The median interval between visits to a vet by cat owners is 11.5 months; a big 21% take them less often than that, and fully 24% never take their cats to the vet at all. Those who do, do so for shots (45%), a yearly physical (22%), because of illness or accident (15%), for surgery (14%), or for boarding (3%).

While nearly all animal owners buy regular animal food for their pets, a sizable amount of indulgence takes place in the form of treats and snacks owners buy. Among dog owners, 87% say they buy special treats for their dogs, mostly biscuits (57%), chew snacks such as rawhide (29%), soft snacks such as jerkies (14%), crackers (4%), and meat-based snacks (5%).

But perhaps the best insight into what goes on in homes with dogs emerges in the fact that fully 80% report they indulge their dogs by giving them human food, especially table scraps.

For cats, a much lower 53% of owners buy special snacks and treats. And a lower 69% report giving their cats human food or table scraps as a treat. Again, cats finish a relatively poor second to dogs.

However, cats begin to come into their own more in the case of litter boxes. An even 50% of all cat owners report that their cats scrupulously use a litter box, and another 24% say they mostly use a litter box, but sometimes go outside to do their duty. The remaining 26% go outside more often than use a litter box. Litter boxes are literally apt to litter nearly any part of the house, but are mostly found in the basement (39%), the bathroom (16%), the laundry room (15%), a utility room (13%), in the garage (9%), the hallway (8%), the kitchen (6%), the bedroom (5%), a spare room (4%), out on the porch (3%), in the pantry (2%), in the backyard (1%), and in the living room (1%). Clearly, cats have the run of the house if they mind their manners.

OBSERVATION

Over half the homes in the U.S. are inhabited by a dog or a cat or, less often, by fish, birds, or rodents. By and large, dogs are given quite careful attention, with regular visits to the vet, regular feedings, and lots of indulgences, including scraps from the table. Cats seem to be second-class citizens, with roughly one in every two getting a regular checkup from the vet and about half being indulged with special treats and snacks.

But the most predictable nightly ritual in 80 million dog-owning homes and in 69 million cat-owning homes is the animal lying in wait around the supper or dinner table for scraps either to fall from the plate, to be bootlegged by some kindly child, or to be put on a special plate at the end of the meal by the master or mistress. Clearly, this is the payoff by these animal lovers, in return for which they obtain a devotion from their pets scarcely matched by that of mere human beings.

Prevention in America III: Steps People Take—or Fail to Take—for Better Health, conducted by Louis Harris and Associates for *Prevention Magazine,* November 15–26, 1985, among a national cross section of 1,256 adults.

NBC News Poll conducted by NBC News, July 1985, among a national cross section of 1,599 adults.

A Report from the 1985 Consumer Panel: Inquiry on Pets, conducted by *Better Homes and Gardens,* in February 1985.

IS LEISURE TIME ON THE WAY OUT IN AMERICA?

Since 1973 the number of hours worked by Americans has increased by 20%, while the amount of leisure time available to the average person has dropped by 32%.

This trend toward less and less leisure time has been steady and inexorable:

☐ Between 1984 and 1985, available leisure hours dropped from 18.1 to 17.7 hours a week.

☐ Between 1980 and 1984, leisure time declined from 19.2 to 18.1 hours.

☐ Between 1975 and 1980, leisure time for the average American fell from 24.3 hours to 19.2 hours a week.

☐ Between 1973 and 1975, leisure time dropped from 26.2 to 24.3 hours per week.

All in all, from 1973 through 1985, the number of leisure hours available to most Americans dropped from 26.2 hours to 17.7 hours a week, a loss of 8.5 hours every week, or one hour and 12 minutes a day.

At the same time, the rise in median hours worked per week has been steady and unbroken:

☐ Between 1984 and 1985, the number of hours worked went up from 47.3 to 48.8 hours.

☐ Between 1980 and 1985, the number of work hours increased from 46.9 to 48.8 hours a week.

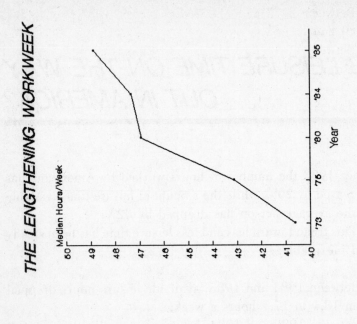

THE LENGTHENING WORKWEEK

Median Hours/Week

Year

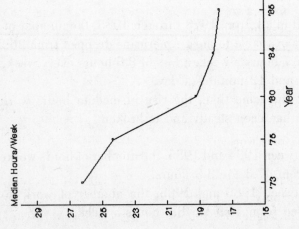

THE DECLINE OF LEISURE

Median Hours/Week

Year

□ Between 1975 and 1980, work hours rose from 43.1 to 46.9 hours per week.

□ Between 1973 and 1975, the number of hours of work went up from 40.6 to 43.1 hours per week.

Taken together, the number of hours the average American spends at work each week has increased from 40.6 in 1973 to a current 48.8, a rise of 8.2 hours a week or one hour and 10 minutes a day.

One key reason for these dramatic shifts in working hours and leisure time can be found in the increasing number of women who are working, now up to an estimated 56% of all adult women. That means that both spouses are spending more time at work and have less time left for leisure. Another is that the country has shifted radically away from blue-collar production to white-collar service jobs. Blue-collar hours of work have remained steady or declined, while white-collar hours of work have risen.

Some segments of society have been caught up more in the squeeze of longer work hours and less leisure time than others:

□ Small-business people, mainly retailers, work an average of 57.3 hours a week and have only 14.3 hours left for leisure.

□ Professional people work 52.2 hours a week and have only 16.9 hours for leisure.

□ Those with incomes of $50,000 and over work 52.4 hours a week and have 17.5 hours for leisure.

□ The baby boom generation works 51.9 hours a week but has only 15.7 hours of leisure time available.

□ Yuppies work 52.7 hours a week and have left only 17.1 hours for leisure time.

□ Women work an average of 48.9 hours a week but report having only 16.4 hours of leisure time. By contrast, men have a much higher 19.0 hours for leisure during the week, even though they work almost the same hours as women. The difference is that women do many more chores around the house that absorb their leisure time.

□ College graduates work 52.9 hours a week and have no more than 18.0 hours of leisure time.

Clearly, a phenomenon has emerged among the country's most affluent sectors: they work the longest hours and have the least time for leisure. This trend toward longer work hours and shorter leisure time runs counter to all the predictions that were made 10 to 20 years ago, when it was widely assumed that automation and technology would shorten the workweek and would give most people more and more leisure time. Precisely the opposite has happened.

OBSERVATION

These results documenting increased time at work and less time for leisure point up the fact that *time* has become a premium in the kind of society emerging in America. Obviously, there is a growing shortage of leisure time, making it a more precious commodity. More people are now considering carefully what to commit their leisure time to, including how to get uninterrupted rest. This means that decisions on time commitment are being made not in terms of the cost of leisure activities but on the basis of the most desirable way to spend scarce hours. In the future, if people want to spend time on something badly enough, they are likely to find the money to do it. Up to now, the assumption has been that if people have the money to do something and want to commit to it, they would find the time.

Of course, these results also have other broad implications. Some might question the stability, balance, and health of a nation that is so absorbed with work that there might not be adequate time left for healthy indulgences, such as creative individual or group work, or for giving growing children enough attention, taking part in community endeavors, or providing spouses with the tender loving care needed to make a marriage work. On the up side, the obvious growing commitment to work should be reflected in positive increases in the nation's productivity and the ability of the U.S. to compete economically.

Americans and the Arts, conducted by Louis Harris and Associates for Philip Morris, Inc., the National Endowment for the Arts, and the American Council for the Arts, January 1973, among a national cross section of 3,005 adults, released 1974; June 1975, among a national cross section of 1,555 adults, released 1976; July 1980, among a national cross section of 1,501 adults, released 1980; March 5 and 18, 1984, among a national cross section of 1,504 adults, released 1984.

The Harris Survey, conducted by Louis Harris and Associates, October 23–27, 1985, among a national cross section of 1,252 adults, released December 26, 1985.

EATING OUT: A REAL TREAT BUT A NUTRITIONAL NIGHTMARE

■ A VERITABLE MOVING FEAST

On any given day, more than one in three American adults (37%) will eat at least one meal away from home. This means that just under 66 million Americans are going out to eat every day, more than the entire population of France, Italy, West Germany, or the United Kingdom.

Most people go out to what is called a family-style restaurant, meaning that it is likely to serve "good old American home cooking" (42%), but almost as many go to a fast-food place (33%). About half the meals eaten out are lunch, another third dinner, and the rest breakfast. Those more likely to dine out are young people, men, college graduates, higher-income people, and employed women—basically the most mobile people, those who can most easily afford the cost, and those with the least time to spare. It is interesting that the incidence of eating out is almost precisely the same in all of the major regions of the country. Obviously, going out to eat is a truly national phenomenon.

■ WHAT PEOPLE ORDER AS AN ENTRÉE

When it comes to the main dish, a substantial 38% report ordering meat, with steak heading the list (19%), followed by roast beef (12%), pork or ham (3%), veal (3%), and lamb (1%); 22% choose fish, followed by shellfish (17%), chicken (11%), and pasta (5%). While higher majorities say they order fish and chicken more frequently than beef and other meat, when asked to recount what they ordered last, fish and chicken are well behind beef. The significance, of course, is that nearly all nutrition authorities advise people to eat more fish and chicken to avoid excessive cholesterol and calorie intake.

■ ETHNIC CHARACTER OF FOODS EATEN OUT

American cooking leads all other types by a wide margin, with a 55% majority reporting that it is their favorite. Far behind comes Italian food (14%), Chinese (12%), Mexican (8%), French (2%), and Japanese (2%). American food dominates most in the South and the Midwest, least on the two coasts. Italian food is most popular on the East Coast, while Chinese and Mexican food rise in popularity in the West.

■ HOME-STYLE FOODS PEOPLE ARE LIKELY TO ORDER

One of the common notions about eating out is that the most wholesome food to eat in a restaurant should resemble what people ate at home while growing up. After all, it is reasoned, what could be better than "Mom's home cooking"? As a consequence, 86% say they like mashed potatoes, and 49% say they are likely to order that dish when dining out. Close behind are home-fried potatoes, liked by 80% and likely to be ordered by 42%. After that comes beef stew, liked by 73% and likely to be ordered by 18%. Then comes meat loaf, liked by 70% and likely to be ordered by 21%. Following are baked beans, liked by 65% and likely to be ordered by 14%, and stuffed peppers, liked by 58% and likely to be ordered by 19%.

■ BUT NOT A NATION OF DESSERT EATERS

Only 19% report almost always eating a dessert to top off their meal in a restaurant. Another 25% say they eat dessert occasionally, but 56% rarely or never touch it. The reason they

HOME-STYLE FOODS AMERICANS LIKE TO EAT OUT

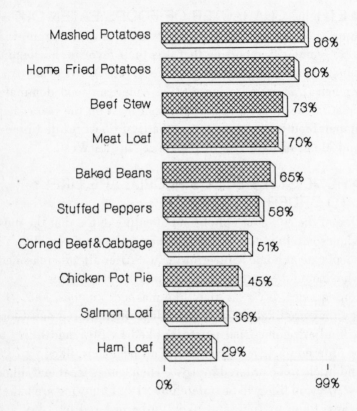

Mashed Potatoes	86%
Home Fried Potatoes	80%
Beef Stew	73%
Meat Loaf	70%
Baked Beans	65%
Stuffed Peppers	58%
Corned Beef&Cabbage	51%
Chicken Pot Pie	45%
Salmon Loaf	36%
Ham Loaf	29%

0%   99%

don't eat dessert is more often that they are just plain too full by then (51%), while another 17% are on a diet, 12% are deterred by the extra cost, 10% say they abstain for health reasons, 10% complain that no desserts on the menu appeal to them, and 9% express a downright dislike for sweets.

However, a substantial 38% say they usually have some wine with their meal. White wine leads as the choice of 57%, followed by red wine (24%) and rosé (18%). Those most likely to order wine are people with the highest income, residents of the East, women who hold down full-time jobs, and Yuppies. Obviously, it is stylish to have wine with a meal.

■ THE RISING POPULARITY OF TAKE-OUT FOOD

A substantial 11% of the adult population, roughly 20 million people, buy take-out food on any given day in America. They are more likely than not to be young people, especially Yuppies, women who work full time and haven't enough time to cook a meal at home, and those with three or more people in their household.

Although nearly nine out of every ten restaurants will now allow customers to take out food, the fast-food places dominate the take-out business, getting 58% of the orders. Therefore, it is hardly surprising that hamburgers (30%) top the list of foods most commonly taken out, followed by beverages (24%), french fries (21%), fried chicken (14%), pizza and pasta (11%), sandwiches (9%), breakfast foods (5%), salads (4%), seafood and fish (4%), Chinese food (4%), hoagies and grinders (4%), desserts other than ice cream (3%), ice cream (3%), and tacos (3%).

Clearly, take-out food largely means junk food.

■ FAST-GROWING MICROWAVE-OVEN OWNERSHIP

Just since 1977 the number of homes with microwave ovens has shot up from 4% to 13% by 1980 to 25% by 1983, 36%

in 1984, and 45% in 1985. If the current trend continues, a solid majority of the American people seem destined to own microwave ovens.

Owners buy foods especially designed for microwave use at about the same rate as people buy fast food. On any given day, 12% will be buying food for use in their microwave ovens. It is not surprising that the owners of microwave ovens tend to be young, affluent, well-educated, and busy marrieds in households where both spouses work and have children at home. Microwave ovens are touted for cutting cooking time to a minimum. In effect, they make it possible to produce fast food literally in your own home.

OBSERVATION

The picture that emerges is of a nation in which a growing minority of close to four in every ten have neither the patience nor the time to prepare meals at home. As a result, they go out to eat or take home ready-to-eat cooked food or food that can be cooked rapidly in microwave ovens.

If this all adds up to a portrait of frenetic baby boom and younger generations gulping down lots of junk food or calorie-ridden "home-style" fare, such as mashed or home-fried potatoes, baked beans, or stuffed peppers, then the hard facts bear it all out. It means that for all the protestations about eating nutritious and low-calorie foods, and having healthful, balanced meals, a sizable portion of the population is on a junk-food binge. It is little wonder that the number of people who would like to see more "all-you-can-eat" specials in restaurants they go to has risen from 30% to 37% of the entire adult population over the past 10 years. By contrast, the number who want more "dieter's specials" has declined from 18% to 16% over the same period.

Nearly every nutrition and diet authority agrees that the keys to controlling weight are food intake and proper exercise. As reported elsewhere in this book, the number of the overweight is going up and the number of those who exercise is falling off. And the sad truth about food intake is that it is simply not true that Americans are on the verge of finally turning toward nutritious and slimming food. To the contrary, indiscriminate indulgence in eating is the order of the day for the mainstream of people under 50. Without doubt, the extravagant price in health consequences inevitably will be paid in the next 10 to 20 years. In some ways it is reminiscent of the last days of the Roman Empire. But this is America in the latter part of the 1980s, where literacy is higher than at any other time in the history of the world, where access to health information has never been greater—and yet where food literacy is not rising and discipline in eating habits appears in fact to be declining.

The 1985/86 Gallup Annual Report on Eating Out: An In-depth Study of People, Foods and Trends of the Eating-Away-from-Home Market, conducted by the Gallup Organization, January–February 1986, among a national cross section of 1,528 adults.

NEW EATING PATTERNS AT HOME

■ CHANGING TASTES IN THE SUPERMARKET

By the mid-1980s the supermarkets of America had to confront the dilemma of how to catch up with the sweeping changes taking place in society or face the possibility of disappearing, as the Mom-and-Pop corner grocery stores had before them. These changes included growing numbers of two-wage families, shrinking leisure time, shopping responsibilities shared by male and female spouses, the fact that only 25% of women wanted to continue being full-time homemakers, and a growing aversion to spending long hours in the kitchen, except occasionally to prepare a deluxe gourmet meal.

By 1986 the roster of things bought at supermarkets would have made the mothers and grandmothers of the baby boom generation think they were visiting another planet:

☐ The most frequently bought products now were what are called delicatessen items, essentially meaning precooked products that can be carried out of the supermarket, taken out of the bag and eaten on the spot. This is the supermarket's answer to the fast-food chains. Fully 54% of consumers say they buy deli foods when they do their food shopping. Leading this trend toward buying precooked, ready-to-eat food are people in the East (64%), where delis were born, blacks (57%), Hispanics (58%), baby boomers (54%), and college graduates (57%).

□ In second place is a category of product that isn't new at all: generic or unbranded items. These are the private-label house brands, which are similar to advertised products but sell for less. Fully 51% of all buyers say they buy these products in supermarkets. Leading the way in these purchases are young people (56%), those with incomes in the $15,000–$25,000 bracket (62%), those who have children (57%), households with five or more people in them (68%), two-wage families with children (57%), blacks (58%), Hispanics (58%), and traditional mothers who don't hold paying jobs and have kids at home (62%).

□ In third place come gourmet or specialty foods, reported to be purchased by 45% during their supermarket expeditions. Most active in indulging themselves in this kind of food are baby boomer types (46%), people 18 to 24 years of age (56%), those who live in the East (51%), and the supermarket big spenders who average $101 or more for each shopping trip (60%).

□ In fourth place (purchased by 43%) is an older type of product—those that are sold in bulk and are also unbranded, allowing the consumer to decide how much to buy. These range from bulk vegetables and fruits to pasta and other carbohydrates, breads and bakery items. The most frequent purchasers of bulk items are lower-income people (50%), small-town residents (49%), and single heads of households who have children (50%). Obviously, bulk buying is associated with more food for the dollar, a necessity for those hard pressed to make ends meet.

□ In fifth place come items from the salad bar, a service utilized by 36% of all supermarket shoppers. Baby boomers (39%), residents of the South (43%), working women (40%), two–wage earner families with kids (43%), single heads of households with children (45%), and those who spend more than $100 a clip at the supermarket (40%) frequent the salad bar more than others. It takes time to make a salad properly.

To be able to pick up the fresh ingredients all peeled and sliced, along with a choice of salad dressing, appeals to harried spouses.

□ The sixth category, growing rapidly, is the purchase of products designed for the microwave, now a practice among 29% of all supermarket shoppers. Leading the way in this category are two–wage earner families without children (42%), high-income people (39%), baby boomers (34%), men (35%), and those who spend more than $100 on each outing to the supermarket (38%).

■ FAVORITE MAIN COURSE AND SNACK-FOOD ITEMS

When asked what dish they feel is their favorite as a main course, a rather high 41% replied that they had no such favorite at all, claiming they liked diversity more than anything else in meal planning. Beef, the traditional leader through the years, though slipping for close to twenty years, is still the top choice of 22%, poultry is the favorite of 17%, pasta of 8%, fish and other seafood of 2%, pork of 2%, and vegetables of 1%. Most of all, a main course becomes a favorite because of taste in the view of 41%, followed by ease of preparation (27%), then nutritional value (23%), economy (20%), calorie content (5%), and texture (1%).

In the case of snack foods, a substantial 46% claim to be abstainers and say they have no favorite. The favorites are nuts, grains, and popcorn, volunteered by 10%, followed by ice cream (8%), fruits and vegetables (8%), chips and pretzels (8%), baked goods (6%), and candy and other sweets (2%). Clearly, a lot of snacks are eaten by many people who simply will not name a favorite. This is a common result of the love-hate relationship that surrounds the recent indulgence in snacks in America. Far and away the biggest appeal of snacks is their taste, followed by claimed nutritional value and ease of preparation. Only a small 6% suggest that calorie content is a major reason for eating a particular snack.

■ WHAT FAMILIES CLAIM THEY ARE CHANGING IN THEIR EATING HABITS

When asked point-blank what they are doing to change their eating habits, here is the roster of diet alterations people report:

☐ 9% volunteer that they are eating less meat—a steady trend since the early 1970s.

☐ An equal 9% say they are eating more vegetables.

☐ 5% report eating more fresh fruits.

☐ 7% say they are eating less in the aggregate.

☐ But 5% also say they are now eating more.

☐ 5% say they are eating less sugar, a fact documented in declines in sugar consumption in recent years.

☐ 4% report eating less salt.

☐ 4% say they are dieting.

☐ 4% report eating less junk food.

☐ 3% say they are now eating more nutritional foods.

☐ 3% report eating less fattening food.

OBSERVATION

From their own words, the American people sound like paragons of virtue with their changes of eating habits. They vow they are trying to avoid fattening, less nutritious foods and are eating more fresh vegetables and fruits, less meat, less salt, and less junk food. (Curiously missing is their eating more fiber.) But the evidence on what is happening to their weight, as reported elsewhere in this book, belies these protestations.

The American people are rapidly picking up the language of healthy food consumption, but in fact their demand for precooked foods, gourmet dishes, and convenience even at the expense of nutrition contradicts their declaration that they have pure eating habits. To paraphrase what Mark Twain once said about smoking, it is very easy for most Americans to break the habit of eating junk foods and those laden with calories and non-nutritious content; they have done it hundreds of times—and they'll do it hundreds of times more in the future.

Trends—Consumer Attitudes and the Supermarket: 1985 Update, conducted by Louis Harris and Associates for the Food Marketing Institute, January 10–21, 1985, among a national cross section of 1,005 supermarket shoppers, released March 1985.

A SENSE OF POWERLESSNESS IS STILL PERVASIVE AMONG THE AMERICAN PEOPLE

■ ALIENATED FROM THE CENTERS OF POWER

A substantial 60% of the adult population of the United States feel alienated from the power structure. This is up from 56% who felt that way in 1985 and the 55% who shared this feeling in 1984. The all-time high occurred in 1976 and again in 1983, when 62% felt a basic sense of powerlessness.

In the period from 1966 through 1972 a majority of the American people did not feel alienated. Back in 1966 only 29% felt that way. By 1969 it had reached the 36% mark, by 1971 it was at 40%, and by 1972 it hit 44%. Then, in the wake of the Watergate disclosures, the Harris Alienation Index jumped to 55% in 1973. Over the years since, it has ranged from a low of 48% in 1976 with the election of Jimmy Carter to a high of 62% four years later at the end of his term in the White House in 1976 and again in 1983 after a long recession.

Basically, this sense of powerlessness stems from the widespread feeling that there are two tiers of justice, privilege, and affluence—one for those who are insiders in power in Washington, Wall Street, corporate America, and major institutions across the nation, and another for ordinary citizens. The real lesson people felt they learned from Watergate was that if you are powerful, you don't go to jail, but if you're just one of the people, you will be prosecuted all the way.

THE RISE OF ALIENATION

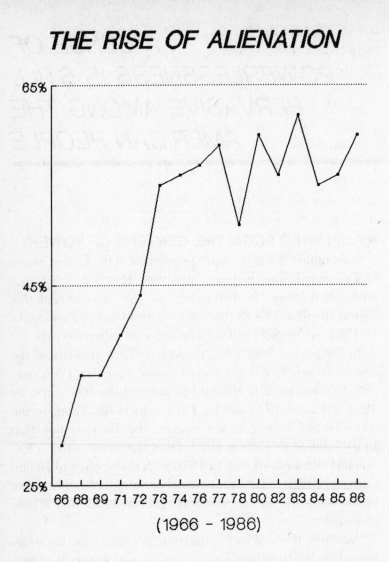

(1966 - 1986)

■ THE COMPONENT PARTS OF ALIENATION

Here is how the American people feel about each of the five specifics that make up the Harris Alienation Index:

☐ 81% of the public believe that "the rich get richer and the poor get poorer," the highest number ever recorded since this item was first asked in 1966. Back then, 45% agreed with that claim. The previous highs (79%) for this item occurred in both 1974 and 1983. The record high score now is the result of the scandals that have surfaced over insider trading on Wall Street, the prominent people in the Reagan administration who have been involved in cases where making money from peddling influence has been charged, and the scandals among defense contractors on cost overruns and use of defense funds for personal gain. There is also a widespread feeling that the Reagan administration has a callous attitude toward helping the poor and minorities. By 3 to 1, the American people are opposed to further cuts in spending from programs that help the poor and the disadvantaged.

☐ 66% of the public feel that "most people with power try to take advantage of people like myself." These latest results are double the 33% who felt the same way back in 1971, and they are also the highest ever recorded. The previous high was 65% in 1983. The heart of this item is that the establishment, whether predatory politicians or business interests, will find ways to make the rank and file pay, while the privileged do not. A prime example of this is the tax system, which is widely perceived as allowing loopholes for the rich and for corporations, but which automatically deducts withholding taxes from the paychecks of most working people.

☐ 60% of the public say their feelings are summed up in the charge that "what I think doesn't count much anymore." Back in 1966 only 37% of the American people shared the same view. The record high for this item (64%) took place in 1976 after the pardon of Richard Nixon.

☐ 55% of the nation are convinced that "the people running the country don't really care what happens to me." This is more than double the 26% who felt that way back in 1966. But it is below the high-water mark of 1976, when 64% shared that view. Most Americans identify and empathize with other people who are visited by misery and often imagine that they themselves may be next to be hit.

☐ 37% of the public say they feel they are "left out of things going on around me," more than four times the 9% who felt this way 20 years ago. This is the most extreme item in the Index, since a person feeling this way is saying he or she feels totally cut off from the mainstream. The peak for this sentiment was reached in both 1980 and 1983, when 48% felt this way.

■ LEVELS OF ALIENATION AMONG KEY GROUPS

Although the national average of those who feel alienated is 60%, it ranges from a low of 48% for those in the $50,000 and over income bracket to a high of 67% among skilled blue-collar laborers. Significantly, a higher percentage of skilled workers feel alienated than the unskilled, 63% of whom feel that way. The skilled workers feel particularly depressed, as it dawns on them that the manufacturing industries they work in are largely being exported abroad. There is a deepening sense that they are being betrayed by those in charge of the economic and political establishment.

Here are other groups whose sense of alienation from the power centers runs particularly high:

☐ 71% of blacks feel alienated. Throughout the years, this group has felt more powerless than any other. The highest their alienation reached was 77% in 1983 and 1984. Back in 1966, just after President Johnson led the drive to pass basic civil rights legislation in Congress, a much lower 33% of blacks felt this sense of powerlessness. But through the years their alienation grew, until it reached 69% in 1973, dipped to 63% during the Carter years, and then rose sharply when Ronald Reagan came to office. In contrast, a much lower 59% of all whites feel alienated, although the fact that a majority of them feel powerless is indicative of how deep this feeling pervades all groups in the country.

□ 64% of those aged 65 and over feel alienated, the highest ever among the elderly. Back in 1966 only 32% felt powerless. One of the ironies of the 65 and over group is that they worry about the possible erosion of Social Security and Medicare, on the one hand, but also feel a pinch from the decline in interest rates, on the other. Many of them had counted on high interest rates on certificates of deposit and other fixed-income instruments, and now they feel they are in trouble as interest rates have declined and the yields many live on have gone down with them.

□ Other groups who feel more alienated than the national average are women (62%), those earning $7,500 or less (68%), and union members (65%).

OBSERVATION

After more than three years of good times the rise of alienation back to levels realized during the recession in the early 1980s indicates that this phenomenon is deep-seated in modern American society. Undoubtedly part of the reason is the complex structure that puts so many layers between the establishment leadership and the broad mass of the public. As an isolated individual, it is not hard to feel a sense of remoteness from those who are running the leading institutions.

But the persistence of this feeling of powerlessness by the majority, now into its second decade, is profoundly disturbing for the country. President Reagan is as effective a communicator as has sat in the White House since Franklin D. Roosevelt. Yet he has made virtually no dent in the high level of alienation. This would indicate that it will take something more than inspirational communication to bring back to the American people a sense of belonging.

What appears to be needed is both a national capability to allow the people some redress to their government and to the major institutions and some reassurance that those at the helm of major institutions really care about the lot of ordinary people. The price that might be paid if the alienated ever became openly hostile could be enormous, with overtones that would be traumatic. The trouble is that no one really knows what the breaking point might be for these literally millions of people. But when over 100 million adults say they feel alienated from the establishment leadership, a national condition exists that cannot continue to be ignored.

The Harris Survey, conducted by Louis Harris and Associates, April 1966, released August 15, 1966; August 5–11, 1986, among a national cross section of 1,248 adults, released September 8, 1986.

A SOMETIMES THING
CALLED HAPPINESS

■ HOW MANY SAY LIFE IS REALLY SATISFYING?

At first glance, the fact that 63% of the American people say they are "very satisfied" with their life might be taken to mean that America in the late 1980s is one happy land, as U.S. boosters, many politicians, advertising people, chambers of commerce, and others would have you believe. On second thought, though, the fact that 35% report that they are something less than really satisfied with their lives means that fully 62 million adults feel that life is not entirely fulfilling.

■ WHO'S HAPPY AND WHO'S NOT

Satisfaction with life varies widely with a host of factors:

□ By age, the older a person gets, the more satisfied he or she is with life. Only 53% of young people 18 to 24 express satisfaction. This rises to 59% among those 25 to 34 years of age, 62% among those 35 to 39, to 73% among those 50 to 64, and levels out at 72% among those 65 and older. Clearly, the older people get, the more likely they are to have come to terms with themselves and their lives. Put another way, with age, a number of fulfillments take place along with a lowering of expectations. In turn, this leads to greater adjustment and satisfaction with one's lot.

□ By sex, 66% of all men say they are satisfied with their lives, compared with a lower 61% of all women. A lower 57%

of employed mothers express satisfaction with their lives. The pressures of coping with work, a home and raising children at the same time are not wholly conducive to a sense of high personal satisfaction, even though American society obviously is committed to that goal.

□ By income, there is little doubt that the more money you make, the more likely you are to feel satisfied with your lot. Only 47% of those earning $7,500 or under express satisfaction with their lives, compared with 66% in the $25,000–$35,000 income bracket, and a big 73% among those earning $50,000 and over. The saying that money can't buy happiness may be at best only a half-truth.

□ Whites (64%) are more pleased with their lives than blacks, only 58% of whom express satisfaction.

When people are asked to choose what they feel is the greatest single source of happiness—"great wealth," "good health," or "personal satisfaction from accomplishment," good health wins with 46%, followed closely by (44%) satisfaction from personal achievement. Great wealth trails far in the rear at 6%, though, as just seen, not having enough money can quickly unravel a sense of satisfaction with one's condition. Those who put a high premium on good health are the elderly, single people, homeowners, and women. Getting happiness more from their accomplishments are young people, particularly Yuppies, the college-educated, and people with children.

For all of the sustained and continuing good times in America in recent years and the much-reported upbeat feelings from the revival of patriotism, there is solid evidence that, compared with the 1970s, satisfaction with key aspects of personal life is declining:

□ Those pleased with their friendships has declined over the same period from 70% to 65%.

□ The number satisfied with their health and physical condition has dropped from 61% to 55%.

□ Those happy about their nonwork, leisure-time activities have dropped from 56% to 52%.

□ Finally, the number pleased with the city or the place where they live has declined from 48% to 43%.

OBSERVATION

It is abundantly clear that what starts out as an upbeat report about happiness in the U.S. during the latter part of the 1980s turns out *not* to be entirely the case upon closer inspection. Indeed, when asked bluntly if their happiness has been going up over the past 5 years, 55% say it has, while fully 44% say it has not. Those with higher incomes, the better-educated, whites, those with jobs, people with kids and bigger families all report being more happy. Older people, working women, the less well educated, single people, those without children, and lower-income people all say they are less happy now.

Indeed, as in so many other ways, the privileged tend to get more satisfaction out of life than those who are not privileged. A modicum of affluence appears to be a necessary precondition for a reasonably happy life in the U.S. in the late 1980s.

But as the decade of the 1980s has unfolded, affluence has grown apace during the long and sustained good times. Why, then, should all the signs point to a decline in personal satisfaction across the land?

The answer is found dramatically in the fact that satisfaction with one's life varies more sharply with how much stress people live under than any other single factor. Among those who experience low stress, 74% report being really satisfied with their lives. Among those with moderate stress as a regular diet, 55% are pleased with their lot. Among those with high stress, a lowly 32% express satisfaction with life.

The great irony, of course, is that, as reported elsewhere in this book, the most affluent are the most stress-ridden in America in the late 1980s. It is a fact that higher-income people are more satisfied with life than lower-income types. But many of the privileged are robbed of real satisfaction with life because they are also plagued by excessive stress, a price many pay to achieve affluence.

Obviously, the happiest people in America, then, should be people of means who live under little stress. Unfortunately, such a breed appears to be diminishing from the land—and at a fairly rapid rate.

The Nuprin Pain Report, conducted by Louis Harris and Associates for Bristol-Myers Company, July 19–30, 1985, among a national cross section of 1,254 adults, released September 1985.

America in the Eighties, conducted by R.H. Bruskin Associates, November 1985, among a national cross section of 1,900 adults.

General Social Surveys 1972–1986, conducted by National Opinion Research Center, February–April 1972–82 and 1985–86, among national cross sections of 12,013 and 3,004 adults, released July 1986.

SOCIALIZING: IF YOU ARE SHY YOU MAY BE MORE TYPICAL THAN YOU THINK

■ PATTERNS OF VISITING FRIENDS, NEIGHBORS, AND RELATIVES

The U.S. seems to be, at first glance, a sociable country. Fully 50% say they visit a friend, a neighbor, or a relative more than twice a week, which seems like a lot of socializing. Another 17% visit people close to them twice a week. An equal 17% visit once a week, and the remaining 16% hardly socialize at all. So one might conclude that two thirds of the people lead relatively busy social lives.

Upon closer inspection, however, wide disparities in the extent of social visiting exist among key segments of American life. For example, far more socializing takes place among the very young and the very old than among age groups in between. Fully 72% of young people under 25 visit friends three or more times a week, as do 59% of those 65 and over, 63% of all retirees, 56% of those employed part time, and 55% of homemakers who hold no paying jobs. By contrast, no more than 39% of all professional people, 43% of all college graduates, 37% of people 35 to 49 years old, and 42% of those employed full time visit friends three or more times a week.

Bluntly stated, there may be less than meets the eye on the degree to which Americans are the visiting kind. There is a lot of socializing over the back fence, so to speak, among homemakers, retired people, and those with time on their hands. But busy people must make sacrifices. Work commands much of their time. As the length of the workweek continues to go up, it would appear that social visits tend to decline. Logically, the people who work the least socialize the most.

■ INTROSPECTION ABOUT THE SOCIALIZING PROCESS

As it turns out, a goodly majority of the American people are just not that keen on entertaining others or being entertained. By 61% to 38% report that they like to entertain "not at all" or "only a little." Less inclined to entertain are men, people 50 to 64 years of age, lower-income people (who just can't afford it), and those with young children. Young people, women who are homemakers, single people, big city dwellers, and residents of the two coasts tend to like entertaining more.

In-depth surveying reveals that a clear majority of people are shy and even uncomfortable in many social situations:

□ By a substantial 69% to 31%, a better than 2 to 1 majority say they "do not like to take the lead in talking" in social situations.
□ By an almost identical 68% to 31%, a majority say they "do not like to have others notice and comment on my appearance."
□ By an even larger 83% to 16%, an overwhelming majority report that they just "do not like to be the center of attention."

While these results point up an innate shyness and anything but an extroverted nature in most Americans, they should not be taken to mean that people in this country are averse to having a good time or want to deny themselves real fun: by a convincing 69% to 31%, a solid majority acknowledge that they "believe in having as much fun out of life as possible."

MOST PEOPLE ARE SHY

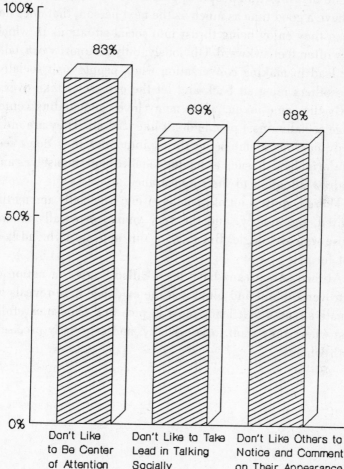

OBSERVATION

While the American people appear to be saying that they like to have a good time as much as the next person, that does not mean they enjoy being thrust into social situations in which they often feel awkward. Obviously, only a minority *can* take the lead in making conversation when people visit socially. The others must sit back and let the extroverts take over.

By the same token, while many love commanding center stage socially, most people don't like it at all. They are obviously nervous about being thrust into roles they don't feel comfortable with, such as having to talk about themselves and to draw attention to their appearance.

There is quite a lot of casual visiting, especially among the retired, the elderly, and the very young, especially among those who are single. But most of this appears to be ad hoc, not formal.

Abroad, Americans have been called "ugly," a nation of extroverts, blunt and bluff. Yet the evidence here reveals an innate shyness that leads most to pick and choose carefully just where they want to be socially, and especially precisely with whom.

The Nuprin Pain Report, conducted by Louis Harris and Associates for Bristol-Myers Company, July 19–30, 1985, among a national cross section of 1,254 adults, released September 1985.

America in the Eighties, conducted by R.H. Bruskin Associates, November 1985, among a national cross section of 1,900 adults.

THE VALUES PARENTS WOULD IMPOSE ON CHILDREN

■ ATTRIBUTES DEEMED DESIRABLE FOR CHILDREN TO HAVE

Each generation of parents determines for itself the proper way to raise their children. There is much interest today in just what values the baby boom generation will pass on to their progeny. The 1960s witnessed a mass revolt by teenagers against their parents, followed by an equally massive swing toward political and social conservatism in the 1970s and 1980s. The parents of the 1960s generation were accused of being too permissive, of having taken John Dewey too seriously.

So there is particular interest in what values today's parents think should be transferred to the new crop of children as they approach the critical stages of growth.

When presented with a list of thirteen attributes that might be desirable for children to have, the American people had no trouble sorting out just what ought to be passed on to the new generation and what should not:

☐ Heading the list is "A child should be honest," singled out by 28% as the most important value to be instilled into offspring.

☐ Not far behind, cited by 19%, was "A child should have good sense and sound judgment."

☐ In third place emerged an interesting answer, selected by

17%: "A child should obey his or her parents well." This is fascinating because it obviously marks a complete turnabout from the once popular notion that by not demanding strict obedience, a parent will allow a child to bloom most fully.
□ Far behind these top three attributes, two other qualities tied for fourth place, each selected by 8%. One was that "a child should learn to be considerate of others"; the other, that "a child should learn to be responsible."

The other eight items finished with only minor mentions. In some cases, the fact that they did *not* attract much support is significant:

□ No more than 4% thought that one of the most desirable goals for children is "to try hard to succeed." Some will see in the weak showing of this quality a confirmation of the failure of American will to be dedicated to raising productivity. Others will be relieved that today's parents and society in general do not want children to be taught to make it at any cost.
□ Another 4% say it is highly desirable to have "a child interested in how and why things happen." The low score for this item will make some worry that instilling a basic intellectual curiosity in children does not seem to be of much concern.
□ A very small 2% singled out "a child being a good student" as an essential attribute. This result is surprising in that it may mean that parents and society alike do not feel any real urgency for children to achieve excellence in studies. This is not a sign of a nation prepared for a much-publicized overhaul of its education system. Of course, others will welcome this de-emphasis on scholastic achievement.
□ Another small 2% selected "a child getting along well with other children" as a highly desirable quality for children to have.

☐ Only 2% cited "a child who has self-control" as a desirable attribute.

☐ A small 2% also picked "a child having good manners" as highly desirable. However, this should not be taken to mean that people want offspring with bad manners; it is simply a reflection of the times, where manners are not a major focus of emphasis.

☐ Two final qualities that were listed were mentioned by less than one percent. One was "A child is neat and clean." Again, this low showing should not be interpreted to mean that parents want their kids to be slobs, but rather that not many have a fetish about cleanliness. The other scarcely mentioned item was that "He acts like a boy and she acts like a girl." This was an effort on the part of the researchers at the National Opinion Research Center (NORC) to test subtly how worried parents are that their children might turn out to be homosexuals. Obviously, there were not many takers.

■ MOST IMPORTANT IN PREPARING A CHILD FOR LATER LIFE

In a somewhat different exercise, the cross section of respondents was also presented with a list of six qualities and asked to choose which one would be most important in preparing a child for later life:

☐ Far and away the most important, cited by 26%, is that "a child should be able to think for himself or herself"—in other words, for a child to have the wits to figure out what to do. Some will hope that this reply signals a public emphasis on turning out students who have the capacity to sort out the larger meaning and significance of what they are learning, but this might be reading too much into it.

☐ In second place, mentioned by 11%, was that "a child should learn to obey."

☐ In third place came "a child should learn to help others when they need help," selected by 7%.

☐ In fourth place was "a child should learn to work hard," picked by 6%.

☐ And in last place, less than 1% chose "a child should learn to be well liked or popular."

OBSERVATION

Of course, a good case could be made for the sound judgment of a people who would bequeath to a new generation a sense of honesty to build character, and an ability to think for themselves as the key to getting ahead in later life. Together, these qualities suggest a model child who combines integrity and mental alertness, a rather formidable formula.

But throughout these results runs a strong belief that children had better learn how to behave or else. Obey your parents, be responsible, don't be too questioning of the basic assumptions of the society in which you are being raised, and don't be too concerned about helping those who might need help the most.

Basically, the message is quite narrow and quite restrictive. In large measure, however, it is reflective of some of the preachings and pronouncements of the dominant national figure of the 1980s, Ronald Reagan himself.

The offspring of the generation accused of being too permissive turned in revolt against their parents in the 1960s. It will be interesting to see if a comparable revolt takes place between the mid-1990s and the turn of the century.

General Social Surveys 1972–1986, conducted by the National Opinion Research Center, February–April 1984 and 1986, among a national cross section of 2,203 adults, released July 1986.

THE RADICALLY CHANGED
WORK ENVIRONMENT

■ THE WORK'S FINE, BUT WHY BE WEDDED TO THIS JOB?

By every measure, job satisfaction is reasonably high among the work force in America. A substantial 88%–12% majority express satisfaction with their jobs. There is every indication that this satisfaction has remained stable over the past 15 years. The basic point is that there is no real sign on the horizon that American workers are deep down dissatisfied with their jobs. To be sure, no more than 50% say they are *very* satisfied with what they do, and 38% say they are only "somewhat satisfied," but this is not the stuff from which worker revolts are born.

Given this high level of satisfaction, it would seem that most employees would therefore be prepared to settle into their jobs for the long haul, and to make a real commitment to a given career track. Yet that is not the way it is with workers in America in the latter part of the 1980s. To the contrary, only 39% say that five years from now they intend to hold the same job they do now. Another 31% say they plan to leave their current work, and the remaining 25% simply don't know what they will be doing in the way of a job five years from now.

This lack of commitment for the long haul raises serious questions about the ability of the U.S. economy to compete effectively in the world. In Korea, Singapore, Mexico, Taiwan, and other countries, employers are able to recruit dedicated workers who can be trained to do mass-production jobs reasonably well at only a fraction of the pay U.S. workers receive. This means that manufacturing jobs will continue to be exported at an increasing rate. Indeed, as reported elsewhere in this volume, it increases the urgent necessity for this country to radically revamp its education system to turn out more highly skilled workers who are able and committed to holding down much more sophisticated jobs producing the products and services that will once again make the U.S. unique and competitive. So the stakes are high in what America does to cope with the take-it-or-leave-it attitude most people have about their jobs.

■ LEVELS OF JOB SATISFACTION BY TYPE OF WORK

Although more than two thirds of every category of worker express more satisfaction than dissatisfaction with their work, nonetheless there are some significant differences by type of work. The tip-off is to be found in the extent to which those in different job categories say they are "very satisfied" with their current employment:

☐ Compared with an average 50% of all workers who are very satisfied with their jobs, a higher 60% of those with management jobs are highly pleased with their work situation.
☐ 55% of all professionals are very satisfied with their present employment.
☐ 53% of skilled blue-collar workers say they are highly satisfied with their jobs.
☐ However, a much lower 42% of all sales personnel express the same job satisfaction.
☐ An even lower 40% of unskilled blue-collar workers are very pleased with the jobs they now have.
☐ Only 39% of all service workers express high job satisfaction.

Clearly, people in professional and executive positions are more likely to be well satisfied with what they are doing. By the same token, at the bottom of the heap—in unskilled and service jobs that range from working in fast-food franchises to doing heavy manual labor or performing elementary cleaning and maintenance chores—there is much less real job satisfaction. Curious is the case of salespeople, who, though generally well compensated, have never received a positive reception from the rest of society (the *Death of a Salesman* and "You wouldn't trust a used car salesman, would you?" syndrome). Sales personnel fall far below the norm in job satisfaction. Interestingly enough, two out of the three relatively "down" categories in job satisfaction are drawn from the white-collar and service sectors of the job market (office workers), not from the ranks of blue-collar workers.

■ GETTING ANOTHER JOB IS NO GREAT HASSLE

Perhaps the single most revealing key to the radical change that has overtaken the job market is the sense that most employees have that it would not be too difficult to find other employment. When asked directly, only 27% said they would find it "very difficult" to get another job that would be as good or better than the one they now have. A much higher 72% say they would have at best moderate or not too much difficulty in getting other employment.

And, despite the serious recession in the oil and textile industries in the Sunbelt and continuing tough times in agriculture, 87% do not expect to be laid off in the next year.

The relative optimism about their current job security and about the possibility of getting another job explains why American workers in the last quarter of the twentieth century feel little compunction about contemplating leaving jobs they think are reasonably satisfactory.

■ WHAT WORKERS WANT ON THE JOB

The other radical change that has taken place stems from a new orientation among workers with respect to what they are looking for in a job. It used to be that most workers wanted good pay and security from unjust firing. But priorities have changed. This was evident when workers were asked to choose which one of five major work attractions was most important to them:

☐ Well at the head of the list, singled out by 48%, was that "the work be important and give you a real feeling of accomplishment." This sense of a job having a larger meaning is obviously critically important in today's job market.

☐ Next is "the chance to advance," with 20%. Getting ahead is important.

☐ Close behind is the former number one motivator, high pay, now singled out by only 19% as most important.

☐ Far down the list, at only 7%, is "no danger of being fired," a former sacred cow.

☐ Finally, cited by only 3%, is "to be able to work shorter hours in order to have lots of free time."

OBSERVATION

Once upon a time, back in the first third of this century, most people spent their entire lives in the community in which they were born. Their families were there, their roots were deep. The notion of going to another community to work, let alone another part of the country, was almost unheard of. As a consequence, a young person had to make it in his or her hometown or not at all.

This meant that getting a job where you lived was the name of the game. And in many small industrial communities there might be only one big employer. That boss had the power to keep pay down and to keep workers in fear of being fired. Of course, it was just such conditions that produced organized

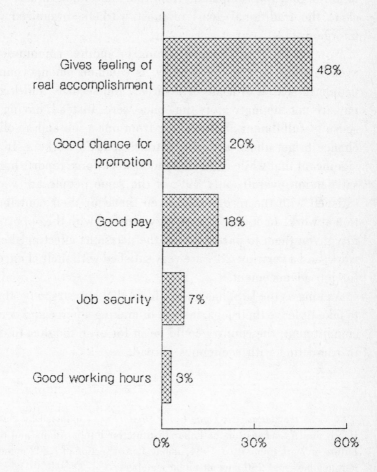

WHY WE WORK

Gives feeling of
real accomplishment — 48%

Good chance for
promotion — 20%

Good pay — 18%

Job security — 7%

Good working hours — 3%

0%   30%   60%

labor and drove the labor movement in the 1930s in America. Good pay and job security became the rallying cry for all union organizing campaigns from that time forward and became the traditional goals of most workers, organized or unorganized.

Now all this has changed. Going to another community, even another part of the country, is common among young people in search of a job or a career. Job security and high pay are not the motivators they once were. Instead, having a sense of fulfillment and meaning from one's job and a solid chance to get ahead are what attracts today's workers. It is significant that while 50% of the total work force reports high satisfaction overall, only 39% of the same people are very satisfied with the recognition given them for their contribution at work, an equal 39% are very satisfied with the opportunity given them to participate in the decisions affecting their work, and a very low 28% are very satisfied with their chances for job advancement.

As long as the U.S. has a work force that appears to be able to take or leave their jobs, instead of making a fierce and deep commitment, the country could be in for even tougher times in competing with economies abroad.

A Study on the Outlook for Trade Union Organizing, conducted by Louis Harris and Associates for the Labor Institute for Public Affairs and the Future of Work Committee, 1984, among a cross section of 1,202 nonunion members and 250 current union members.

America in the Eighties, conducted by R.H. Bruskin Associates, November 1985, among a cross section of 1,900 adults.

General Social Surveys 1972–1986, conducted by the National Opinion Research Center, February–April 1984, 1985, and 1986, among national cross sections of 3,007 (1984–85) and 1,826 (1985–86) adults, released July 1984, 1985 and 1986.

SLEEP: BLISSFUL OR TROUBLED?

■ PATTERNS OF SLEEP

Most adult Americans (64%) sleep 7 to 8 hours a night. However, substantial minorities deviate from this norm. For example, 1% regularly get no more than 5 hours' sleep a night, 5% make it on 5 hours' sleep, and 20% regularly get 6 hours' sleep. Thus, better than one in every four people do not need or regularly have more than 6 hours' sleep.

At the other end of the spectrum, 5% report sleeping 9 hours a night and 4% sleep 10 or more hours a night. This adds up to 9% who sleep 9 or more hours a night.

But although the bulk of people get 7 hours (32%) and 8 hours (32%) of sleep a night, looked at another way, a clear majority of 58% of the entire adult population (103 million people) sleep 7 hours or less a night. This means that a majority regularly get less than the traditional "eight hours of sleep" long viewed as ideal for human beings. Indeed, sleep researchers have long questioned the wisdom of the magical eight hours. Basically, experts now say that the proper amount of sleep can vary greatly, depending on the psychological, neurological, and physiological makeup of an individual.

■ TROUBLED SLEEPERS

Fully 43% of the American people (76 million) say they have trouble sleeping. A nearly identical 40% of the adult population suffer from stress nearly every day of their lives and find they can sleep no more than 6 hours a night. Clearly, they are the chronic stress types whose tensions follow them to bed every night and prevent them from getting to sleep and then staying asleep throughout the night. Others who get the least sleep a night are those who feel compulsive about paying attention to every last detail, those who say they just don't have enough hours in the day to get their work done, those who in fact take the least care of their health, those who are least interested in proper nutrition, and those who are less than very satisfied with their life.

■ WHO GETS THE MOST AND LEAST SLEEP
However, before concluding that people who get less sleep are all severely emotionally stressed and disturbed, some other evidence must be examined. Among the groups who sleep the least are also those with four years of college or better, those in the baby boom generation, professional and top managerial types, and those who expect their health to change for the better over the next 20 years. These people tend to be the high performers, those who not only work the longest hours but are also the most productive citizens in terms of work output.

Thus, it can be concluded that the majority who get 7 hours or less sleep a night divide into the most disturbed and troubled people, on the one hand, and some of the most successful, on the other.

By key groups, others who get less sleep are residents of the East, blacks, men, and those who have a limiting disability or physical handicap.

On the other side of the coin is quite a different roster of types. Those who get the most sleep on an average night include residents of the South and West, small-town and rural folk, those with incomes under $15,000, those with the least education, people 65 and over, women, and blue-collar workers. The mark of these people is that they are far more relaxed, suffer much less from stress, and feel much less put upon by the outside world and their own problems adjusting to it. However, they are also much less likely to be the achievers, the movers and shakers who get things done.

OBSERVATION

Most Americans in the latter quarter of the twentieth century get along on less than 7 hours' sleep a night. This is partly because the stress most live under directly affects their capacity for sleep. But it is also because those who get the most done simply do not have much time to spend on sleep in their busy lives. Clearly, some high achievers also are high-stress types who are candidates for burnout not long into the future. For them, perhaps a dose of more relaxing sleep would prolong their productivity and longevity. But those who get the most sleep are clearly not the achievers. They are more apt to say they get high satisfaction from life, however, and by every measure appear to be more at one with themselves and their circumstances, which are often quite modest, indeed.

Prevention in America III: Steps People Take—or Fail to Take—for Better Health, conducted by Louis Harris and Associates for *Prevention Magazine*, November 15–26, 1985, among a national cross section of 1,256 adults.

Prevention in America IV: Steps People Take—or Fail to Take—for Better Health, conducted by Louis Harris and Associates for *Prevention Magazine* November 14–30, 1986, among a national cross section of 1,250 adults, released May 1987.

The National Survey of Antecedents, Mediators and Consequences of Stress, conducted by Louis Harris and Associates, January–March 1984, among a national cross section of 2,387 adults, released April 1985.

A SOCIETY OF 28 MILLION ALCOHOLICS

■ THE MAGNITUDE OF THE PROBLEM

A nearly unanimous 93% of the American people readily acknowledge that heavy drinking is a serious problem in the United States, with 64% calling it "very serious." It should be added that this estimate by the public basically has not changed over the past 15 years.

Alcoholism is a phenomenon that is all too familiar. Fully 55% of the public report knowing someone who "drinks too much." And the person most know is not the stereotypical town drunk. On the contrary, six in ten who know someone with a drinking problem say that the troubled person "is close to me."

The significant fact is that 32% of the nation's households have someone at home with a drinking problem. This comes to 28 million homes where drinking troubles exist, with at least one alcoholic person in the family. This is undoubtedly a conservative estimate, since quite often alcoholism is found among several members of a family. In addition, these results are based on surveys of the adult population only and do not entirely reflect the growing number of young people who have acquired serious drinking problems over the past several years, during which many parents took to encouraging their young to drink alcoholic beverages instead of trying illegal drugs.

The 32% incidence is largely confirmed by another answer given by the same sample: 30% report that their "life has been affected in a major way by someone who drinks too much."

■ WHERE EXCESSIVE DRINKING STRIKES HOME MOST

Although 32% nationwide report a drinking problem in their family, among a number of segments in the population the rate of alcoholism is much higher:

☐ By region, easily the heaviest drinking area of the country is the West, where 40% report an immediate family member who drinks too much. Next is the South at 34%, then the Midwest at 31%, and the East at 25%.

☐ By age, alcoholism is most noted by the young, with 37% of all people under 30 reporting families beset with drinking problems. A lower 27% of those in the 50–64 age group report excessive drinking, as does a lower 21% among those 65 and over. This pattern reflects a long-standing fact that the drinking of alcoholic beverages tends to taper off as people get older. But it also reflects the trend among young people in recent years to turn toward alcohol as a substitute for drugs. A high 40% of Yuppies report having a real drinking problem. However, among those 18 to 20 years of age, an even higher 44% report alcohol troubles, the highest incidence in the population.

☐ By sex, men have a more serious drinking problem than women, with 35% of males reporting excessive drinking, compared with 30% of women. Significantly, however, more women than men say their lives have been affected in a major way by someone who drinks too much, which may be reflective of the miseries of women with children whose husbands have a drinking problem.

☐ By income, excessive drinking is found most among those earning $35,000 to $50,000 a year, with 37% reporting problems. This tends to confirm the realization in recent years that alcoholism is very much a middle-income and probably even more an upper-middle-income affliction.

Most affected in a major way by someone with a drinking problem are residents of the West and South, big-city dwellers, those in the 30–49 age group, women, Hispanics, the $35,000–$50,000 income group, and Yuppies. These results largely confirm the patterns of people directly reporting someone "close to them" with a drinking problem.

■ WHAT CAN BE DONE ABOUT IT?

Much has been done in recent years to try to come to grips with the widespread drinking problem in the U.S. However, the American people are prepared to go well beyond the current laws in combating excessive drinking:

☐ An overwhelming 89%–9% majority favors taking away the license of a person arrested for the second time for drunk driving. A substantial 68% are convinced that such crackdowns will have a major effect in increasing auto safety.

☐ By 85% to 12%, a sizable majority supports making the legal age for the purchase of alcoholic beverages 21 years of age or over. An increasing number of states have been adopting such drinking laws.

☐ By 65% to 29%, another big majority favors sentencing drunk drivers to jail, even if they have not caused an accident.

☐ By 70% to 27%, an even higher majority supports having police set up roadblocks to catch drunk drivers.

☐ By 57% to 37%, a majority would favor banning all advertising of beer and wine from radio and television. By a narrow 49% to 46%, a plurality believes such a ban would discourage alcohol consumption, especially among teenagers.

Nonetheless, four other possible drastic actions to curb excessive drinking meet with rejection by the public:

□ A substantial 61%–37% majority is opposed to automatically taking away the license of a person arrested for the first time for drunk driving, a sharp contrast with the nine in ten who want to strip a driver of his license after a second arrest. Most people are willing to give first offenders a second chance.

□ By 60% to 34%, a majority rejects the notion of making the host of a party liable if a drunken guest kills or injures someone on the road.

□ By 55% to 39%, a majority also rejects the proposal to make bartenders and bar owners liable if someone leaves their bar drunk and then kills or injures someone in a driving accident.

□ By a narrow 47% to 45%, a plurality rejects the suggestion that happy hours at bars be made illegal. Significantly, a 54%–36% majority of nondrinkers support this move, but are barely outweighed by a 56%–38% majority of drinkers who oppose it.

■ ALCOHOL CONSUMPTION IS GOING DOWN IN THE U.S.

As a result of heightened public awareness of drinking problems and a growing desire to crack down on drunk driving and other aberrant behavior by excessive drinkers, consumption of alcoholic beverages is down in the country.

Here are the signs:

□ 33% of the adult public reported having drunk beer in the previous month before the survey. But this is down from a comparable 37% over 10 years ago.

□ 27% report drinking wine in the previous month, but this is down from 38% who said the same 11 years before.

□ 25% report having drunk hard liquor in the previous month, but this is down from a comparable 48% over a decade ago.

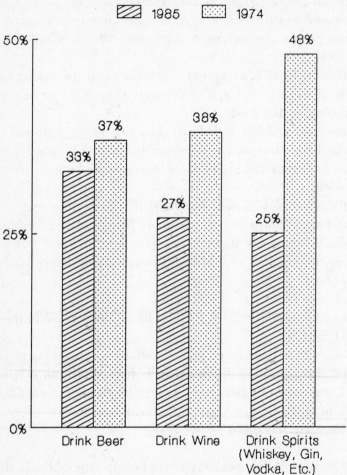

DRINKING TRENDS

1985   1974

This absolute decline over the past decade, confirmed in official industry trade numbers, is a well-known fact to drinkers of alcoholic beverages. A big 45% of all drinkers say they are now drinking less than they were five years ago, compared with only 13% who report drinking more and 41% who say there has been no change. Back in the early 1970s, a lower 31% said they were drinking less. Today when those drinking less were asked why, 39% gave health reasons; 24% said that drinking and driving don't mix, indicative of the impact of the campaign to discourage driving when drinking; 15% thought a cutback in drinking helped them in their jobs; and 11% admitted that drinking is now less fashionable than it once was.

OBSERVATION

Alcoholism still is probably the most serious drug problem in the country, with at least 28 million afflicted by it. It is an illness that strikes most at middle-income families, especially among the young. It erodes health, destroys productivity on the job, and wreaks havoc on families.

But there are real signs that in the late 1980s American society is beginning to come to grips with the alcohol problem. Public support for decisive measures and crackdowns, such as raising the legal drinking age to 21 and automatically taking away licenses from second-offense drunk drivers, are sure signs that people are finally playing for keeps on the issue.

In fact, the approach of American society to alcoholism may well be indicative of a dovetailing of public and private efforts. The private sector has generated several highly visible organizations that have conducted major campaigns to cut down on drunk driving. In turn, the media have picked up the messages of these efforts and have conducted public service campaigns of their own. At the same time, a number of states have passed tougher laws against drunk driving and are beginning to move into other areas to crack down on those under the influence. Basically, the effort is a joint one between the public and private sectors.

Perhaps the most incisive effect, however, may well end up being a long-term decline in the number of Americans who drink alcoholic beverages. Self-imposed abstinence is a growing practice of Americans. Since the early 1970s people are eating less red meat because of concern with cholesterol, and since the early 1980s, people are consuming less sugar, out of concern with its fattening effects.

It would be ironic, indeed, if the alcoholism rate was drastically reduced because of a further extension of this new-found self-discipline.

Business Week/Harris Poll, conducted by Louis Harris and Associates for *Business Week,* February 6–10, 1985, among a national cross section of 1,254 adults, released February 25, 1985.

A GOD-FEARING COUNTRY?

A nearly unanimous 95% of the American people say they believe in God. Yet, a clear-cut 58% of these same people are not at all regular church or synagogue attenders. On the surface, this seeming contradiction would indicate either that individuals in this country want to worship privately for the most part, or that only a minority of the people harbor anything approximating deep religious feeling.

■ RELIGIOUS ATTENDANCE: NO GREAT REVIVAL HERE

For many years the Gallup Organization has been the unofficial keeper of the record on church attendance. In recent times the high-water mark for religious attendance occurred in 1958, when 49% said they had attended a church or synagogue at least once in the past seven days. It should be noted, however, that even in that peak year a slim majority could not be classified as regular attendees.

From 1958 onward, there was a steady decline in church attendance. By 1960 it was down to 47%, by 1967 down to 43%, then to 42% in 1970, 41% in 1977, and 40% in 1980. It went up to 41% in 1981, back down to 40% in 1983, and in 1985 went up to 42% only to drop back to 40% in 1986. Statistically, it must be concluded that, by and large, church attendance has plateaued in America, despite the periodic claims by some politicians and preachers that "a great religious revival is sweeping the country." If such a surge was in fact taking place, then surely church attendance would also be rising.

■ SEPARATING THE CHURCHGOERS FROM THE ABSTAINERS

Big differences in church attendance exist by age, sex, region of the country, race, and specific religious denomination:

☐ By age, older people tend to go to church much more often than their younger offspring. Those 50 and over attend to the tune of 48%, compared with 39% for the group 30 to 49 years old and a lower 33% for those under 30. Maybe it's a matter of age bringing one closer to God. Or, lower attendance by the young might be a harbinger that attendance is likely to fall off more in the years ahead.

☐ By sex, there is no doubt that women are far more religious than men. A substantial 46% of women are regular attenders of church, compared with a much lower 33% of men. This is not a new development at all, but has been the case for many years.

☐ By region, the heaviest churchgoers are to be found in the South, where 43% attend regularly, followed by the Midwest at 42%, the East at 39%, and the West at a very low 35%.

☐ Among the three main religious groups, more Catholics attend church than any of the others. A substantial 49% of all Catholics report going to services at least once a week, compared with 41% of Protestants and 20% of Jews. Among the various Protestant denominations, there are wide differences. The most frequent attenders are members of the Church of Jesus Christ of Latter Day Saints, 53% of whom regularly attend, followed by 39% among Baptists, 36%

among Lutherans and Presbyterians, 34% among Episcopalians, and 36% among Methodists.

Despite all the waves of immigration and the melting-pot character of the country, the United States remains essentially a Protestant nation, with 65% having been born into that denomination, 28% into the Catholic Church, and 2% as Jews. Another 3% have never been associated with any religion, and another 2% belong to some other sect. To the same overwhelming extent that they express belief in God, nearly everyone in the country reports being born into some religion.

■ IN THE IMAGE OF GOD

Exactly what God, a divine figure in nearly all religions, means to worshipers might have remained strictly in the eye of each beholder, had not the National Opinion Research Center in 1986 asked an intriguing series of questions. To find out what the dominant view of God was in the minds of the American people, NORC put a cross section through the rigors of what is called a series of paired comparisons. On this scale, people were asked to say if God to them was more like a father or a mother, a master or a spouse, a judge or a lover, a friend or a king, a creator or a healer, a redeemer or a liberator.

Here are the results:

□ A substantial 68% say that in their mind God is much more like a master than a spouse, which only 8% opt for. Another 18% say God can be both to them.
□ Nearly two out of every three, 65%, say that to them God comes far closer to being a father figure than a mother figure, an image that is conjured up for only 7%, although 24% believe God can be a cross between the two.
□ While 17% view God as a lover, a much higher 58% have

an image of God as a judge. Another 22% can see both attributes in God.

□ A clear plurality of 44% say they think of God more as a friend than as a king, whom 27% perceive God to be like. But 26% believe God can mean both to them.

□ A substantial 49% see God as a redeemer, much higher than the 10% who think of the Almighty as a liberator, but a high 36% believe God can be both.

□ Finally, 37% say they view God as a creator rather than as a healer, as 14% view Him. However, in this case, the most sizable group, 45%, thinks of God as both.

OBSERVATION

Association with a religion is as common in the U.S. as nearly any other experience. So is belief in God. By the same token, solid majorities of the American people believe that worship and organized religion must remain a private affair, totally separated from the state. A big 66%–25% majority is wedded to that notion.

Nonetheless, less than half the people who believe in God regularly go to formal worship in a church or synagogue. Despite an increase of 2% in church attendance this past year, there is no sign that a wave of religious sentiment has engulfed the country. As reported elsewhere in this book, there is solid evidence that populist evangelical preachers, such as Jerry Falwell, appear to be antagonizing the eight in ten people who are not their followers and creating a backlash against clergy of the Moral Majority type.

God does have personal meaning for most Americans, emerging as a father figure, a kind of master of the universe, who passes judgment on moral, ethical, and faith-related matters, but who is also a friend in need, a creator and a healer.

The evidence is that America is religious, but neither

demonstratively nor with heavily ritualistic tastes. Religious belief may well run deep, but it is likely to be contained within the individual rather than reflected in a slavish loyalty to church attendance or to the letter of the dicta of a particular religion. It seems that religion is practiced in a way that makes it thoroughly compatible with a nation founded on the principles of pluralism and religious freedom.

––––––––––––

Religion in America 50 Years: 1935–1985, conducted by the Gallup Organization, January–December 1985, yearlong survey among a national cross section of 5,093 adults.

Media General-Associated Press Poll, conducted by Media General and Associated Press, September 1–7 1985, among a national cross section of 1,412 adults.

General Social Surveys: 1972–1986, conducted by the National Opinion Research Center, February–April 1986, among a national cross section of 1,470 adults, released July 1986.

The Gallup Poll, conducted by the Gallup Organization periodically in 1986 among a national cross section of 6,633 adults, released December 28, 1986.

The Gallup Poll as reported in the U.S. Bureau of Census, *Statistical Abstract of the United States, 1986* (Washington, D.C. 1985), Table 77: Church Attendance 1958 to 1984, and by Selected Characteristics: 1984, p. 51.

PREGNANT WOMEN: A SPECIAL MOMENT OF LIFE

■ TRYING TO TAKE NO CHANCES

In recent years, wide attention has been given to numerous studies pointing up the deleterious effects upon new babies of dietary, drinking, smoking, and drug habits of mothers. Physicians have been urged to warn pregnant women to avoid practices that might have a harmful impact on the new baby.

Fully 93% of all recent mothers say they began seeing a doctor during their first three months of pregnancy. A substantial 81% report that their physician gave them detailed health advice. A nearly unanimous 94% say they changed their health habits as a consequence of this advice. Basically, most women in pregnancy now appear to want to take no chances with medication or habits that might harm their new offspring.

■ CHANGES PREGNANT WOMEN MAKE

Here is the roster of changes made and precautions taken by women once they realized they were pregnant:

□ In the case of prescription medicines, a big 87% say they took steps to make sure those medicines would be safe for the fetus. Much the same happened with nonprescription drugs: 88% said they took steps to make sure the ones they were using would have no harmful effect on their child. One in ten (10%) of these mothers said they used recreational drugs before pregnancy. One percent said they used less recreational drugs, while the same number reported using the same amount or more; but 8% percent said they stopped using all recreational drugs during their pregnancy.

□ A sizable majority (82%) reported taking special care with their own nutrition upon becoming pregnant. As a consequence, 63% say they were able to stay close to the recommended weight gain during their pregnancy. However, 25% reported gaining too much weight, while 11% could not gain enough. After their babies were born, 46% of all new mothers breast-fed them, which was yet another incentive to be mindful of their health practices.

□ One in three (32%) of these mothers was a smoker before pregnancy. However, once they found out they were pregnant, four in ten of the smokers gave it up, another four in ten smoked less, but the remaining two in ten said they smoked the same amount or even more.

□ A substantial 59% were drinkers of alcoholic beverages before pregnancy. However, close to six in ten of the drinkers gave it up for the duration, and another one in three cut down on alcohol consumption. The remaining one in twelve kept on drinking during the pregnancy.

□ A high 88% said they drank beverages containing caffeine, such as coffee, tea, and soft drinks before their pregnancy. However, only one in seven gave them up for the duration, although a much higher 56% cut back on coffee, tea, and soft drinks. But over one in three kept on drinking such beverages at the same rate.

OBSERVATION

It is apparent that pregnant women are by and large heeding many of the warnings by health authorities about the risks involved in taking medication and drugs and smoking and drinking during pregnancy. Indeed, the record here of either outright abstinence or cutting back on drinking, smoking, or recreational drugs, and taking precautions with medication, must be viewed as a tribute to mass health education efforts. The one area remaining in which a majority of mothers still remain unconvinced of risk is the case of drinking beverages containing caffeine. Many mothers explained that they simply felt they needed the stimulation that they reported such products gave them.

Prevention in America II: Steps People Take—or Fail to Take—for Better Health, conducted by Louis Harris and Associates for *Prevention Magazine*, November 15–29, 1984, among a national cross section of 1,715 adults.

DRUGS: A MONSTER IN OUR MIDST

■ SOME SOBER FACTS ABOUT DRUG USAGE

For a generation now, the U.S. has been deeply concerned about what has been viewed as the spreading use of and addiction to illicit drugs among the nation's young people. During the past few years, in which a seeming explosion of cocaine use has descended on the country, the worries have been extended to certain sectors of the adult population, ranging from Wall Street brokers to professional athletes and to government employees in sensitive security positions.

Carefully conducted surveys by the federal government have tracked the use of drugs, especially among high school students. The trends indeed show an increase in illicit drug usage over the past 10 years, but notably not quite as spectacular an exlosion as the media and some authorities would suggest. This is not to say that the situation is not serious, when 4 in 10 teenagers regularly use marijuana, almost 1 in 5 use stimulants or uppers, 1 in 9 use cocaine, 1 in 12 are using hallucinogens, 1 in 12 inhalants, 1 in 14 illegal sedatives or downers, and 1 in 17 illicit tranquilizers. Obviously, anyone might justifiably be frightened and even alarmed at the penetration of illicit drugs into the mainstream of American society. There is no guarantee of immunity for any family.

With respect to marijuana, the most widely used illicit drug, extensive federal government surveys yield some inter-

USE OF DRUGS BY HIGH SCHOOL SENIORS

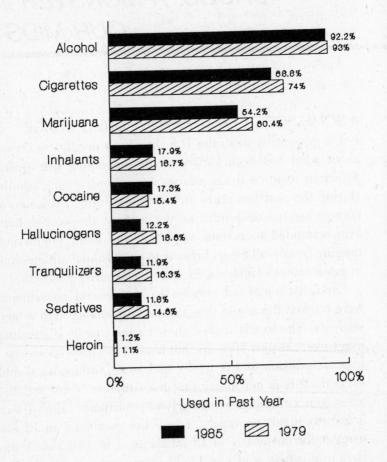

Alcohol	92.2%	93%
Cigarettes	68.8%	74%
Marijuana	54.2%	60.4%
Inhalants	17.9%	18.7%
Cocaine	17.3%	15.4%
Hallucinogens	12.2%	18.6%
Tranquilizers	11.9%	16.3%
Sedatives	11.8%	14.6%
Heroin	1.2%	1.1%

0%   50%   100%

Used in Past Year

■ 1985   ▨ 1979

esting breakdowns by key groups. By sex, more men than women use the drug. By race, the rate of usage is higher among white youths aged 12 to 17 than among blacks and other minorities, but higher among minorities aged 18 to 25 and among minority adults in general. Clearly, marijuana usage is much higher in big cities than in the suburbs, small towns and rural areas.

Among the high school population, the trends over the past 10 years are quite revealing and unexpected in light of reports given by the media or by political leaders:

☐ The National Institute on Drug Abuse (NIDA) surveys of roughly 16,000 high school seniors annually show that as of 1985, the latest data available, the use of marijuana has steadily declined among teenagers since 1981. Back in 1975, 47% of high school students reported ever using marijuana. This rose to 53% in 1976, 56% in 1977, 59% in 1978, and then peaked at 60% in 1979, 1980, and 1981. Then it went down to 59% in 1982, 57% in 1983, 55% in 1984, and 54% in 1985. Since 1981 the number of high school students who have ever used marijuana has declined 5%. Those who reported using that drug in the last 12 months declined from a peak of 51% in 1979 a full 10 points, to a current 41%. This translates into a decrease of 20% in current marijuana use among high school students.

☐ In the use of hallucinogens, stimulants, sedatives, and tranquilizers, there has been a corresponding decline over the past 10 years. The University of Michigan Institute for Social Research scholars who actually conduct the NIDA surveys also report that over the same period the length of the "highs" reported by high school students has declined as well.

☐ The survey results for the same period show no change in the pattern of heroin usage, a slight increase in the use of inhalants, and a sizable rise in the use of cocaine. Since 1975 the number of high school students who have tried cocaine went up from 9% to 17%, an increase of 89%. Those teenagers who currently use cocaine increased from 6% to 13%, a jump of 117%. Just in the past year the rise in current cocaine usage among these young people went from 12% to 13%, or up 15% in 12 months. And these figures do not fully reflect the recently reported heavy increases in the use of crack, a form of cocaine. Obviously, the growing drug of choice to which high school students are most vulnerable is cocaine.

■ THE DRUG ENVIRONMENT FOR TEENAGERS

When asked how often they have been around people who were taking illicit substances "to get high" or "for kicks," 24% said this was often the case with respect to marijuana, 7% with amphetamines, 7% with cocaine (up from 3% in 10 years), 2% with barbiturates and the same number with tranquilizers, 2% with LSD, another 1% with other psychedelics, and 1% with heroin. Just about the same percentages reported that friends of their use these drugs. However, dwarfing all this reported usage of illicit drugs was the fact that 60% of high school seniors reported often being around people who were getting drunk on alcoholic beverages. A 1979 private survey conducted by the Harris firm that utilized a secret ballot showed a 64% correlation between regular use of illicit drugs and relatively heavy use of alcohol. The affinity between the two is close and undeniable.

Drugs are available in substantial quantities to high school students. For example, 86% say that marijuana is easy to get, 66% say the same for amphetamines, 55% for tranquilizers, 51% for barbiturates, 49% for cocaine, 31% for LSD, 26% for other psychedelics, 21% for heroin, and 33% for other narcotics, including methadone.

■ HIGH SCHOOL SENIORS' VIEWS ABOUT DRUG USE

Substantial numbers of high school students disapprove of regular use of all illicit drugs, alcohol, and cigarette smoking: 98% frown on using heroin regularly, 97% on using LSD frequently, 94% on using cocaine regularly, 92% on having four or five drinks nearly every day, 96% on taking barbiturates regularly, 93% on taking amphetamines often, 86% on smoking marijuana regularly, 72% on smoking a pack of cigarettes a day, and 60% on having five or more drinks once or twice each weekend.

Obviously, young people are aware of the dangers of addiction and of regular use of any of these licit and illicit substances. It is equally apparent that they feel highly knowledgeable about the existence and availability of them all. Clearly, all have been the subject of intense discussion among their peers.

However, the nub of the problem becomes clear when high school seniors are asked how much risk is involved in different dosages of these substances:

□ In the case of cocaine, the drug rising fastest in popularity, 79% see "great risk" in using it regularly, indicating that most high school seniors are aware of its addictive qualities. However, only 34% feel that "trying cocaine once or twice" is "a great risk."

□ The same pattern exists for most of the other legal and illegal substances. In the case of using marijuana regularly, 70% say that it poses high risk, but smoking it occasionally seems a big risk to only 25%, and using it only once or twice is a serious risk to 15%. Or LSD: taking it regularly is a huge risk in the minds of 83%, but trying it once or twice, to only 44%. Taking heroin regularly is a "great risk" to 86%, taking it occasionally a big risk to 70%, but trying it once or twice

is viewed as high risk by only 47%. Again, taking amphetamines regularly seems a high risk to 67%, but trying them
once or twice seems a big risk to only 25%. And taking
barbiturates regularly is thought a great risk by 68%, but
trying them once or twice seems risky to only 26%. But, then,
only 43% see big risk in having five or more drinks once or
twice each weekend, and no more than 70% see high risk in
drinking four or five drinks every day.

OBSERVATION

The irony is that high school students are well aware of the
dangers of getting hooked on illicit or licit substances, but
they are also wide open to trying just about anything once or
twice. In other words, they have been well warned that taking
just about any of these drugs regularly can be dangerous or
even fatal—most undoubtedly know of cases where it has
been.

But youth is an experimental time of life. The temptation
to "see what it's like" is almost more than teenagers can
resist. Implicit in their answers is a built-in confidence that
they can try anything and walk away from it, just as built into
their parents' worst fears is the conviction that if their children try drugs, they are likely to end up being junkies.

The problem appears to center on what might be called the
wide-open "entry" for drugs, already abundantly available to
high school students, to be pushed to a willing audience. The
pusher's seductive come-on, "Just try it once and see how it
feels," is made to order for the teenage mind-set.

This means that while the vast majority of high school
students undoubtedly avoid dope addiction and alcoholism, a
considerable number will also fall prey to the wiles of those
who urge them to experiment.

The adult public in 1986 sharply toughened its line on
drugs, with big majorities favoring periodic drug screening

tests for high school teachers, high school students, airline pilots, police officers, TV, film, recording stars, professional athletes, and government workers. On the other hand, most do not want to fire drug takers, but instead to require that they enter drug treatment programs. They correctly see crack and other forms of cocaine as the growing menace.

But when asked to name the most important step to take in the war against drug abuse, easily their first choice was to "teach young people about the dangers of drugs." Teaching the dangers is one thing. Persuading the young not to experiment even a little would be a monumental achievement.

Use of Licit and Illicit Drugs by American High School Seniors, College Students, and other Young Adults: National Trends through 1985, a continuing survey of 16,000 high school seniors annually conducted by the University of Michigan Institute for Social Research, under the direction of Dr. Lloyd D. Johnston, Dr. Patrick M. O'Malley, and Dr. Jerald G. Bachman, under grants from the National Institute for Drug Abuse, released January 1986.

Newsweek Poll, conducted by the Gallup Organization for *Newsweek*, July 31–August 1, 1986, among a national cross section of 758 adults, released August 11, 1986.

SEX EDUCATION TODAY, AVOID UNWANTED PREGNANCY TOMORROW

■ HOW KIDS LEARN ABOUT SEX

Probably throughout the ages, learning about sex has been partly a matter of self-discovery at the first signs of puberty, partly an inevitable result of furtive talk among children, and partly a somewhat fumbling effort by parents to have serious discussions about "the facts of life." But it is really quite strange that a subject as basic as sex has been largely left to chance, a kind of catch-as-catch-can proposition—even in the mid to late 1980s.

When asked directly how they first learned about sex, fully 40% of all adults confess they heard about it from "friends." This is the case particularly among men and among Catholics. Eager and superstitious talk among friends between the ages of 8 and 11 often will center on sex. The evidence shows that much of what is passed on as the gospel truth is specious and downright misleading. Yet most children still find out about sex in precisely this way.

Parents are also a major source, with 26% reporting they first heard about sex from their mother or father. A much higher 21% remember hearing about sex from their mother, compared with only 5% who say their father told them about it first. However, 33% of all women report that their mothers told them, compared with only 10% of men who say their father revealed the critical facts of life. Virtually no young girls were informed about sex from their fathers, but 8% of boys heard about it from their mothers.

When the one third of all parents in the country who have a child between 6 and 18 are asked about it, 76% say they have talked with their offspring about sex. A smaller 67% of Catholics say they've discussed it with their kids. The median age at which parents finally broach the subject is just after the child's tenth birthday. Nearly one third do not talk to their children until after puberty. Yet, in these discussions about sex, only 33% of the parents report having talked with their children about birth control or how to avoid unwanted pregnancies. On the face of it, most parents have real difficulty mustering the courage to talk with their kids about sex. It is simply a difficult and awkward subject. And chances are the child knows about it before the parent ever says a word, although rarely will either party acknowledge that fact.

A significant 10% of all adults confess that they first learned about sex from a sexual partner. This is more often the case among men and white born-again Christians than other groups. Another 8% report first having learned about sex through formal sex education courses in schools. However, it should be noted that one in every six young people under 30 report having learned about sex in a school course, compared with less than 3% of those aged 50 and over. Other ways young people hear about sex are from books and magazines and from siblings or other relatives.

∎ THE POWERFUL MANDATE FOR SEX EDUCATION IN THE PUBLIC SCHOOLS

Only 53% of the parents of children between 6 and 18 report that sex education is available in the school system where they send their children. A lower 47% of blacks and 52% of Hispanics say that sex education for their kids is taught at their schools. But, for almost half the country, formal sex education is virtually nonexistent, leaving those children to learn about it the way youngsters did 50 or 100 years ago.

Yet, when asked if sex education should be made available

in the schools, an overwhelming 85%–14% majority nation-wide say it should. What is more, 64% of all adults and 67% of those with children aged 6 to 18 feel very strongly that such courses should be made available. By religion, 61% of all Protestants and 71% of all Catholics (but only 47% of white born-again Christians) strongly favor making such teaching available. Nonetheless, a 68%–30% majority of the white born-again Christians favor rather than oppose sex education in the schools, a stand most of their preachers adamantly oppose. Indeed, 80% of all conservatives, 82% of all Republicans, and 77% of all small-town and rural people support formal sex education for children.

In fact, 54% of the country sees a direct connection be-tween sex education in the schools and the number of un-wanted teenage pregnancies. They conclude that if sex education was eliminated from the schools today, it would definitely lead to more pregnancies among teenagers. Only 16% endorse the position of the New Right that doing away with sex education in the schools would result in fewer rather than more pregnancies. The remaining three in ten feel there would be little or no change in the teenage pregnancy rate if sex education was abolished. Significantly, among Catholics, 60% believe that elimination of sex education would lead to more pregnancies, and a plurality of 41% of white born-again Christians agree with that estimate.

But most of the country wants to go much further than simply establishing sex education courses in every school in the land. A lopsided 67%–29% majority nationwide also fa-vors having public schools establish direct links with family planning clinics, "in order to make sure that young people learn about sex and birth control." Even a 52%–41% major-ity of white born-again Christians favor such a link, a view shared by a much higher 70%–27% majority of Catholics. Parents who have young people in the public schools support such close ties with birth control clinics by 69% to 29%.

OBSERVATION

Sex education in the schools has been a subject of constant controversy and contention. But these results clearly demonstrate that as far as the people themselves are concerned, the issue has been settled. A nearly unanimous 85% want sex education in the schools. There are 1.1 million unwanted teen pregnancies take place each year, representing 11% of all teens aged 15 to 19. It is obvious that most mothers of teenage girls live in quiet desperation over the possibility of their daughters becoming pregnant. These mothers want help from any and all sources—churches, friends, families, *and* schools—in teaching their children all the facts about sex.

Indeed, a solid majority of seven in ten parents want to go further. They would like to see a link between the public schools and family planning clinics. What they want, above all, is to have their children fully informed about sex. Most parents are willing to trust their boys and girls, provided they understand the implications and consequences of sex. The real enemy, they feel, is ignorance. As a nation, the methods used to inform roughly half the young people on sex are archaic. As sex education becomes more firmly established in the education system, the conviction is that teenage pregnancies will decline. The people themselves keenly want the media and the schools to embark on a major campaign to get the facts out once and for all. There are some signs that this is one area where change is highly likely to take place.

Public Attitudes About Sex Education, Family Planning and Abortion in the United States, conducted by Louis Harris and Associates for the Planned Parenthood Federation of America, Inc., August 13–25 and September 13–17, 1985, among a national cross section of 2,510 adults, released October 1985.

COPING WITH MARRIAGE, DIVORCE, AND WHO KEEPS THE KIDS

■ CONVENTIONAL WISDOM AND SOME FACTS

A careful examination of marriage and divorce statistics reveals that divorce may well be on the decline in the U.S., while marriage is not. These facts, compiled by the U.S. Center for Health Statistics, are directly contrary to the media's loud proclamation that one out of every two marriages now will end in divorce.

The fact is that in 1981 the number of divorces did hit a record total of 1,213,000. Marriages also reached a record 2,422,000. Some quick-read experts then put the two set of facts together and concluded that since there were half as many divorces as marriages, it could be concluded that half the marriages were doomed to failure. But the facts show that only 10% of all ever-married men and a slightly higher 13% of all ever-married women are divorced. This in turn means that almost 90% of all marriages survive.

Moreover, a further look at the facts shows that since 1981 the number of marriages has gone up 3% nationwide, while the number of divorces has declined 5%—the first time this has happened in modern times. While it would be sound to wait a few more years before drawing conclusions, the evidence strongly suggests that marriage just might be making a strong comeback and divorce might be on the wane. Such a conclusion, of course, flies wildly in the face of all conventional wisdom.

■ MARRIAGE HAS CHANGED IN THE EYE OF THE BEHOLDER

Views of what constitutes the most satisfying kind of marriage have undergone radical change over the past decade. Back in 1974, by 49% to 45%, both men and women considered best "a traditional marriage with the husband assuming responsibility for providing for the family and the wife running the home and taking care of the children." But in 1985, only 11 years later, a big 57%–37% majority of women and a closer 50%–43% plurality of men were convinced that a better marriage is one "where the husband and wife share responsibilities more—both work, share the housekeeping and the child responsibilities."

Clearly, as women have moved away from the traditional status of homemaker and have gone out to seek employment, notions of what a marriage should be have changed to accommodate the new reality. It has also meant a blurring of the traditional roles played by husband and wife. Above all else, it has meant recognition of the growing independence of women both in society and in the home.

With this accommodation on the part of both men and women, there are sure signs that marriage as an institution may in fact be firming up and gaining strength, although most are wary about saying that too loudly. When asked who is happier, a big 65%–18% majority of the entire adult public say married people, as opposed to singles. And when asked if they would remarry their spouse if they had to do it all over again, 85% of married people say they would. Contrary to what might be expected, however, 87% of men say they would remarry their wife, while a somewhat lower 76% of women say they would remarry their husband. These results do not suggest an institution that is on the way out. Somehow the bonds of marriage are stronger than conventional wisdom would have it, and, for all the strains and vagaries, marriage has much going for it. Indeed, the number of marriages appears to be increasing and the number of divorces decreasing since 1981, when the divorce rate reached the 50% mark. Since 1981, the number of divorces in the U.S. has declined each year, while the number of marriages has not. It is entirely possible that the worst for marriage may be over.

■ WHY DO PEOPLE GET MARRIED AND WHAT MAKES A GOOD MARRIAGE?

Over the years, the reasons people give for getting married and then their explanations for what makes a successful marriage have not changed much at all. In addition, men and women are by and large agreed on the optimum ingredients for a good marriage.

Here is what both men and women say are the compelling reasons why a man and a woman get married:

☐ "Love" is far and away the key, say a substantial 83%. Obviously, this has not changed much over the long spill of time; it still remains the indispensable impetus, nearly everyone believes, for getting married in the first place.

☐ "To like to be with a particular person" is a major reason given by 55% for getting married.

☐ "To have children" is a key, according to 44%.

☐ Other reasons are given far less frequently: 24% say that "it's an easier, more comfortable life, sharing responsibilities and income"; 21% that "it's a better way of living than being on your own"; 17%, "it's better than being lonely"; 11% believe it brings "economic security"; 14% do it to achieve "a satisfactory sexual relationship"; and 6% say "married couples have a better social life."

Many of the same themes can be seen in what people say makes a "good marriage":

☐ At the top of the list is "being in love," cited by 90% as the magic potion that holds marriages together.

☐ "Being able to talk about your feelings," reinforces the reason for marrying in the view of 84%.

☐ "Spousal sexual fidelity" is cited by 80% as a key to a good marriage.

☐ "Being able to see the humorous side of things" is important, according to 74%. Significantly, more women (77%) than men (71%) think you need to be able to laugh at yourself to survive in a marriage.

☐ Another 75% say the key is "to keep romance alive."

☐ 71% cite the importance of "having a good sexual relationship."

☐ 68% say a real key is "having similar ideas on raising children."

☐ 63% give importance to "your spouse understanding what you do every day."

☐ 64% believe a key is "having similar ideas on how to handle money."

☐ And 62% cite "having the same kind of life, activities, and friends."

☐ Then 56% believe a real key is "financial security."

☐ Curiously, two other items are cited by less than 50% as essential ingredients for a successful marriage. No more than 46% think that "having children" is a major criterion, and only 25% believe "having similar backgrounds" is critical.

■ DIVORCE AND WHO SHOULD KEEP
THE CHILDREN

Despite the popular, though mistaken, notion kept alive by the media, that divorce keeps increasing each year and marriage is its obvious victim, there is solid evidence that attitudes toward divorce are changing. For example, while 43%

of the country think that divorces should be no more difficult to get today than in the past, almost as many, 39%, think it should be more difficult to get divorced now, compared with 14% who say it should be easier. In addition, there is evidence that the acceptability of divorce as a way to resolve marital problems may have peaked back in 1980. Fifteen years ago 53% thought that divorce was an acceptable alternative. This rose to 60% in 1974 and stayed at that level through 1980. But by 1985 acceptability of divorce had dropped back to 56%.

The other change in opinion that has taken place is over who should get custody of the children in the event of a divorce. Back in 1974, 56% said that the mother and the father should be equally considered for custody and that a decision should be made to give the kids to one or the other parent. But a decade later, the number who felt that one parent or the other should be granted sole custody had dropped to a much lower 41%. Similarly, back in the mid-1970s, 21% thought that the mother should automatically get custody of all the children. But now that has dropped to 15%.

A new consensus, that the mother and the father should get joint custody is emerging, currently preferred by 27%. Significantly, more women (28%) opt for this solution than men (25%). This is a reflection of the real change in the role models that men and women were supposed to play in married life according to long tradition. The newfound independence of women obviously is being recognized.

OBSERVATION

It is perfectly obvious that as mobility has increased, as societal disapproval of broken marriages has faded away, as divorce has become a much more common and accepted event, the institution of marriage has come under enormous pressure. Yet the unexpected appears to be happening. With women moving inexorably into the workplace, with men having to share more of the burdens of running the household and raising the children, with both spouses in constant time binds over how to manage both work and family life, something inside both spouses appears to be surfacing that makes them dig in to make marriage work. Divorce is beginning to look more like a cop-out, while staying married seems more desirable. Women are probably the major key, in that they see marriage as an anchor point in an uncertain and ever-changing world both outside the home and in it. Men contribute to sustaining the marriage by demonstrating a real desire to stay married to the same woman and also in their feeling more than women that they are not capable of facing the loneliness of divorced status. All in all, the institution of marriage is far from shattered, and it is entirely likely that the divorce rate will continue to gradually decline.

America in the Eighties, conducted by R. H. Bruskin Associates, November 1985, among a national cross section of 1,900 adults.

Los Angeles Times Poll, conducted by the *Los Angeles Times,* December 5–12, 1985, among a national cross section of 2,308 adults.

The Virginia Slims American Women's Opinion Poll, conducted by the Roper Organization for Philip Morris Inc., among 3,000 women and 1,000 men, released 1985.

U.S. National Center for Health Statistics, *Vital Statistics of the United States,* annual and *Monthly Vital Statistics Report* as reported in U.S. Bureau of the Census, *Statistical Abstract of the United States, 1986* (Washington D.C., 1985), Table 124, Marriages and Divorces, 1960 to 1982, p. 79; Table 125, Marriages—Number and Rate by State, 1970 to 1983, p. 80; Table 126, Divorces and Annulments—Number and Rate, by State, 1970 to 1983, p. 81.

PARENTHOOD: A DIFFICULT STAGE OF LIFE

■ MAKING OUT AS A PARENT IN A DIFFERENT WORLD

At last count, the U.S. Census estimates that an even 50% of all households in the country have children under 18 years of age. In fully 41% of the households both the husband and the wife work.

But the flood of married women in the workplace has just begun. When working mothers are asked what they would do if family finances were not an issue, an overwhelming 82% say they would work anyway. Among nonworking women, fully 71% say they would prefer to be working, although roughly half would like part-time employment or the chance to do work in their own home. The point, however, is that there is every likelihood that by the 1990s, a majority of both spouses will be holding down full-time jobs. And by the turn of the century, as many as eight in ten of all families will have both husbands and wives working.

Making this trend virtually inevitable is the additional fact that with the slowdown in the birthrate, it is generally agreed by work force experts that the U.S. will face a serious shortage of available labor. In turn, this will necessitate the further tapping of two sources of new labor: women and the elderly.

With these facts, the bottom line for parenthood in the future suddenly becomes clear. The typical family will consist of both spouses working, with both taking periodic maternity and paternity leaves to raise children. But the central challenge will be how to keep a marriage going well, how to take care of home chores while both hold down jobs, and how to still find time to raise a family responsibly—in other words, how not only to satisfy the deep and natural desire to be a parent but also to find the time to give children the loving care and attention that will allow them to blossom into full and well-adjusted human beings.

■ CHILDREN: TO HAVE OR NOT TO HAVE

One of the very real pressures that are felt more keenly today than ever by young married people is just how to cope with children. This means planning carefully whether to have children or not, and if so, just how many to have and, finally, when to have them—early or late?

The thought of not having kids at all has passed through the minds of almost all young people soon after they marry. In fact, a big 78%–17% majority of both men and women concede that a childless marriage can be a happy one. So it is considered possible not to have to face the growing pressures of being a parent and still to have a good marriage.

But the underlying truth surfaces when both men and women are asked what would be the ideal number of children to have in a family, if financial and other problems were not a consideration. Only a bare 1 percent say that it would be ideal to have no children at all. Among the remaining 99%, the median ideal number now would be 2.8 children. This is down sharply from the 3.7 children thought to be ideal back in 1941.

Of course, what is ideal undoubtedly is not practical. So when both mothers and fathers are asked to give a realistic estimate of how many children they have or plan to have, the median is a somewhat lower 2.4. However, this barely tells the story. Among those 40 and over in age, the number of children they have or want rises to 2.7, then declines sharply to 2.2 among those 30 to 39, and down to 2.1 among those 18 to 29.

This means that among young marrieds, there is every likelihood that as more wives work, there will be fewer children. But the indelible fact remains: there will be children, and the job of being an effective and responsible parent has to be faced. This makes parenthood an increasingly difficult stage of life.

■ HAVING BABIES AND WORKING, TOO

Since 1974 there has been a dramatic increase in the number of women who have made a deliberate decision to approach married life far differently from their parents. Now a substantial 63% of all adult women say they want to "combine marriage, a career, and children," up from 52% who felt that way just over a decade earlier. By the same token, the number of women who opt for "marrying, having children, and no career" has dropped sharply from 38% to 26%. Even more significant is the fact that among those aged 30 to 49, a higher 66% say they want marriage, a career, and children, and among those under 30, an even higher 70% feel this way. This can only mean that the commitment to marrying, working, and bearing children will continue to grow into the future.

The strains on the mothers, however, are inevitable and telltale:

☐ By 2 to 1, they recognize the hard fact that "we would have a hard time economically if I didn't work."
☐ But by almost 3 to 1, they also add that "I feel I am a more interesting person to my husband or mate because I work."
☐ And by close to 3 to 1, they believe that "I may spend less

time with my children because I work, but I feel I give them as much as nonworking mothers because of the way I spend my time with them."

Today's women also stoutly deny some of the claims made by their critics:

☐ By 3 to 1, they reject the notion that "I feel I would be a better mother if I didn't work."
☐ By 6 to 1, they deny that "I feel that I would be a better wife if I didn't work."
☐ However, the real strain of it all shows when they divide almost evenly on the claim that "when I'm home I try to make up to my family for being away at work, and as a result I rarely have any time for myself."

■ PROBLEMS FOR WORKING MOTHERS TO COPE WITH

When a working mother has children, the issue of just who will care for the offspring while the mother is at work must be squarely faced early on. And it is never an easy matter.

Here is the way America's families with both spouses working solve the problem of who looks after the children: 25% leave the child with grandparents or other relatives; 21% report that the husband and wife work different hours so that one is always home to care for the kids; another 10% take their kids to a day-care center; 11% have a housekeeper at home to look after the children, 10% get a neighbor or friend to take the child; 8% report that one spouse works at home in order to be with the child; 7% have an older sister or brother look after the younger ones; 6% say that the kids take care of themselves after school until one of the parents gets home from work; and 5% send them off to nursery school.

Despite the publicity given some scandals at day-care centers in recent years, 96% of working parents nonetheless express satisfaction with the way child-care arrangements work out for their children and themselves. And a ringing 80%–11% majority say they favor the establishment of more day-care centers, up from 56% to 31% in 1970. Significantly, 42% of all nonworking women say they would look for work if there were more day-care centers where they live.

OBSERVATION

Clearly, the basic decision of women in America to undertake a career and not be content simply to get married and stay at home raising kids is changing the home environment and the institution of marriage radically in the 1980s. In fact, the changes will be even more acute and more universal by the 1990s.

Fundamentally, by exercising their option to pursue a career, get married, and have children, working women are placing upon themselves a burden that no other generation has assumed. Time obviously becomes the most important commodity. Yet it is not just a matter of juggling the job, the marital responsibilities, and the care of the children. The real art lies in making a significant contribution at work, fully satisfying the needs of a mate, and giving fully to children so that they grow up to be well-balanced and attractive people.

So far, young working mothers have not cracked under the strain. Husbands have not shouted out that they are being neglected. Children seem willing by and large to adapt to very different home circumstances. On the surface, at least, it seems to be working. However, it might take another five or ten years to really know how this truly heroic effort by young American women will work out.

But, make no mistake about it, the determination, the

resolve to do it and to make it work, burns deep in the new women growing up in the U.S. today. It now appears that the country is witnessing a radical and even revolutionary change in the basic role of women within the family unit.

Newsweek Poll, conducted by the Gallup Organization for *Newsweek,* February 5–11, 1986, among 1,009 women, released March 31, 1986.

Virginia Slims American Women's Opinion Poll, conducted by the Roper Organization for Philip Morris, Inc., among 3,000 women and 1,000 men, released 1985.

U.S. Bureau of Labor Statistics, *Employment and Earnings,* monthly and unpublished data as reported in U.S. Bureau of the Census, *Statistical Abstract of the United States, 1986* (Washington, D.C., 1985), Table: Employed Civilians by Selected Characteristics—1970 to 1984, p. 394.

HOW NICE TO HAVE A MAN AROUND THE HOUSE—IF HE SHARES THE CHORES

■ **SHARING IN ALL WAYS IS THE NEW NAME OF THE GAME**

Traditionally, the husband was always the breadwinner who brought home the family-support money. He was the king of the castle. And when he arrived home, not only was he given all due respect, but he would rarely lift a finger to do a household chore. Outdoor work, heavy labor, *manly* matters, of course, were his province. But the dirty work of cleaning up, cooking, washing dishes, changing baby's diapers, and a thousand other chores were simply not expected of the man of the house.

But beginning in the 1970s and now accelerating in the 1980s, a drastically changing environment has now overtaken the home. With a majority of adult women now at work, taking care of the home and children must be a shared responsibility. Solid majorities of both men and women say that is the case.

Of course, getting it all to happen is something else again. When asked directly about who does the household chores today, 41% of all women report that they do, another 41% say they do a lot and their husbands help some, 15% report the chores being evenly divided, and 2% say the husbands do more. Clearly, there is a gap between the recognition that equal sharing should be the name of the game and the reality of who in fact gets it all done.

However, it must be noted that in families where both

spouses are employed, among husbands a much lower 24% say the wife does nearly all the work around the house, a much higher 42% that the wife does the bulk of it but the husband helps some, and a lower 28% report that the work is evenly divided, and 5% that he actually does more around the house. This pattern of far greater sharing also is more prevalent among young married families under 30 years of age and among those who are college-educated.

■ SOME SIGNS OF THINGS TO COME

When both spouses work, 79% of both men and women report that both salaries are combined and used for all household expenses, personal expenses, and savings. Only 15% of men whose wives work say that they have an arrangement under which each contributes a part of their salaries for household and living expenses and savings, and then keeps the rest for themselves. Obviously, on financial matters, equal sharing of both salaries and expenses has become the order of the day. And the chances are high that this newfound equality will spread to other areas.

A completely radical idea is that ultimately some men will switch roles with women: the woman will become the breadwinner and the man will stay home and tend to the household chores. This extreme prospect has been surveyed since 1970. Back then, 63% said they would respect less a husband who stayed home, only 8% would respect him more, and 15% said it would make very little difference. By 1980 things had begun to change. A much lower 41% said they would respect the stay-at-home husband less, 6% more, but 42% about the same. By 1985 only 25% said they would respect a man who stayed home to do household chores less, 12% more, and a big 50% said the same.

Thus, the number who claim they would think less of a husband who switches roles with his wife and stays home to manage the household has dropped dramatically from 63% to

25% over a generation's time. What is more, the younger and more affluent men and women are, the less they are likely to say they will respect a stay-at-home husband less.

■ THE WAVE OF THE FUTURE: TEENAGERS LOOK AT SHARING CHORES

Attitudes toward change are usually formed early in life or no later than the teens. Therefore, it is significant to find that teenagers today have become convinced that the sharing of almost all household and child-rearing chores is what both young women and young men look forward to in married life.

Here is the lineup on household chores:

□ On vacuuming the house, only 40% of all teenagers think this should be the responsibility of the wife, compared with 38% who say both should do it, 2% who think the husband should do it, and 20% who believe it doesn't matter who does it. The point is that a 60%–40% majority does not think it is the duty of the wife to vacuum the house.

□ On mopping the house, an even 50% think that is solely a woman's chore, but an equal 50% do not think that should be the practice.

□ On preparing meals, 39% of the teenagers think this is a wife's responsibility, but a higher 46% see cooking as a distinctly shared future responsibility, 2% see it as primarily a man's task, and the remaining 13% say it doesn't matter.

□ On washing dishes, only 26% believe this is a woman's chore, compared with a much higher 60% who believe it is a duty to be shared equally.

□ On washing clothes, in other generations almost exclusively a woman's domain, no more than 54% of teenagers believe this is a wife's task, and 46%, nearly as many, do not agree with this assignment of duty.

□ On washing the car, traditionally a man's duty, now only 40% of all teenagers think the husband should do it. A

substantial 39% think the chore should be equally borne by both, led by 49% of teenage girls who feel this way; 2% think the woman should do it, and the rest say it doesn't matter.
□ On mowing the lawn, almost always the man's job around the house, a goodly 64% still agree with tradition and say let the husband do it. But 15% of the young men and a much higher 43% of young women simply don't agree with that. It is significant that teenage girls lead the way in feeling that many traditional men's chores should now be shared by women.

On caring for young children, the prevailing teenage view is that the chores should be shared all the way:

□ 91% of all teenagers are convinced that playing with children should be an equal responsibility of husbands and wives.
□ 71% are convinced that feeding babies and young children should be a joint duty of husbands and wives.
□ 64% of all teens believe that changing diapers should be shared all the way, although a much higher 78% of teenage girls think this, compared with a lower 50% of teenage boys.
□ 87% are convinced that disciplining young children should be a responsibility shared between men and women.
□ 56% believe that bathing a baby should be the equal and joint responsibility of husband and wife.
□ 73% think that putting the baby to bed should be done just as often by husbands as by wives.
□ 68% of all teenagers hold the view that putting a toddler to bed must be the shared responsibility of both spouses in a good marriage.

OBSERVATION

The U.S. has always taken a certain amount of justified pride in breaking the mold to bring about changes. Yet, one of the least recognized traditions in American culture is the introduction of radical and even permanent change without a bitter struggle over principle, but rather through pragmatic accommodation.

On the face of it, the public believes, it is very difficult for a young mother to work, take care of the household, and be primarily responsible for raising children. Patently, there simply is not enough time to do it all. And there is no doubt that most women in the future are going to opt to work, marry, and be mothers. Therefore, they conclude, tradition must give way and male spouses must step up and assume responsibilities that many of their fathers and certainly their grandfathers would have scoffed at and would have adamantly refused to do at all.

Women, especially young women, are determined to see the change come about. Even more fascinating is that males, particularly teenage boys, are coming around to agreeing with the women.

The significance of this trend is that right in the home, day in and day out, the reality of equality between the sexes is being forged. This newfound sharing is not simply a pious pronouncement of words and objectives. It is nothing less than the consummation of a revolution.

Jeanne Warren Lindsay, *Teens Look at Marriage: Rainbows, Roles and Reality* (Buena Park, Cal.: Morning Glory Press, 1985), a survey of a national cross section of 2,345 young women and 673 young men.

The Virginia Slims American Women's Opinion Poll, conducted by the Roper Organization among a national cross section of 3,000 women and 1,000 men, released 1985.

SMOKING: A SCOURGE BUT ALSO A CIVIL RIGHT?

■ THE STEADY DECLINE OF CIGARETTE SMOKING IN THE U.S.

Over the past two decades the number of people who smoke cigarettes has declined from 45% back in 1954 to a current 30% of all adult Americans. Fully two in every ten people who used to be regular smokers have now given up the habit. The falloff has been fairly uniform among all key groups in the population except young working women, among whom smoking has not only continued but has risen. The reason commonly cited for this phenomenon is that young women who aspire to hold down executive or professional jobs find themselves under unaccustomed stress and find some relief in smoking, that there is a perceived status associated with smoking, and that they believe that smoking kills appetite and calories, allowing a weight-conscious woman to stay thin. The only group among whom lung cancer is now rising is young women.

The cause of the decline in smoking is not hard to find: a nearly unanimous 94%–4% majority of the American people are convinced, as the labels say, that "cigarettes are harmful to your health."

■ THE DRIVE TO ISOLATE SMOKERS

As the antismoking campaign has gained momentum in the country, so have various local ordinances that would restrict smoking in the presence of nonsmokers. These have ranged from the outright prohibition of smoking in public places to isolating smokers on airplanes, at work, and in public places, theaters, and elsewhere.

Yet, in the fervor of this abolitionist movement, few have suggested an outright ban on smoking. Indeed, no more than 8% would ban all smoking in the workplace, for example. And virtually no one has seriously suggested banning the sale of cigarettes and other smoking materials. Whenever a total ban on smoking has been proposed, majorities of between seven and eight out of every ten have consistently opposed it. The reason most commonly given is that "people ought to have the right to kill themselves from smoking if that is their choice." Much the same reasoning is given for the equally pronounced opposition to the proposal of banning the sale of alcoholic beverages.

If it is the case that Americans do not want to outlaw the sale of cigarettes, pipes, tobacco, and cigars, then the issue comes down to just how far people want to go to restrict, isolate, or confine people when they smoke.

■ RESTRICTIONS ON WHERE PEOPLE CAN SMOKE

The number of Americans who agree that smokers should refrain from smoking in the presence of nonsmokers has risen from a 69%–25% majority in 1983 to a current 75% to 24%. However, it is important to note that the number who feel very strongly about restricting smokers' rights comes to no more than 33%, up only 2 points in the past two years. This would indicate that while the basic set of public opinion is decidedly in the camp of the antismokers, nonetheless smoking does not appear to arouse a deep antipathy among any number close to a majority. At the same time, the pro-smoking cause obviously has by now clearly lost the battle to allow no restraints or restrictions on the right of people to smoke.

Even a 62%–37% majority of current smokers is willing to accept restrictions on where and when they can smoke.

Yet, oddly enough, despite the overwhelming view that smoking is harmful to one's health and the clear mandate for restraining the rights of smokers to indulge their habit, there is only one place where a clear majority support in fact restricting smoking. That is in an enclosed public gathering place, where a 62% majority of the entire adult population favors forcing people to refrain from smoking.

No more than 34% of the entire public favors forcing smokers to refrain from smoking at work. And only 19% would like to restrict the right to smoke in the home. Even among those who have never smoked, the group most likely to be hostile, only 38% would request smokers to refrain from their habit at work, and only 24% would restrict people's right to smoke in the home.

The solution that the public obviously opts for is to assign certain areas at work for smokers to indulge their habit. Fully 79% of the public nationwide would favor this solution, although 12% would be against any such policy. But no more than 8% would place a flat ban on smoking, including only 12% of nonsmokers.

■ THE QUESTION OF CIGARETTE ADVERTISING

When asked directly, no more than 32% of the American public would put a total ban on all advertising of cigarettes. There is a current ban on television and radio advertising of cigarettes, but no ban in the other media. Recently a movement has been started to lobby for that total ban, but at the moment, that group has two thirds of the American people against it.

Instead, 36% of the public would favor curbing some types or forms of cigarette advertising, presumably those ads which suggest that good things are associated with smoking. But a significantly high 31% of the public wants no ban at all on smoking acts and might even welcome a return of cigarette advertising on TV and radio. Even among nonsmokers, only 39% favor a total ban on cigarette advertising.

OBSERVATION

It is obviously clear that a sizable majority of Americans eschew cigarette smoking and want no part of it for themselves. Almost everyone in the country is convinced that cigarettes are harmful to one's health. There is no contention whatsoever over requiring health warnings in all cigarette advertising and on all packs that are sold.

The antismoking drive has placed the entire tobacco industry on the defensive, to the point where it seems it is fighting for its very life. Yet, when asked about an outright ban on smoking, only 8% nationwide are takers. And when asked about asking or even forcing smokers to refrain from smoking, only in the case of public places can a majority be mustered, and that comes to 62%, while 34% would support a similar ban on smoking at work. But only a small 19% minority would place similar bans on smoking in the home.

In other words, while sizable majorities say they back restraints on smokers, when it comes down to it the restrictions desired appear to be highly limited and even mild. The latest charges that smoke exhaled by smokers can cause lung cancer have not yet achieved real currency. No more than 33% of the public appear to be intensely concerned about the smoking issue, despite the steady falloff in smoking and the fact that less than one third of the adult public indulge in the habit.

What seems to be the case is that the American people feel strongly about the right of people to smoke if they want to. This is the deep-seated sense of pluralism rising to the surface. Most Americans are wedded to the notion that people ought to have the freedom to choose many different pathways, depending on what suits their tastes. The only restrictions people basically place upon others is when their practice jeopardizes the capacity of others to enjoy their freedom of choice. Even though 94% think smoking is harmful to the health of those who do it, it is apparent that the vast majority today do not want to prohibit the minority who want to indulge in it. Their attitude is very much like the attitude toward prohibition of alcoholic beverages, which led to repeal.

It is strange to think of smoking as a civil right, but that seems to be precisely how the American people see it. They want to confine smoking to smaller and smaller areas, but they will not opt to take from smokers their right to smoke.

Survey of Attitudes Toward Smoking, conducted by the Gallup Organization for the American Lung Association, July 1985, among a national cross section of 1,540 adults.

The Harris Survey, conducted by Louis Harris and Associates, September 4–7, 1986, among a national cross section of 1,255 adults, unreleased.

DO MOST AMERICANS ENVY THE CROOKED YUPPIE INSIDE TRADERS?

■ A MATTER OF PURE GREED

Why would a 33-year-old investment banker making a million dollars a year and with $10 million in the bank—a man who knew federal investigators were closing in on him—keep making illegal insider trades, testing his luck and testing the system? Dennis Levine did just this. He was caught and pleaded guilty, and now his career is destroyed. Several other young Wall Street bankers and lawyers have also been indicted for insider trading.

The legal status of insider trading is simple: it is against the law for someone to make a profit from confidential information about a company that is not available to other potential investors—such as that it is about to be acquired, is the object of a takeover bid, or is poised for a major change in its fortunes.

When a cross section of the American people were asked why the Yuppies on Wall Street did it, 56% of them answered, "Pure greed"; 21% said, "Many others on Wall Street were doing the same thing"; 11% thought it was because "they made too much money at an early age." Only 6% thought they were "criminal by nature."

Two pervasive assumptions emerged in the survey. One belief, shared by a 63%–26% majority of the country, is that such insider trading on Wall Street is a common occurrence.

Indeed, Dennis Levine kept telling his accomplices, "Don't worry about it, everybody's doing it." In other words, don't miss the boat, get on board, get it while it lasts. The other is that somehow the country has bred a generation of Yuppies whose lust for making it big is so powerful that virtually nothing, legal or not, will stand in the way of their realizing their ambition—a view subscribed to by 44% of the public.

However it is described, it adds up to nothing less than a dominant theme of the 1980s: Make it fast, make it now, get it all. Pure greed.

■ WOULD YOU DO IT IF YOU HAD THE CHANCE?

A cross section of the American people were faced with this proposition: "Suppose someone got a tip from a friend that the company he or she works for was going to be purchased for a lot more money than its current stock price." When asked what they think *most* Americans would do in that situation, a big 82% to 14% said most people would buy the stock—even though they knew it was illegal to do so.

Finally, the same people were asked what they themselves would do. Without much hesitation, a 53%–42% majority said they would buy it, too—even though they knew it was illegal to do so. A much higher 64% of those earning $50,000 a year and over would make such a buy, as would 61% of all men, 60% of college graduates, 61% of those who now own stock, and 58% of the Yuppies. In other words, the more affluent people are, the more privileged, the higher their status in society, the more they potentially have to lose by being sent to jail like Dennis Levine, the more likely they would be to engage in insider stock trading.

No wonder that 84% of the public concluded that the whole insider scandal had not given them a lower opinion of the ethics of those who work on Wall Street. Indeed, even among the minority who said they would not engage in insider trad-

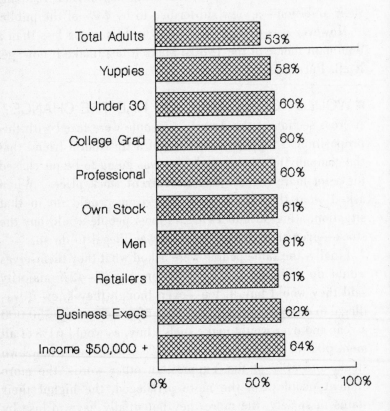

WOULD YOU ENGAGE IN ILLEGAL INSIDE TRADING IF YOU GOT A TIP?

Total Adults	53%
Yuppies	58%
Under 30	60%
College Grad	60%
Professional	60%
Own Stock	61%
Men	61%
Retailers	61%
Business Execs	62%
Income $50,000 +	64%

0% 50% 100%

ing, 37% said the reason was that "the tip might not be any good." No more than an equal 37% could bring themselves to say that "it's just plain wrong to do it."

In fact, after having thought hard about the insider issue, having pondered the illegality of it all, when the same cross section was asked which of six key types in society has the lowest ethical standards, those who work on Wall Street finished better than all but one. Only 7% billed them most unethical, while doctors were named by an even lower 5%. Heading the list were politicians at 43%, then lawyers at 16%, reporters at 10%, and corporate executives at 8%.

OBSERVATION

By the latter half of the 1980s, it is patent that making a lot of money has become so accepted and common an American goal that traditional ethical standards appear to have become its casualty. More surprising, perhaps, than the fact that a clear majority would opt to commit an illegal act is that only a small minority is shocked and dismayed by cases like that of Dennis Levine. Indeed, the overtones of the responses suggest that the only thing wrong with Levine and the other young men was that they got caught. Otherwise, it is equally evident that they might well be among the more admired people in their generation—because they were making it big in the money world.

But it would be unfair to single out young Wall Street investment bankers as the arch-villains of the piece. After all, according to the American people themselves, politicians, lawyers, reporters, and top businessmen are all less ethical than Wall Street types, who are perceived by two out of every three Americans as insider traders.

The country has had similar binges of wanting to strike it rich quick, most notably in the late 1920s, just before the stock market crash of 1929. Whether or not this latest surge of greed is a prelude to another crash and another sobering up remains to be seen. But one thing is sure: making a lot of money is viewed as one of the pure, unmitigated pleasures. Just one caveat: *Don't get caught.*

Business Week/Harris Poll, conducted by Louis Harris and Associates, August 5–11, 1986, among a national cross section of 1,248 adults, released August 25, 1986.

MASSIVE NEGLECT OF CHILDREN: IT'S NO JOKE WHEN WE TAKE W. C. FIELD'S NOSTRUMS SERIOUSLY

■ THE AMERICAN PEOPLE ASSESS THE LOT OF CHILDREN

In the stress-ridden, alienated, and frenetic times that are the 1980s, the older people get, the more they are likely to compare the present with the good old days when they were growing up. Sizable numbers of people currently believe that many things have become worse since they were young. For example, 33% think that the quality of education is now worse, 43% say unemployment has grown worse, and 52% believe family life is worse today.

But the worsening of all of these problems pales before yet another: 74% of the American people are convinced that the problems affecting children have grown worse compared with what they were when they themselves were young. Two groups feel most keenly about this: women, 79% of whom believe it, and blacks, 84% of whom think the lot of children has deteriorated. Significantly, parents and nonparents do not differ much in their assessment of the status of children.

Not only are the problems of children in contemporary America viewed as serious and getting worse, but sizable numbers feel that the troubles of young people have been largely tucked out of sight, in a kind of massive studied avoidance. People were asked if society spends too little, too much, or about the right amount of effort on the problems of various groups:

□ 73% think the U.S. spends too little effort on the problems of the elderly.

□ 67% believe too little effort has been devoted to the problems of the poor.

□ 63% say that too little effort has been directed toward the problems of children.

In their own intuitive way, the American people have identified precisely those pockets of humanity—the poor and children—as the objects of particular neglect. Indeed, children who live in conditions of poverty stand out in stunning contrast to the affluence that is the singular mark of postindustrial America.

The latest Census Bureau estimates (1985) describe the impact of poverty upon the lot of children. An estimated 33 million people live below the poverty line. Among all families with no children 5.5% are classified as living in poverty. But among all those families with related children under 18, a much higher 20% are living in poverty. This means that for a child under 18, the chances are nearly three times as great of living in poverty as for an adult.

■ HOW CHILDREN SUFFER

The perceived shortchanging of children by contemporary American society emerges sharply when people are asked about it:

□ No more than 40% of all adults feel that children get a good education.

□ Only 36% think that most children live in a safe neighborhood.

□ No more than 58% believe that most children get medical treatment when they need it.

□ Only a bare 53% think most children have loving parents.

□ And only 48% believe that most children are basically happy.

And significant numbers think that the problems children face are rising, not declining:

□ 40% hold the view that hunger, certainly one of the most degrading experiences of the human race, is increasing for children.

□ 57% believe that physical abuse of children by parents is on the rise.

□ 71% are convinced that sexual assault of children is increasing.

□ 72% believe that kidnapping of children by strangers is going up.

□ 76% think that child prostitution is on the rise.

□ 80% feel that child pornography is increasing.

Studies by committees of Congress, particularly those conducted by Congressman George Miller (D. Cal.), strikingly bear out the impressions of the public: the problems of children have accelerated and multiplied, growing progressively worse with each passing year.

■ THE TARGETS OF PUBLIC WRATH OVER THE NEGLECT OF CHILDREN

The public was asked to assess the efforts of key groups in meeting their responsibilities to children:

□ Churches far and away are thought to be doing the best job, but only a bare 53%–42% majority rates church efforts positive.

□ Community organizations come up only a barely 50% to 47% positive on their efforts to help children.

□ Parents are given a negative rating of 55% to 43% in their efforts to meet their responsibilities toward their offspring.

□ Local government is accorded a negative rating of 65% to 34% in caring about children.

□ At the bottom of the heap in meeting its responsibilities to children is the federal government, given a big 69% to 28% negative.

■ THE CENTRAL ROLE OF GOVERNMENT IN HELPING CHILDREN

The American people are hardly at a loss to come up with remedies. In an era not marked by public attempts to find governmental solutions to many problems, in the case of children, people are so desperate that they are calling out for government to step into the breach in many ways:

□ By 93% to 5%, they want government to institute national tracing for missing children.

□ By 90% to 9%, they want government to provide more health coverage for children who cannot get health insurance.

□ By 88% to 11%, a big majority wants government to provide day-care services for children of poor working mothers.

□ By 70% to 29%, they want government to provide birth control services for teenagers.

Specifically, most Americans have very clear ideas on what they want government to spend more money on in order to reverse the neglect of young people:

□ 72% support spending more government funds on job training for teenagers.

□ 60% want to spend more government funds on the public schools.

□ 56% favor spending more government money on prenatal care for poor mothers.

□ 51% want to spend more government money on immunization for children.

□ A plurality of 42% wants to spend more government funds on welfare assistance for poor families with children, such as those on Aid to Families with Dependent Children (AFDC).

Nor is this public request for higher government expenditures an irresponsible pie-in-the-sky expression of sympathy that people hold as long as it won't cost them a thing. By 76% to 22%, a majority would be willing to increase their own taxes to give more money to the public schools. By 73% to 26%, a majority would pay higher taxes to provide more day-care programs.

OBSERVATION

It is obvious from these results that the American people have come to a new consciousness about children, a long-forgotten minority that has been largely without a voice. These results indicate clearly that the public is ready for leadership to emerge that will call upon them to make those sacrifices necessary for government and the private sector to take action in behalf of children.

Striking is the fact that big majorities want to help not only children generally, but particularly those who are living in poverty. It is highly doubtful that such results as these could have been obtained in a poll 5 or 6 years ago. But it is evident the times are changing more rapidly than might have been imagined. Politicians who ignore these pleadings from the American people do so at their own peril. This is a poignant and plaintive demand that simply will not go away.

Children's Needs and Public Responsibilities: A Survey of American Attitudes about the Problems and Prospects of American Children, conducted by Louis Harris and Associates for Group W—Westinghouse Broadcasting Company, July 29–August 7, 1987, among a national cross section of 1,254 adults released September 1986.

U.S. Department of the Census, *The Current Population Reports: Consumer Income,* Series P60, no. 154, "Money, Income and Poverty Status of Families and Persons in the U.S.: 1985."

THE STRESSFUL BUT HOPEFUL STATE OF ALL THINGS NEAR AND DEAR TO US AS INDIVIDUALS

■ WHAT A DIFFERENCE TWENTY YEARS CAN MAKE

In the last half of the 1980s the baby boom generation is no longer young but is rapidly approaching middle age. The hippies of the 1960s have turned into the Yuppies of the 1980s.

Twenty years ago young people claimed they had no use for the affluence their parents' generation had worked so hard to achieve. Of course, underneath that façade of antimaterialism and antiestablishment sentiment, young people insisted on not giving up the wheels that got them around and they needed money to buy the latest rock tapes. The language was antimaterialist, but the habits stemmed from basic and deep commitments to materialism.

It is important to recognize this continuity in the acquisition of goods and services, for it is the basis of postindustrial society. Indeed, the singular mark of this society, which now primarily earns its living not from the production of basic goods, but instead from rendering services in the financial, health, educational, governmental, and other services areas, is that most physical needs are easily satisfied and will be readily accommodated.

Much was written a generation ago about a "me" generation, which was only concerned with ego involvements and ego fulfillments. The claim was that self-indulgence was so rampant that a sense of a larger community and an obligation to help one's fellow human beings would soon perish from the U.S. There are some today who would claim that the "me" phenomenon of yesterday produced the Yuppie phenomenon of today and a whole generation of young people has been created whose material aspirations dominate their own lives and those of the rest of society.

■ MAKING IT BIG

In the results reported in this book, there certainly is ample evidence that the importance of making it big, even making it big and greedy, is close to a given in today's society. Prevailing sentiment is widely recognized by eight in ten people and can be summed up thus: to make a lot of money is not only desirable, it is the "in" thing to do. To make money by skirting the intent and even the letter of the law is in itself a vicarious thrill. In a 1984 *Business Week/Harris Poll* 53% of all Yuppies admitted that they did their own income taxes so that they could cheat—no CPA or tax consultant would countersign their IRA returns. A big 82% of the entire adult population are convinced that if most Americans had the chance, they would engage in insider trading on Wall Street, even though it is illegal. A solid majority also agree with convicted Yuppie Dennis Levine, who justified his making $12.6 million from illegal insider trading by saying, "Why, everybody is doing it."

It has reached the point that 53% of the adult public say they would take the risk and try to make a killing by buying stock through inside information. More startling is that 64% of those in the highest income group would engage in insider trading, as would 61% of all those who currently own stock and 58% of all Yuppies.

The era has produced the kind of leadership that encourages attitudes such as these, and these attitudes in turn spawn new leadership that makes the notion of making it big at any cost more deeply ingrained.

Put bluntly, in these Reagan years especially, society has put a premium on making it big, not being a bit shy about flaunting wealth and high style, and making as big a splash as possible in personal appearance and life-style.

■ MAKING SURE OTHERS THINK YOU LOOK GREAT

Back in the 1960s, today's baby boom generation revolutionized the dress of the nation by taking to long hair and jeans, and eschewing neckties and formal clothing. All in all, they staged a full-fledged revolt against the gray flannel suits and bow ties worn by daddy. After a score of years the jeans have survived but they are now expensive designer jeans. Long hair for men perished when Middle Americans assumed the look, so now short hair is back in style. The dress of the 1960s was meant to shock a generation of parents. The dress of the 1980s is meant partly to shock by bringing attention to Yuppie women's clothes by the most fashionable department stores and boutiques. Young women then become the mirror image of the ads and the mannequins in the store windows.

Now, 20 years later, people are showing more signs of individual vanity than at any time since the 1920s. Two out of every three people in the country are literally obsessed with how they look. Many more women than men possess this concern, as might be expected. But a majority of 54% of men feel this way, too. Given these statistics, it should come as no surprise at all that this deep concern about physical appearance has led 94% of all men and 99% of all women to wish they could change something about their physical appearance.

Both men and women would like to change their weight,

which is almost always higher than desired. That means changing their waistlines, too. Women also worry about the size of their thighs and buttocks; men, in turn, worry about not having enough muscle on their bodies. But almost as serious a concern, especially for women, is to find ways that will cover up any and all signs of aging. Wrinkles are a symbol of defeat—except in a linen suit, where they are a mark of distinction.

In the past, materialism and vanity were taken as sure signs of the decline and fall of a civilization. Yet the pressures of conformity in the 1980s strongly encourage women and men to be concerned with their looks and to measure their progress by their money funds, their financial assets, and, above all, by how affluent they *look*. The *look* has become every bit as important as the substance of the life itself. And even more important than making lots of money is making it in a way that beats the establishment, even the law.

What is more, this contagion is spreading from the baby boom generation to those who were born in the mid- to late-1960s. Materialism and good looks, affluence and preppy smartness, acquisitions that are *not* traditional possessions and high skill in playing Trivial Pursuit, living well and, above all, having people *know* you are living well—therein lies the key to what you are supposed to be in the latter part of the 1980s.

As has probably been true for all generations and in all times, the leavened truth, the reality, is quite different. Indeed, the signs all indicate that a massive revolt is in the offing that will kick over the vestiges of excessive materialism and showy demeanor—once again.

■ THE PRICE OF LIVING UP TO WHAT YOU'RE SUPPOSED TO BE

To make it big means to work hard. There's no easy or quick fix, even for business school or law school hotshots who can begin their careers these days with a Wall Street investment or law firm at as high as $100,000 a year. Even though there may be a pot of gold at the end of the rainbow, long hours, dislocation of family life, and enormous application of talent and training are all bedrock requirements.

In turn, the pressure to succeed means that the workweek in the U.S. has grown longer, not shorter. The dream of previous generations that everyone would end up working 35-hour weeks, then 30-hour weeks—a vision highly popular with certain academics in the late 1940s and 1950s—obviously has perished. The work week has risen from an average 40.6 hours per week spent at work in 1973 to a current 48.8 hours, a rise of 20%—8.2 hours per week or one hour and 10 minutes a day.

The people who work the hardest and the longest are not those at the bottom of the wage ladder, but rather are executives, professionals and retailers—those who make the most money and live the most prosperous lives. Small-business executives work over 57 hours a week; professional people, Yuppies, and those earning $50,000 and over, more than 52 hours a week.

By the same token, leisure time is rapidly slipping away. Between 1973 and 1985 it dropped from 26.2 to 17.7 hours per week, a loss of 8.5 hours a week or one hour and 12 minutes a day. And the very same people whose work hours have increased the most have paid for it by having their leisure hours eroded the most.

This trend means more work and less play. But it also means more time away from home and therefore, now that more wives are working, less time to get the chores done. And it means less time to spend with one's spouse. In short, it means packing much more into a day at work and at home, and especially into the limited time available for vital human relationships with spouses, children, and friends.

■ THE PERVASIVENESS OF STRESS

The price of these pressures is not hard to find. Stress is now a mass phenomenon in American society. Fully 90% of all adult Americans, a substantial 158 million people, report experiencing high stress, with as many as six in every ten reporting "great stress" at least once or twice every week.

It should be noted well that close to twice as many high-income as low-income people suffer from stress. The more educated people are, the more certain they are to be afflicted with stress. Whites feel more stressed than blacks, although the latter have much cause to feel stress in the 1980s. Professional and executive types suffer more from stress than those in any other type of occupation.

Stress means misery to nearly everyone who has it: seizures of anxiety, tension, nervousness, headaches, anger, irritability, fatigue, depression, muscle aches, stomachaches, an increased heartbeat, insomnia, a rise in blood pressure, compulsive eating, loss of appetite, a pervasive sense of upset. Fully 40% of all those with stress report having trouble getting enough sleep at night.

The braver but perhaps the more foolish among the professional types ignore stress. They view it as just part of the baggage you agree to carry if you want to make it. But more sober types try to cope with it, girding themselves for the onslaught when it comes, taking physical steps to relieve it, or engaging in studied avoidance of stressful situations. They coach themselves *not* to get all stressed out when crises occur, they escape into hobbies to get away from it all, they read or create, they try to focus on what really is cause of their anxiety, they meditate or pray, they play or listen to music. They learn breathing exercises, slow down their physical pace, learn to relax in a hurry. They seek out friends who soothe rather than bruise their egos, stay away from social situations that re-create the same stressful conditions they confront at work, and quietly seek counsel to spill out their woes.

Stress has become a common denominator in modern American society. Obviously, it is taking a severe physical, mental, and emotional toll on the movers and shakers of society and the literally millions more who have set their sights on qualifying for that rarefied status.

■ CASUALTIES IN THE SOCIAL ARENA

There are still other costs of our current life-style, not always apparent. Patterns of socializing with friends, relatives, and neighbors are affected by the hours people work. The more we work, of course, the less time we have for socializing. Yet the people who work the longest hours also generate the most stress on themselves and therefore most need the relaxation of spending time with friends in a stress-free environment.

But our attitudes about social visiting are also ambivalent. While young people, singles, and women who are homemakers like to entertain, a majority of people are not comfortable in many social settings and even find them stressful. For example, seven in ten say that they feel uncomfortable being thrust into conversational roles and that they worry about others judging how they look, and a higher eight in ten just don't like to be the center of attention.

Just below the surface, there is an innate shyness in the vast majority of Americans, particularly in social situations. Yet, in the bang-bang world of making it big, with leisure sharply curtailed, people must endure strong pressure to "perform" in social situations, which, of course, is likely to generate more stress. The net effect is to reduce drastically the social opportunities for genuine relaxation and pleasure. Obviously, too many people, particularly in the more affluent sectors of society, move from a high-stress setting at work right into high-stress social situations.

■ IN A SEA OF AFFLUENCE, A DEEP SENSE OF POWERLESSNESS

In the frenetic environment into which most Americans are now thrust, where the pressures are immense to get many things done in too little time, it is obviously difficult at best to feel a sense of having deep roots, of belonging, and of making a contribution to the larger community in which one lives. The singular mark of modern society is that it is so complex, that the gap between the power centers where leaders make far-reaching decisions and the arenas in which most people live out their ordinary lives is so great that many simply feel left out of it all. The high irony is that no previous generation has had so much of the world at its doorstep, on television and in print, so many opportunities to travel to places other generations never dreamed of visiting, such affluence as Americans have today. Yet, in a sea of ambition and affluence, the vast majority of Americans feel a deep and pervasive sense of being powerless.

A substantial 60% of the adult public feel this sense of alienation, up sharply from only 29% who felt that way 20 years ago. There is a deep belief that American society has two tiers of justice, privilege, and affluence—one for the rank and file and another for the "insiders" in the seats of power in Washington, Wall Street, and corporate boardrooms. Watergate indelibly burned into a whole generation's consciousness the lesson that if you are rich or powerful, you go scot-free, but if you are not, you'll get hounded all the way. Obviously, groups like blue-collar workers, 67% of whom feel alienated, or blacks, 71% of whom feel powerless, or the elderly, 64% of whom feel that way, are more affected than the more affluent. But a substantial 48% of those earning the highest incomes, $50,000 and over, also feel alienated—a figure that has more than quadrupled over the past two decades.

■ THE BOTTOM LINE OF SATISFACTION

While on the surface, a healthy 63% of the American people report that their life is highly satisfying, another 35%, some 62 million people, say their life is not a very happy lot. The older people get, however, the more satisfied they are. Young people tend to be far less happy, as are women, particularly working mothers, lower-income people, and racial minorities.

Good health and personal achievement are widely seen as the keys to happiness, with wealth trailing far behind. However, it should be noted that those in economic trouble express far less satisfaction with their lives. On a whole series of key dimensions there are now distinct signs of deterioration in our satisfaction with life: the numbers of us who are pleased with our friendships, health and physical condition, leisure activities, and place of residence have all been declining over the past decade.

But the distinction between those who are satisfied with their lot and those who are not lies not so much with specific aspects of happiness. The real divider is stress. A big 74% of those with low stress report being really satisfied with their lives; among those with high stress, no more than 32% are satisfied. This means that as long as stress seemingly goes hand in hand with economic success and making it big, then real happiness will be an elusive and ephemeral goal for many in the U.S. The happiest people are those with the least stress, but they are a disappearing breed in America in the latter part of the 1980s.

■ OUT OF SHAPE AND NUTRITIONALLY BACKWARD

Most people think they are not much overweight—but they are wrong. When you don't ask them about it, but simply plot their height and weight on charts that indicate what authorities believe are acceptable weights, 62%, 109 million adults, are overweight—and at considerable risk for a variety of health problems. Predictably, those who are overweight tend to have the least nutritious diets and also get the least exercise.

This evidence flies in the face of widespread reports that an increasing number of Americans lately have begun to learn how to exercise properly and that at long last the country is emerging from nutritional illiteracy. Little appears to have been learned. And little of what has been learned has been applied.

A substantial 77% of Americans claim they exercise regularly. But a closer look at the regimen they follow cuts their ranks to no more than 30% who really take serious exercise. A majority of 58% is sedentary.

At home, Americans' favorite food is still beef, even though beef consumption has been declining for 20 years. Beef is followed by poultry, pasta, fish and other seafood, pork, and vegetables. Taste and ease of preparation are the prime considerations in picking a favorite food, with nutritional value third.

But our choice of a favorite main course hardly begins to tell the story of food habits in the American home. A majority of 54% report regularly eating snack foods, with nuts, grains, and popcorn most popular, followed by ice cream, fruits and vegetables, chips and pretzels, baked goods, and candy and sweets. Taste is the trigger reason people pick a snack food, followed by nutritional value.

American people really give away their state of nutrition, though, when they relate what they eat when they go to a restaurant for what most call a "treat." A high 37% of all adults eat one meal a day away from home. The two most popular places to eat are "family-style restaurants" and fast-food places. Higher-income people, young people, and employed women eat out most often.

When eating out, people order meat most often, led by steak or roast beef, followed by fish, shellfish, chicken, and pasta. But the real clue to food tastes emerged when people were asked to name their favorite dishes in "home-style restaurants." At the top of the list was mashed potatoes, followed by home-fried potatoes, then beef stew, meat loaf, baked beans, and stuffed peppers.

Finally, a growing practice, especially with working mothers and young people, is to order take-out food for eating at home—usually hamburgers, soda pop, french fries, fried chicken, and pizza—by and large junk food from fast-food chains.

Ironically, when asked what they *should* be eating, a majority of people are able to come up with a goodly and healthy mix of chicken and fish, fresh vegetables and fruits, not a lot of fried foods and cholesterol-laden dishes. But much of this appears to be lip service. When they get inside a supermarket or especially when they go out to eat, the American people revert to what can only be viewed as a nutritionally disastrous diet. When such eating habits are combined with rising stress, the chances of cutting the rate of heart attacks, high blood pressure, and other health problems that decrease the life span would appear to be slim at best.

There is one notable exception to the general pattern, one group who are taking seriously what nutrition and health authorities have to say: pregnant women. Better than eight in ten say they take special care of their diet during pregnancy, with two in every three reporting they achieve the weight goals set for them by their physicians. Roughly half now breast-feed their babies, yet another health incentive. Sizable numbers of pregnant women also report giving up smoking, alcoholic beverages, drinks with caffeine. They may not follow all the instructions to the letter, but, by and large, pregnant women are doing a highly creditable job of taking care of themselves. Would that the remainder of the population followed their example. Unfortunately, that is just not the case; in their food and exercise habits, the U.S. clearly is a nation at risk.

■ THE STATE OF OUR UNIONS

It is popular among many sociologists and other "experts" to continue making the sweeping generalization that has been prevalent for close to a generation, that the American family is crumbling, that divorce and separation are on a long-term rise, and that the institution of marriage is in deep trouble.

This conventional wisdom does not square with the actual trends of the past five years. Some so-called authorities say that the period from 1981 to 1985 is an artifact, only a temporary blip in a much longer pattern. It is my view that social scientists must make a hard choice: Either go by the data or get out of the business.

And the hard evidence shows some significant and surprising trends: the divorce rate is coming down steadily and the rate of marriage is steady or even rising. The record also shows that 90% of all marriages survive. This does not mean that marriage as an institution is out of trouble. But neither can it be said blithely that marriage is on the way out or that divorce has taken over, as so many claim. The evidence, albeit from only a four-year period, indicates just the opposite.

The evidence also suggests some reasons why lasting marriages may be on the upswing. Now a majority of married people are convinced that marriage is no longer an arrangement whereby the husband assumes the breadwinning responsibilities and the wife takes over the household management and childrearing. To the contrary, both men and women are now convinced that a marriage in which both husband and wife work and share the housekeeping and child care is a better one. Both married and single people overwhelmingly prefer marriage to single status. More than eight in ten, and a higher percentage of men than women, would remarry their current spouse if they could do it all over again. Conventional wisdom would have it that as mobility increases, as more and more women have to work, husbands and wives will inevitably drift apart, especially given the necessity of coping with children and household chores in more limited time. Yet the unexpected appears to be happening. Hard-pressed spouses are digging in and working all the harder to keep their marriages intact and to care for their children in a responsible manner. Women are the key to making it work, and they appear to be gearing their attitudes and behavior to make a go of it. To declare the demise of the institution of marriage would, it seems, be vastly premature.

■ THE CRISIS OVER CHILDREN

For nearly a generation now, there has been a gradual but steady decline in the attention that society has paid to children. The public school system, beset with lower enrollments because of the lower birthrate, attracted a poorer quality of teachers who in turn delivered a poorer quality of education to students who learned less and dropped out more. Less heed was paid to drug usage among young people as the use of marijuana, heroin, uppers, and downers seemed to level out and even decline somewhat. Young people were having children later, so that the centerpiece of family life was not the kids, but how to cope with both spouses working.

At the same time, seemingly out of benign neglect, the *real* problems of children began to soar. The phenomenon of missing children coincided with young people turning up on big-city streets, having become involved in pornography or prostitution—often after having been taken in by shelters for wayward children. After much attention to the family and the workplace in the late 1970s, there seemed to be a decline in emphasis on the need for child-care facilities for the offspring of working mothers. Government-sponsored lunch programs for poor children were cut back. Campaigns were mounted against sex education in the schools, birth control services for teenagers, and spending for immunization programs for young schoolchildren. There seemed not to be a significant constituency speaking consistently for children. Those organizations advocating help for children seemed to be distant voices almost from another era.

But as happened with the elderly early in the 1970s and blacks in the 1960s, somehow out of this neglect there has arisen a public recognition of the plight of children, which promises to become a major and lasting public concern.

Here are some of the key facts: 74% of all adults think the problems now besetting children have grown worse. A substantial 63% believe too little effort has been made to solve those problems. Only 4 in 10 think most children are getting a good education, only a little over 1 in 3 feel that most children live in safe neighborhoods, fewer than 6 in 10 think they receive adequate and timely medical care, only slightly more than 5 in 10 think most children have loving parents, and less than half think most children are basically happy. At the same time, sizable numbers also believe that all the problems facing children are increasing: hunger, sexual assault, kidnapping, child prostitution, and child pornography. Authorities confirm that this impression is correct.

As often happens when the public suddenly awakens to find itself confronted with a crisis, it levels a withering barrage of criticism at those institutions that have been failing in their responsibilities: parents, local and federal governments, churches, and community organizations. And as often also happens, when things get bad enough, the public unhesitatingly turns to government for leadership, even when it does not trust government to take the lead in many areas. People now want government to take over the tracing of missing children, and to provide health care for those who are not covered by insurance, day-care services for children of

poor working mothers, sex education, birth control services
and job training for teenagers, prenatal care for poor mothers,
and immunization for all children.

In one fell swoop, the American people, parents and nonparents alike, suddenly became aware of the deteriorated
condition of both children and the poor. Doing something for
the children of poverty is suddenly becoming a high national
priority. The bottom line which the public is now seeing is
that 20% of all families with children 18 years of age and
under are in the poverty category, compared with only 5.5%
of families with just adults in them. As Senator Daniel Patrick
Moynihan has pointed out, the U.S. is perhaps the only country in modern history to treat its children worse than it treats
adults.

■ COPING WITH DRUGS, ALCOHOL, AND TOBACCO

Perhaps it is sheer coincidence, but at one and the same time,
32% of the nation's households acknowledge that someone in
their family has a drinking problem, 41% of teenagers are
using marijuana, and the number of those who still smoke
totals 32% of the adult population. Put in context, this means
that over the past decade, marijuana usage has remained
steady or declined a little, alcohol problems have leveled off
at a high rate (even though alcohol consumption shows signs
of declining), and cigarette smoking is in decline.

Yet, under the impetus of an enormous media campaign,
especially in the cities, drugs have become the number one
issue in the minds of the public, mainly because of the reported sharp rise in the use of "crack," a cheap form of
cocaine. The best available statistics, however, indicate that
among high school students the only drug on the rise usage
is cocaine; the use of drugs in general has leveled off or
declined. Meanwhile, efforts are being made to restrict where
people can smoke, but a substantial seven in every ten Ameri-

cans are opposed to banning the use of cigarettes, even though almost all see a definite connection between smoking and lung cancer. The fact is that in a pluralistic country, the public does not want to deny people the option to smoke or to use alcoholic beverages, even if both might well be deleterious to their health. In the case of illicit drugs, the public has asked for draconian governmental measures, though these will likely not see the light of day because most cannot pass the test of constitutionality.

The chances are that Americans will continue to struggle with what to do with these legal and illegal substances, which plainly create serious health problems, but which are also widely used. It is unlikely that cigarette smoking or alcoholic beverages will be made illegal, although it is highly likely that usage of both will decline. By the same token, it is also unlikely that the flow of illicit drugs will be stemmed or that pious hopes for a drug-free environment will be realized. Nonetheless, with the increased attention being given to the problems of children, it will probably be a long time before parents again urge their offspring to turn to drinking instead of drugs, as happened in the early 1980s, and a long time before parents again tell themselves that their own children could not possibly be experimenting with drugs, or before people believe smoking cigarettes are a symbol of macho in men or sophistication in women.

■ A FINAL NOTE

The veneer of vanity and materialism that appears to be the hallmark of the 1980s is surface-thin. Beneath it can be found a growing sense that many human concerns, especially for those less able to fend for themselves, such as children, have been neglected and are in sore need of attention. Slowly but surely, Americans may be making the connection between good nutrition and what they in fact eat, between a sound regimen of exercise and how they actually care for their bodies, between invoking greater discipline in order to perform well and fully in the home and on the job and fighting hard to keep fragile marriages together, between pursuing individual interests and identifying increasingly with the larger community.

The signs indicate that there will be a reaction in the late 1980s to the indulgences of the early 1980s. In short, a return to conscience appears to be growing across the U.S., and with it a greater self-respect, a respect for the integrity and fulfillment in the heart of an individual who feels at one with herself or himself in a free society.

PART TWO

COMMUNITY

GENETIC ENGINEERING: PLAYING GOD OR SAVING HUMAN LIVES?

■ A POSITIVE RESPONSE TO GENE SPLICING

Perhaps the most dramatic industry to be born in recent years is genetic engineering. By examining the genes, scientists are now able to find out whether certain people are likely to come down with such incurable ailments as Huntington's disease. These scientists are convinced that they are close to being able to cure people with such genetic diseases as cystic fibrosis by altering the genes that determine basic characteristics.

In many respects, genetic engineering is the ultimate step in man's quest to artificially reproduce life cells. Some scientists believe that the American people's positive response to genetic engineering would be a sign that they are truly commited to science and its applications. But other people believe that genetic engineering comes close to playing God.

To determine what people think about genetic engineering, it was explained to a national cross section of adults that it now might be possible to cure people with fatal diseases by altering their genes. They were also told that changing the basic structure of a human being comes close to playing God. Yet, when the choice was laid on the line, a decisive 64%–24% majority gave genetic engineering a green light.

But the overall results cloak major differences in reaction by age and sex. For example, while an overwhelming 74%–19% majority of people under 30 want genetic engineering to go forward, a bare 51%–27% majority of those 65 and over agree with them. Compared with a 71%–21% majority of men who back genetic engineering, a lesser 58%–27% majority of women share the same view. Throughout the survey, young people and men are far more in favor of genetic engineering than are older people and women.

■ GETTING PERSONAL ABOUT GENETIC ENGINEERING

Of course, it is one thing to agree in general that genetic engineering should go forward, but it is quite another to be willing to participate personally in some of its applications. Yet, when asked directly what their response would be in basic situations, solid majorities opted to try out the new and largely untried science:

□ By 57% to 33%, a majority of the American people say that if they were told after an examination of their own genes that they were likely to get an incurable disease that genetic engineering might help them avoid, they would go ahead with the treatment. Again, age and sex were decisive. While 67% of young people under 30 would undergo the treatment, as would 62% of those 30 to 49, people 50 to 64 divide down the middle, 45% to 45%, on the issue, and those 65 and over would refuse any such treatment by 45% to 41%. While 63% of all men would undergo the genetic change, a smaller 52% of women would agree to it.

□ The other case was what geneticists call a classic situation. It was explained to them that some people can be carriers of a genetic disease but not come down with it themselves, although they can pass it on to their children. They were asked whether, if tests showed they were carriers of a genetic disease, they would choose to have their genes altered to correct that condition not only for their own children but for future generations. By a decisive 62% to 29%, a majority said they would choose to have their genes altered. Again, 70% of the young would do so, compared with no more than 52% of the elderly. But men and women came up much the same, with 64% of the men and 60% of the women agreeing to undergo such a basic alteration. Both men and women, it appears, would do so for the sake of their children.

■ WHERE PEOPLE WOULD DRAW THE LINE

While majorities are willing to utilize genetic engineering for their own health purposes, nonetheless they fiercely draw the line at institutionalizing genetic tests as a matter of broad policy:

□ By an overwhelming 92% to 6%, almost every American rejected the proposal that the government test people to find out if they are carriers of fatal diseases, and, if they are, that they be required to have their genes changed. No way, people say: Leave the decision strictly to the individual.

□ By 84% to 13%, another lopsided majority rejected the proposal that people who are carriers of genetic diseases not be allowed to have children.

□ By just as decisive a margin, 88% to 9%, a big majority also felt that genetic engineering would go too far if it made it possible for individuals to have their genes changed to make their children smarter, physically stronger, or better-looking. No such engineering of a master race, say the American people.

□ The results are just as negative when people are asked about the rights of employers in the future to utilize genetic tests on employees. By 86% to 11%, people rejected the notion that employers should have the right to make such tests to determine whether employees are prone to genetic diseases. By 82% to 15%, people also turned down the proposition that an employer have the right to refuse to hire someone who tests showed was likely to develop a genetic disease in the future. And by 73% to 23%, people also gave a flat negative to allowing employers the right to include the results of such genetic tests in people's personnel files.

□ Finally, by 75% to 21%, another decisive majority felt that insurance companies would not be justified in refusing to insure the lives of people who such tests indicated were likely to develop a serious disease later on in life.

OBSERVATION

The reaction of the American people to the arrival of the genetic engineering era is clear-cut. People are eager for the industry to continue its research and to come up with products and services that can make gene changes work for humanity. Most people also are quite willing to become the personal beneficiaries of such scientific breakthroughs—most would undergo gene changes to avoid a fatal genetic disease later in life and would be willing to acquire new genes in order to have children without genetic defects.

But, above all else, the American people insist that the use of genetic engineering advances be left up to the individual. Under no condition will they allow any rules, laws, or practices that would violate their pluralistic right to accept or reject the techniques that are developed. They do not want any kind of governmental or private sector fiats that would impose a genetic imperative on society. They are appalled at the prospect of any kind of discrimination, restriction, or penalty against people who might be carriers of genetic diseases.

As an indication of their underlying views on the matter, when asked if they would take a test to see whether they might develop an incurable disease later in life, a narrow 50%–44% plurality said they would. When asked what they would do if the test indicated they were going to come down with a fatal genetic disease 10 or 20 years from now, a big majority of 79% to 16% rejected the notion that they would prefer to die rather than to wait for the inevitable. By the same token, by 61% to 35% they also turned down the notion that they would then stop doing what they are doing now and would start doing all the things they ever dreamed of doing. Instead, a nearly unanimous 86% to 12% said they would continue to live the way they do now.

———————————

Business Week/Harris Poll, conducted by Louis Harris and Associates for *Business Week,* November 1–4, 1985, among a national cross section of 1,254 adults, released November 18, 1985.

GUN CONTROL: WHAT PEOPLE THINK DOESN'T SEEM TO MATTER

■ THE PHENOMENON OF THE GUN LOBBY

By any measure, the American people are convinced that the sale and use of guns is out of control. For every person who wants to see less strict control of guns in the country, there are seven who want tougher laws. Yet, over the years, public opinion has had little impact on the gun control laws passed by Congress. In 1986, the U.S. Senate repealed major portions of the 1968 gun control law passed after the assassination of Martin Luther King, Jr., and Robert Kennedy. The House restored some of the controls, but the gun lobby, headed by the National Rifle Association (NRA), basically showed once more than it is fully capable of dominating the shaping of laws governing the sale and use of guns in the U.S.

The threat used so effectively by the NRA is to pour funds and manpower into districts and states where a senator or congressman has dared to vote for tighter gun control laws. The NRA points to several campaigns in which it claims to have delivered money and votes that upended incumbents who favored gun control. These threats seem to be enough to carry the day in Congress. Indeed, with Ronald Reagan as president, the gun lobby has had a good friend in the White House. He has steadfastly opposed laws that would have either outlawed handguns or required their registration or strengthened existing national gun control laws.

Yet the firm, even fierce set of public opinion continues to be on the side of tougher laws controlling guns.

■ 38 MILLION GUN-TOTING CITIZENS

Our Constitution gives the citizenry the right to bear arms. The success of the American Revolution was partly predicated on the fact that citizens took up arms to overthrow British rule. To the Founding Fathers, it seemed fully appropriate to recognize that people should have the right and the means to take matters into their own hands if it came to it. After all, the Declaration of Independence stated the eternal right of the citizenry to overthrow their government when it oppressed them. The radical and revolutionary origin of the American republic is often forgotten.

However, the U.S. has taken its right to bear arms so seriously that it is literally an armed camp compared with any other developed country on the face of the earth. And it also leads the world by far in murders, armed assaults, armed robberies, and gun-related accidents.

In all, 44% of the 87 million households in the land possess a gun. This comes to 38 million homes with guns in them. The South leads, with 54% of all households owning guns, followed by the Midwest at 46%, the West at 44%, and the East far down at 29%. More whites than nonwhites own guns. Far more skilled workers and manual workers own guns than professional or white-collar types. More high school than college graduates own guns, as do more older than younger people, and more higher- than lower-income people, although peak ownership is among households with incomes between $25,000 and $35,000. Politically, 47% of Republican homes have guns, 46% of homes where Independents live, and a lesser 41% of Democratic homes. Since 1972 there has been virtually no change in the overall rate—40% to 45%—of gun ownership in the country.

Types of guns owned are fairly evenly divided among rifles (found in 60% of the gun-owning households), shotguns (found in 55% of the homes), and pistols (found in 49% of the households). This means that there are close to two guns in each gun-owning home. Since 1972 there has been no increase in ownership of rifles or shotguns. But the possession of handguns has risen sharply, from 36% to 49%. Pistols will soon become the most common firearms in the American home, and since handguns are not widely used for sport, they are basically owned as weapons against people.

■ ATTITUDES TOWARD GUN CONTROL

When asked about handgun laws, 60% say they should be made more strict, only 8% say less strict, and 30% say make no change. Women want tougher laws more than men do, blacks more than whites, college-educated more than those with less education, Easterners more than residents of any other region, and, obviously, non-gun owners more than gun owners. However, even among gun owners, 41% want stricter control of handgun sales, only 15% want less strict laws, and 43% want no change.

A key law that is under attack is the federal statute that prohibits the sale of handguns to a citizen of another state. The Senate repealed this law earlier in 1986, but the House refused to go along. By a clear-cut 67% to 23%, a sizable majority of the American people believe the interstate handgun sales ban should be continued. Handgun owners favor the law by 60% to 32%.

By 70% to 25%, another big majority would favor the registration of all handguns. Sentiment for such a federal law has risen since the early part of the decade. There is no significant segment of the population that is opposed to such a handgun registration law.

In recent years a number of communities have passed laws prohibiting the ownership of handguns. Nationwide, the country splits down the middle on that one, with 47% favoring such a ban and 47% opposing it. Again, the pattern is familiar, with women, blacks, the college-educated, residents of the East, and nonowners of guns favoring such a law. Gun owners oppose it by 64% to 31% and handgun owners are even more against such a law, by 71% to 26%.

OBSERVATION

Clearly, the preponderance of public opinion in the country favors much tighter control over gun ownership, especially handguns. Yet, aside from some isolated communities where handguns have been banned or where they must be registered, there has been remarkably little movement toward stricter control. Indeed, whatever modest gun control laws are on the books have come under increasing attack from anti-gun-control forces.

The plain truth is that the gun lobby is extraordinarily well organized, while the anti-gun lobby is not. It is still viewed as an act of political courage in most places for a political leader to press hard for gun control. The establishment has been effectively intimidated by a well-organized minority. Police chiefs, law enforcement officials, and other authorities may be for stricter gun control, but this is one area where expert opinion counts very little.

After Martin Luther King, Jr., and Robert Kennedy were shot and killed within a few months of each other in 1968, the Harris Survey asked a cross section of the American people if they thought America was wrong in allowing unrestricted sale of handguns. A massive 71%–23% majority agreed. The frontier rules have not changed much since the early founding days. Sadly, however, the weapons that the nation's forefathers thought were necessary to protect against political oppressors now more often than not are used by one set of citizens against another. And the United States remains the most murdering country on the face of the earth.

The Harris Survey, conducted by Louis Harris and Associates, among a national cross section of 1,634 adults, released April 22, 1968.

The Gallup Poll, conducted by the Gallup Organization, April 12–15, 1985, among a national cross section of 1,525 adults, released May 26, 1985; April 11–14, 1986, among a national cross section of 1,552 adults, released May 11, 1986.

YUPPIES: LATELY SPAWNED AND NOW SCORNED

■ WHO ARE YUPPIES, AND WHERE ARE THEY?

Discovered in 1984, they were first defined as young upwardly mobile types. The literal-minded *New York Times* insisted for too long that they were "Yumpies," but "Yuppies" stuck. The claim was that they were a materialistic lot, a far cry from the generation in revolt in the late 1960s. This "on the make" generation had largely replaced the "on the road" beatniks and hippies as the symbol of young people in America.

For survey purposes, we decided that a fair definition of a Yuppie was someone 18 to 39 years of age who had had at least some college education. Altogether, this group comes to 29% of the adult population, or 51 million young Americans. These Yuppies are not evenly distributed among the population. They are more likely to populate the highly mobile East and West coasts and the big urban centers, and are more often male than female, more likely to be professionals and business executives, earning distinctly higher income, being less unionized, more Republican, partisan of Ronald Reagan but more moderate in political philosophy than the rest of the population. Significantly, they tend to turn out to vote more than the rest of their generation.

■ MATERIALISTIC IN HEAVY DOSES

Back during the 1970s energy shortage, it was widely predicted that America would lead the world in a return to simplicity, a rejection of material acquisitions—back to basics. The young were supposed to be in the vanguard of this movement, even though throughout the late 1960s, teenagers never lost their taste for spending money on jeans, records, and cars. Nonetheless, there was some substance to the claim that antimaterialism had begun to take over. By 5 to 1, people felt that to learn to live with the basics was more important than reaching higher living standards. The same majority also believed that it was more important to get pleasure from nonmaterial things than to satisfy needs for more goods and services. And by 2 to 1, it was thought more important to appreciate human rather than material values and that it was not necessary to find ways to create more jobs by producing more goods.

But by the mid-1980s this sentiment had changed, especially among young people, many of whom were encountering trouble finding jobs in the recession. The number who gave priority to creating more jobs by producing more goods jumped 16 points among the public as a whole, but 21 points among young people. Young people advocating the goal of satisfying the needs for more goods and services jumped 14 points. And those who opted for higher standards of living instead of a simple existence went up 10 points among the young. Clearly, by the mid-1980s, the American people were far more oriented toward economic growth and materialism than before. Most significant, young people were leading the charge back to material values. Yuppie power was alive and right at the cutting edge.

■ PERCEPTIONS OF YUPPIES TURN SOUR

Yet a 1986 survey indicates that as awareness of Yuppies has spread, most people downright didn't like them, including Yuppies themselves:

□ By 73% to 18%, a big majority is convinced that Yuppies are intent on making as much money as fast as possible. An even higher 81%–17% majority of Yuppies confirms this notion. But a 59%–36% majority of the public also finds this quality in Yuppies unattractive. Even Yuppies themselves find it unappetizing by 57% to 40%.

□ By 72% to 18%, a big majority of the public is also convinced that Yuppies are more concerned with their own needs than other people's. Yuppies agree with this characterization by 72% to 25%, and 87% of the public and 90% of the Yuppies themselves find this egocentric tendency to be singularly unattractive.

□ By 70% to 20%, another big majority of the public believes that Yuppies are inclined to buy showy clothes and autos that set them apart from other people. A higher 81% to 17% among Yuppies agree. But by 75% to 20%, a majority of the public and a 72%–24% majority of Yuppies think such tastes are unattractive.

OBSERVATION

As the symbol of an ascendant new generation, Yuppies now appear to be fading fast—almost as fast as hula hoops and other fads of yesteryear. A presidential candidate who stakes out a claim for the Yuppie vote might even run into a backlash now—it's possible that Yuppies themselves might vote against him. The irony, of course, is that while the perception of Yuppies might have tumbled, the materialism of this newer generation is highly unlikely to disappear overnight, irrespective of what people or Yuppies continue to think of Yuppies. Yuppies won't mind being cursed all the way to the bank.

The Harris Survey, conducted by Louis Harris and Associates, 1977, among a national cross section of 1,501 adults; January 24–27, 1985, among a national cross section of 1,254 adults, released March 28, 1985; January 3–7, 1986, among a national cross section of 1,254 adults, released February 3, 1986.

PORNOGRAPHY: A DELICATE BALANCE IN A FREE SOCIETY

■ AWARENESS AND EXPOSURE TO
  PORNOGRAPHIC MATERIALS

Only a minority of the adult public in the U.S. reports buying, reading, or viewing what might be called pornographic materials. A substantial 37% say they "sometimes" buy or read magazines like *Playboy*. While a minority, this amounts to a substantial 53 million adults. A much lower 13% report buying magazines like *Hustler*, 7% say they went to an X-rated movie in the past year, and 9% report having rented an X-rated movie or cassette during the same period of time.

But these movies and publications are not the only, nor perhaps even the most serious, focus of the worries the public has about pornography. A 51%–44% majority is offended by the sexual content of top Hollywood movies. An even higher 55% to 44% report being offended by sexual displays in advertising. A comparable 53% to 45% is in turn offended by the sexual content of top TV shows. An exception: a solid 66% to 27% are not offended by the sexual depictions in contemporary novels.

It is evident that a slight majority of people in the country is uneasy and uncomfortable with highly suggestive displays of sex in the mass media.

■ REACTIONS TO SEXUALLY EXPLICIT MAGAZINES, MOVIES, AND BOOKS

In the case of sexually explicit magazines, movies, and books, public opinion is surprisingly mixed. For example, a 67%–29% majority holds the view that such explicit presentations lead to a breakdown of public morals. An even higher 73% to 22% are convinced that they "lead some people to commit rape or sexual violence." A big 76% to 20% believe they "lead some people to lose respect for women." And by 55% to 34%, a majority denies the claim that they provide "a safe outlet for people with sexual problems."

But there is another side. The majority understands how such explicit renderings of sex can benefit some people. For example, by 61% to 35%, a goodly majority believes they provide entertainment. By 52% to 43%, a majority is convinced that such magazines, movies, and books "provide information about sex." And by a narrow 47% to 46%, a plurality of the adult public believes they "can help improve the sex lives of some couples."

■ TO BAN OR NOT TO BAN SEXUALLY EXPLICIT MATERIALS

Despite its somewhat mixed view of pornographic matter, the public is quite clear on just what it wants banned and what should be allowed to be circulated:

□ By 69% to 29%, a big majority is opposed to banning magazines "that show nudity."

□ By 54% to 43%, a majority is opposed to banning "theaters that show X-rated movies."

□ In a 49%–49% standoff, people are divided on banning "magazines that show adults having sexual relations."

□ By 62% to 36%, a substantial majority is opposed to banning "the sale or rental of X-rated video cassettes for home viewing."

By the same token, however, majorities do favor banning certain kinds of explicit sexual materials:

☐ By 74% to 24%, a solid majority supports banning "theaters showing movies that depict sexual violence."

☐ By 76% to 22%, an even higher majority favors banning "magazines that show sexual violence."

☐ And by 73% to 25%, a majority also would back a ban on "the sale or rental of X-rated video cassettes featuring sexual violence."

It is evident that the public sharply draws the line at depictions of sexual violence. At the same time, as long as they are available only to adults, for private enjoyment, most Americans are willing to tolerate the sale and rental of sexually explicit materials.

OBSERVATION

Public attitudes toward sexually explicit magazines, films, and books clearly indicate that the position of the U.S. Supreme Court is supported by public opinion. As long as there are some restraints to protect minors from open exposure to such materials, and as long as they are largely made available only to adults for private or restricted consumption, most Americans are opposed to a ban on sexually explicit materials. The one exception is magazines, books, and movies that show sexual violence.

These findings have special relevance in light of the concentrated campaign to get magazines such as *Playboy* banned from sale in stores that carry a broad selection of other magazines. The American people are not deeply worried about their own and their neighbors' capacity for sorting out the issue of pornography. To the contrary, there is every indication that most people believe a delicate balance can be struck between protecting the morals of society as a whole and the freedom of the people to make the ultimate selection of what they read and view.

Newsweek Poll, conducted by the Gallup Organization for *Newsweek,* March 6–7, 1985, among a national cross section of 1,020 adults, released March 18, 1985.

The Gallup Poll, conducted by the Gallup Organization, July 11–14, 1986, among a national cross section of 1,539 adults, released August 14, 1986.

THE RISING PUBLIC DEMAND TO LEGALIZE THE RIGHT TO DIE

■ THE AMERICAN PEOPLE OVERWHELMINGLY SUPPORT EUTHANASIA

Back in 1973 a clear-cut 53%–37% majority of the American people said that it was *wrong* "to give a patient who is terminally ill, with no cure in sight, the right to tell the patient's doctor to put the patient out of his or her misery." By 1985, in response to precisely the same question, a resounding 61%–36% majority of the public now said it was *right* to give a patient such a right.

Backing for this position has been steadily rising since 1973. In 1977 a 49%–38% plurality favored it. By 1981 support went to 56% to 41%. In the latest measure, four years later, it rose to 61% to 36%. And the trend lines on the two other basic questions the Harris firm has put to the same cross section of the American people also show a dramatic upsurge in support for making euthanasia legal:

□ When asked about the case of a terminally ill patient who is being sustained on a life-support system, a massive 85%–13% majority now believes that a patient has the right to tell the doctor to pull the plug on the support systems so that the patient can die. Back in 1973 a lower 62%–28% majority favored it. By 1977 this had risen to 71% to 18%, and then to 78% to 19% in 1981. The increase in support is remarkable, in view of the controversy surrounding this issue.

RIGHT OF TERMINALLY ILL PATIENT TO ASK FOR EUTHANASIA

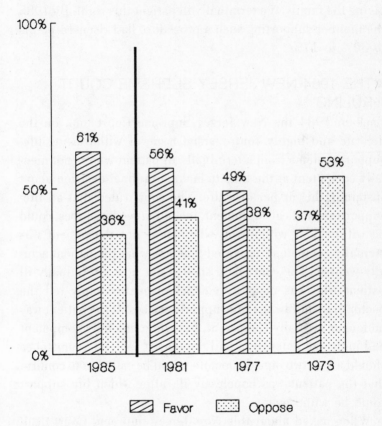

☐ In a third case, "a patient is terminally ill, in a coma and not conscious, with no cure in sight." The question then is whether or not "the family of such a patient has the right to tell the doctors to remove all life-support services and let the patient die." Back in 1977 a 66%–19% majority favored giving the family of a terminally ill patient this right. By 1985 the number supporting such a procedure had risen 14 points to 80% to 17%.

■ THE 1984 NEW JERSEY SUPREME COURT RULING

Back in 1984 the New Jersey Supreme Court took on the delicate and highly controversial issue of withdrawing life-support systems from a terminally ill patient who is not mentally competent at the time to make a rational decision about sustaining his or her own life. The court ruled that all life-supporting medical equipment, including feeding tubes, could be withheld or withdrawn, whether or not the patient was mentally competent, provided that was what the patient actually wanted. The court then spelled out how a terminally ill patient who was mentally competent could simply tell the doctor to withdraw the life-support services. If the patient was no longer mentally competent, but while mentally competent had indicated a desire to pull the plug if such a circumstance should arise, two outside doctors would be called in to confirm that the patient was hopelessly ill, after which life support could be withdrawn.

When asked about this New Jersey Supreme Court decision, an overwhelming 82%–16% majority said they personally favored it. But that court also laid down three important provisions that would have to be met before life-support systems could be withdrawn:

☐ First, it must be determined that the patient's request to remove life support when terminally ill was made while the patient was still mentally competent. An 87%–10% majority agrees with that condition.

□ Another condition specifies that "if there is no evidence of what the patient said, then the family and doctors should measure whether the burdens of the patient's life outweigh the benefits the patient gets from being alive." Another big 80%–18% majority backs this condition.

□ Finally, the New Jersey Supreme court stipulated that it must be determined "that the treatment of keeping the patient alive would involve severe and constant pain so that to keep the patient alive would be inhumane." The public across the country backed that condition by 83% to 15%.

OBSERVATION

What is striking is the strength of the mandate to legalize euthanasia in the United States. These are not 51%–49% hairline divisions. By any reasonable standard, the public's views on the right to die are so decided that the issue would ordinarily not seem to be in doubt. There is no major segment of the public that does not support euthanasia by wide margins. This includes Catholics and members of the Moral Majority whose evangelical preacher leaders vigorously oppose legalizing euthanasia.

But the battle over the issue goes on unabated, and not many states seem inclined to pick up the New Jersey precedent. Indeed, after the New Jersey decision was rendered, the right-to-life movement stated its opposition on the grounds that "allowing the taking of life of terminally ill patients when they want life support removed is a first step toward killing off older citizens who are seen as a burden on family and society." When this statement of opposition was read to the cross section surveyed, an overwhelming 79%–18% majority rejected it out of hand.

This issue, however, is unlikely to go away. In recent years a major incremental increase has taken place in Medicare monies spent to provide medical and hospital services for terminally ill patients. A number of authorities, many of them of a conservative bent, are convinced that the entire Medicare system will be placed in jeopardy unless the cost of support for terminally ill patients is brought under control. Because of this and other issues, whenever those in power get ready to come to grips with the issue of euthanasia, they will find the overwhelming majority of the American people not only in favor of legalizing it, but greatly relieved that at last the leadership has got the message.

The Harris Survey, conducted by Louis Harris and Associates, February 1973, released April 23, 1973; February 1–7, 1977, among a national cross section of 1,466 adults, released March 24, 1977; March 27–April 2, 1981, among a national cross section of 1,253 adults, released May 14, 1981; January 24–27, 1985, among a national cross section of 1,254 adults, released March 4, 1985.

MASS NEED FOR CREATIVE EXPRESSION: THE EXPLOSION OF THE ARTS

■ **THE AMERICAN PEOPLE OPT FOR THE ARTS**

At a time when leisure time is shrinking rapidly, when stress on the individual has been rising, when the incentive to make money has never been more pressing, the American people have reached out and embraced the arts, partly as a respite from all these pressures, partly as an expression of creativity in an era marked by conformity.

The stereotype of the U.S. is that of a people mired in pop culture, and with relatively low-brow tastes shaped by excessive exposure to television, especially to any and all sports events. But not only is it the case that more people attend arts events than attend sports events, but just about as many people go to art museums as to pop concerts. The deep commitment of the American people to the arts is yet another mark of the breadth and versatility of the American people.

■ **TRENDS IN ARTS ATTENDANCE**

From the mid-1970s to the mid-1980s, arts attendance in this country literally exploded:

☐ The number of people who attended the movies went up from 70% to 78%. This adds up to 136 million adults annually who go to the movies. Of course, the movies are particularly popular with younger people. Fully 96% of people under 30 attended the movies, as did 85% of those 30 to 49 years of age, 90% of those with some college education, 88% of college graduates, 87% of those in the $35,000–$50,000 income group, and 88% of those earning $50,000 or more. The audience for the movies is both young and affluent.

□ Attendees at live performances of plays, musical comedies, pantomime, and other forms of theater rose during the same period from 53% to 67%, up to 116 million people a year. Attendance at the theater was highest in the East (74%), among residents of the big cities (72%), and among college graduates (88%).

□ Those going to listen to live music performances by popular singers, bands, and rock groups increased over the decade from 46% to 60%, a total of 104 million attendees. Heaviest attendance at pop concerts was in the South (64%), among people under 30, those with incomes between $35,000 and $50,000 (67%), and those with some college education but not a four-year degree (71%).

□ By contrast, the number going to art museums went up only marginally, from 56% to 58%, which comes to 101 million adults annually. Art museum attendance is highest on the West Coast (65%), in the big cities (66%), among people 18 to 29 (66%), and among those with a college degree (78%) and those with incomes of $50,000 and over (76%).

□ Since 1980, attendance at live performances of the opera or musical theater has risen from 25% to 35%, a yearly total of 61 million. Opera and musical theater draw most heavily in the East (41%) and the big cities (41%), and among those in the 50–64 age group (41%), those with a college degree (55%), and those with incomes of $50,000 and over (58%).

□ The number going to live performances of the ballet, modern dance, and folk or ethnic dance has gone up from 23% to 34% since 1975, up to 59 million per year. Dance is most popular on the West Coast (40%), in the big cities (42%), and among those between 18 and 29 (40%), those with some college education (46%), and those with incomes of $50,000 and over (46%).

□ Increase in attendance at live performances of classical or symphonic music by orchestras and chamber groups has gone up over the decade from 25% to 34%, which comes to 59 million. Classical music followers can be found most often in the big cities (40%), and among those 30 to 49 years of age (39%), college graduates (57%), those earning $35,000 to $50,000 (47%), and those with incomes of $50,000 and over (51%).

It is apparent not only that the arts have grown apace in attracting much bigger audiences, but also that they are thriving on both coasts, among the better-educated and more affluent sectors, in the big cities, and among the young. However, the reach of the arts is not confined exclusively to these groups, but extends in sizable numbers to all ages, almost all economic groups, and to all regions of the country.

■ THE APPETITE FOR ARTS ATTENDANCE HAS HARDLY BEEN SATISFIED

Despite the sharp increase in arts attendance, sizable numbers of the American people report that they feel a need for more presentations of a host of arts fare:

□ A substantial 59% want more children's theater performances where they live.
□ 49% want more outdoor arts festivals in their communities.
□ 47% feel a need for more exhibitions of paintings or sculpture.
□ 45% think there should be more plays, musicals, pantomimes, and other adult theater performances where they live.
□ 43% have an appetite for more ballet and modern dance performances in their area.
□ 42% feel the need for more classical music concerts and recitals.

□ 41% would like to have more folk or ethnic dance performances where they live.

□ A smaller 34% want more pop music concerts.

To put this appetite for more serious arts fare into proper perspective, the survey also asked people about live sports events in the area in which they live. No more than 28% said they feel a need for more. Since 1975, the number who express this desire has declined, in contrast to every category of the arts, with the exception of pop concerts.

■ PARTICIPATION IN THE ARTS IS WAY UP AS WELL

As attendance has exploded in the arts since the mid-1970s, participation in the arts has increased even more:

□ The number who are involved in photography has jumped from 19% in 1975 to a current 47%, which comes to 82 million. Photography is most popular on the West Coast (54%), among those 30 to 49 years of age (53%), people with some college education (55%), college graduates (64%), and men (56%).

□ The rise in those involved in needlepoint, weaving, and other handiwork has been less spectacular, going up from 39% in 1975 to a current 44%, which means that 76 million Americans are engaged in this creative activity. Needlepoint, not surprisingly, appeals to women (69%), people 65 and over (47%), and those who live in small towns and rural areas (48%).

□ The number of adults in this country who play a musical instrument has increased from 18% in 1975 to a current 31%, which comes to 54 million Americans. People under 30 lead the way (40%), though college graduates (40%) are also heavily involved in musical expression.

□ The number of people who are involved in painting, drawing, or the graphic arts has gone up from 22% in 1975 to a current 29%—all in all, a substantial 50 million adults. Again, this form of creative expression is most popular in the West (33%), among people under 30 (39%), and those with at least some college (38%).

□ The number of people who write stories and poems has almost doubled over the past decade, going from 13% to 25% over that period. This means that 43 million Americans are engaged in writing, especially poetry. Leading the way are people who live in the West (29%), those 18 to 29 years of age (35%), those who are college-educated (33%), blacks (34%), and Hispanics (30%). The number of professional black women poets has grown dramatically in recent years.

□ The number of people who sing in choirs or other choral groups has doubled since 1975, from 11% to 22% of the adult population, or 38 million people. Most are people in the South (31%), small-town and rural folk (28%), women (25%), and blacks (47%).

□ An even bigger surge has taken place in participation in ballet and modern dance, up sharply since 1975 from 9% to 21%, a total of 37 million adult Americans. This artistic activity is most heavily participated in by people under 30 (34%) and blacks (33%).

□ Another form of dancing that has grown rapidly is folk and ethnic dance, up from 5% in 1975 to a current 17%, which comes to 30 million Americans. The heaviest participation in such dance groups is among college graduates (22%) and blacks (24%).

□ The number of people who report making pottery or ceramic objects has risen sharply, from 8% to 17% over the past decade. Now a total of 30 million people are actively engaged in such work. Most absorbed in it are women (23%).

□ Over the past decade the number who regularly sculpt or

work with clay has increased from 5% to 9% of the adult population, a total of 16 million people. Hispanics (13%) are very much involved in this kind of creative activity.

☐ Finally, the number who have joined a local theater group has gone from 3% to 7%, which comes to 12 million people. Residents of the West (10%), people under 30 (10%), college graduates (12%), and Hispanics (11%) are most active in this form of the arts.

OBSERVATION

The explosion in public participation in the arts and attendance at arts events has been a phenomenon of modern American life. Clearly, the arts have struck a deep and sensitive chord in literally millions of Americans.

When probed to say in their own words what makes the arts unique, people say that they are a reflection of life, that they are an important outlet to express something of meaning, that they give a real spiritual lift and a memorable time.

But what emerges more than any other fact from this survey is the size of the audience for and participants in the arts. The arts in America in the 1980s have truly become a mass proposition. People have learned that you don't have to be an elitist to appreciate music, ethnic dance, painting, or sculpture or to play a musical instrument seriously. Blacks, for example, who are as low on the economic scale as any other group, nonetheless lead in the number of those writing poetry, singing in choral groups, and participating in ethnic and modern dance.

The arts, incredibly, have met this huge demand for expansion without the resources that other major institutions enjoy. For example, the average artistic director of an arts company, with credentials comparable to those of a university associate professor, is paid 40% less. The arts receive a smaller federal stipend in the U.S. than in any other major Western nation. The sacrifices made by those who present the arts are legion. The country is deeply in the debt of those who keep its arts institutions going and who allow creative genius to express itself.

Americans and the Arts poll, conducted by Louis Harris and Associates for Philip Morris, Inc., the National Endowment for the Arts, and the American Council for the Arts, January 1973, among a national cross section of 3,005 adults, released in 1974; June 1975, among a national cross section of 1,555 adults, released 1976; July 1980, among a national cross section of 1,501 adults, released 1980; March 5–18, 1984, among a national cross section of 1,504 adults, released 1984.

AIDS: DARK SHADOW
OF THE PLAGUE

■ A NATION SHOCKED BY AIDS

It all started a few years ago with the innocuous and technical-sounding name of Acquired Immune Deficiency Syndrome, a little-known disease that seemed to afflict intravenous drug users and homosexuals and that physicians immediately recognized as totally destructive to the immune system. Alarm spread quickly in the medical community, because of two critical aspects of the problem: first, the disease carried an almost certain probability of death, and, second, if it ever spread to the population at large, it could create a modern plague of epidemic proportions.

It did not take long for the rest of the population to get the word about what became popularly known as AIDS. By spring 1986 an almost unanimous 98% of the adult public had heard of it. And 95% felt it was a serious problem for the country, with 73% saying it was "very serious."

Rarely has a disease so quickly captured the imagination of a people. If there was any doubt that the dreadful nature of AIDS was pressing on the national consciousness, the clincher came in early October 1985, when movie idol Rock Hudson died of AIDS in as widely publicized celebrity death as any in modern times.

■ HOW YOU CONTRACT AIDS AND
HOW YOU DON'T

Across the country, nearly every household had a similar conversation at the supper table or after the kids had gone to bed. The subject: How do you catch this dread disease called AIDS? And what should be done by society to contain it? Finally, what should be done to make sure that some cure for AIDS is discovered by medical science? Make no mistake about it, however—the discussions and thinking about AIDS were highly personal in nature. Deep inside, few people felt any real guarantee of immunity.

The situation was ripe for wild and unfounded rumors to take over. Yet this did not happen: on the contrary, majorities of the people found out the facts rapidly—a classic case that gives the lie to those establishment elites who ardently believe in the ignorance of the unwashed masses.

☐ A sizable majority of 96% said it was likely that AIDS could be contracted from homosexual sex acts. Not until late 1986 did word come from medical authorities that the disease could also be contracted from heterosexual sex acts.
☐ 95% knew that AIDS could be caught from transfusions using blood donated or sold to blood banks by those carrying the AIDS virus.
☐ 93% were aware that the disease could be transmitted by the use of contaminated needles in injections of illicit drugs.
☐ 87% thought that AIDS could be contracted by babies one of whose parents had the disease.

And sizable majorities correctly identified a number of ways AIDS is *not* transmitted:

☐ By 67% to 31%, they denied that a child could get the disease by sitting in a classroom with an AIDS victim. A 68%–31% majority rejected the notion that it could be caught by eating in a restaurant where an AIDS victim also was eating. A 67%–30% majority denied it could be contracted by breathing too close to an AIDS victim. By 64% to 35%, another majority did not believe it could be transmitted by being in the same hospital with an AIDS victim. By 62% to 37%, a majority rejected the claim that it could be contracted by working side by side with someone with AIDS.

□ On two other propositions, the division was close. By only 51% to 45%, a majority did not believe AIDS was transmitted by inhaling the air expelled from sneezes and coughs of those with AIDS. And by a close 53% to 44%, a close majority believed that AIDS could not be caught just by living in the same house with an AIDS victim.

The essentially sober reaction and lack of panic among the public was reflected in the 80%–17% majority who firmly said that AIDS victims should *not* be treated as lepers.

■ WHAT TO DO TO PREVENT THE SPREAD OF AIDS

Nor were the people lacking in support for a host of measures designed to minimize exposure to AIDS and to show some compassion for its victims:

□ A nearly unanimous 98% favored testing all blood donated to hospitals and other blood banks to be sure that no blood containing the AIDS virus is accepted. Most hospitals are now doing just this.

□ 87% supported making certain that hospitals in every community would accept AIDS victims and give them full medical care. Slowly, this practice appears to be taking hold, although a number of private hospitals were believed to be slow to embrace it.

□ 86% favored providing government funds to allow anyone who wants to be tested for AIDS to take a free blood test. Such funds have been limited.

□ 80% favored raising significant sums of federal and private money to educate people on how to minimize the risk of

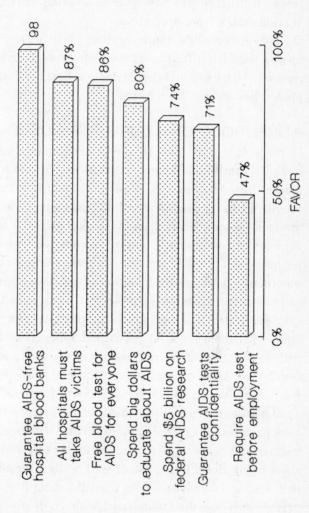

HOW TO MEET THE AIDS CRISIS

Guarantee AIDS-free hospital blood banks — 98

All hospitals must take AIDS victims — 87%

Free blood test for AIDS for everyone — 86%

Spend big dollars to educate about AIDS — 80%

Spend $5 billion on federal AIDS research — 74%

Guarantee AIDS tests confidentiality — 71%

Require AIDS test before employment — 47%

0%   50%   100%

FAVOR

getting AIDS. Much money has been generated for such purposes and many educational programs are under way.

□ 74% favored federal expenditures of $5 billion for crash research programs to find ways of treating, curing, and preventing AIDS from spreading.

□ 71% supported guaranteeing that positive results of AIDS testing would not be passed on without an individual's permission. There are no reliable data on how much this privacy pledge has indeed been kept.

■ LIKELIHOOD OF A CURE FOR AIDS

If there is a soft spot in the American psyche, it is the boundless faith that big majorities almost always have that no matter how terrible the ailment, somehow a cure will be found. When people are asked, for example, if they expect to die from cancer, heart disease, stroke, or many of the other common causes of death, majorities consistently say that they probably will not die from any of them. The reason: By golly, a cure will be discovered before any of those gets me!

Thus it comes as no surprise that when asked whether a cure for AIDS will be found "in the next few years," an 84%–14% majority is at least moderately confident that it will. In fact, scientists were relatively quick to identify and isolate the AIDS virus. Then in the early fall of 1986, the Burroughs Wellcome Company in North Carolina's Research Triangle Center came up with AZT, a substance that showed such promise for extending the lives of AIDS victims that the normal waiting period for drug testing was waived and physicians began distributing the drug. The startling tests showed that among 145 victims who tried the drug over a two-year period, only one died, compared with 16 deaths among 137 subjects who had been taking a placebo over the same period. Scientists were ultracautious in warning that this was not a cure, but merely a possible way to prolong the lives of AIDS victims. Nevertheless, this breakthrough gave an enormous boost to people's faith that medical science would come to the rescue in the nick of time, although medical scientists themselves were not nearly so confident.

OBSERVATION

Without doubt, public response to the AIDS crisis manifested a sobriety, maturity, and intelligence that did credit both to medical science for the way in which people were informed and to the people themselves. Indeed, when asked whether children with AIDS should be allowed to attend classes as usual or be banned from them, a solid 67%–24% majority said that they would send their own children to class with a 14-year-old who had AIDS. (In Indiana, a 14-year-old boy was in fact allowed to attend regular classes and still does, despite initial protests by some parents.)

The public has not lost its head over AIDS, nor has it yet gone overboard by proclaiming that a cure is so imminent that the threat is vastly diminished. Balance, good judgment, and coolness have been the mark of the American people during the AIDS crisis. If there were an explosion in AIDS cases, especially if the disease were to spread widely among non-homosexuals and nonintravenous drug users, as it has in Africa, there is no telling how long the calm would hold out. But up to now the American people are amply demonstrating that they are coming through in the clutch and are rising admirably to the new and dreadful challenge of AIDS.

The Harris Survey, conducted by Louis Harris and Associates September 5–8, 1985, among a national cross section of 1,255 adults, released September 19, 23, and 26, 1985.

The Gallup Poll, conducted by the Gallup Organization, March 7–10, 1987, among a national cross section of 1,004 adults, released April 17, 1986.

A RADICAL PROGRAM FOR REVITALIZING PUBLIC EDUCATION

■ IT MIGHT WELL BE A RARE HISTORIC MOMENT

In the summer of 1986 two reports emerged back to back that may one day be seen as the turning point in public education. One was the report of a task force of the Carnegie Forum on the Economy and Education, and the other the Report on Education issued by the National Governors Association. Each reinforced the other, and together they had a powerful message.

That message in essence was this: the United States can no longer be economically competitive in the world and still maintain its standard of living unless the work force in this country is upgraded to the point that it is capable of producing new products and generating new services that exceed the abilities of the rest of the world. That we are not producing such workers is clear—Japanese high school students are now surpassing American students in scores on math and science tests. To meet the new challenge, the public education system must be completely overhauled. A new breed of students must be turned out, who will have learned math, science, and technology, but will also be able to think for themselves and to know where to go to learn what they don't know.

But to produce such students will require just as radical changes for turning out a new breed of teachers. These teachers must know their subject matter well, be able to teach superbly, and must be willing to assume far more leadership responsibility in helping to plan and to run the public schools. To attract and motivate the best young people to want to go into teaching, teachers must be truly given much more freedom to contribute to the school's agenda and policies, must be paid professional salaries (comparable to those of accountants), and must be treated as professionals, relieved of many of their clerical and other mundane chores. In return, however, teachers will have to agree to be certified nationally, to be paid according to their level of responsibility and competence, and, above all, must be judged by a new bottom line: how well they have taught their students in the classroom.

Basically, the two reports were saying that the real essentials in public education are twofold: the caliber and quality of the teachers who will teach and the effectiveness of the process in educating first-class minds and competent students. All the rest, including the entire bureaucratic structure of public education, is subsidiary to this basic and simple performance standard.

If the public education system in fact adopts this approach, the changes will be no less than revolutionary. But it remains to be seen whether the American people are ready for such a draconian change and are willing to pay for it.

■ PUBLIC REACTION TO THE PROPOSAL FOR RADICAL CHANGE IN EDUCATION

In all, the Carnegie Forum came up with thirteen key recommendations. All of them met with endorsement by a majority of the American people:

☐ A big 87% majority opted for setting up a National Board of Professional Standards, which would establish high standards for what teachers need to know and must do, and would certify teachers who meet those standards.

☐ A nearly unanimous 95% favored requiring teachers to

demonstrate full command of the subject they teach and the ability to communicate that knowledge to students.

□ 93% supported creating incentives to focus the school's entire energies on improving student performance.

□ 77% favored requiring all teachers to obtain a four-year college degree in the subject the teacher will teach before any professional study of teaching, which is not the case today.

□ 88% backed creating a new graduate degree, an M.A. in teaching, through which teachers could master the subjects they teach, understand children's growth and learning capabilities, and learn sound teaching technique.

□ 86% favored creating a new position of lead teacher, to be filled by the most competent teachers, who would be responsible for helping to improve the performance of other teachers and students.

□ 77% opted for adopting a Code of Ethics, with provisions for disciplining violators.

□ 79% agreed with the proposition that if teachers were to be accountable for student progress, they should also be allowed to have real say in what is taught, how materials are used, and how the budgets in their schools are allocated.

□ 54% favored allowing lead teachers to hire school administrators in some cases (current practice is for administrators to hire teachers).

□ 93% supported making teacher salaries and career opportunities competitive with other professions, which means raising teacher pay high enough to attract and keep capable people who may have other opportunities.

□ 82% backed paying teachers on a scale similar to that of accountants, whose average pay ranges from a beginning salary of $20,000 to a high of $60,000 for a full year's work.

□ 72% felt that real emphasis must be put on increasing the number of members of minorities who become teachers.

□ 81% believed that this increased emphasis would mean that graduate fellowships and other forms of financial aid must be provided to needy minority students who are qualified and promise to become teachers.

OBSERVATION

Not the least important of these recommendations are those addressed to the recruitment and education of minority teachers. By the end of the century an estimated one third of all the children in the public schools will come from minority homes. A big 2 to 1 majority of the public is convinced today that these children receive an inferior education. A higher 3 to 1 majority believes that the U.S. cannot compete economically if poor and minority children are badly educated. The American people clearly are ready to give the education of poor and minority children the attention and resources needed to bring them into the mainstream of society. Accomplishing this end, they believe, is essential to the overhaul of public education. In addition, with a labor shortage looming in the 1990s, there will be no way to obtain the work force the country will need without tapping the poor and minorities. Therefore, it will be common in the years ahead to find conservative businessmen leading the demands that the children of the poor and minorities be educated well. These demands will be made out of pragmatism more than of altruism.

But most astounding are the overwhelming numbers who welcome such radical change. There is a reason for this reaction. For most of the life of the republic, the golden dream of each generation has been to hope and expect that their children will do better than they did. What would open that opportunity for their kids was always education. But about 15 years ago, everything about public education suddenly seemed to go sour: dropouts on the rise, illiteracy growing rapidly, unqualified students being graduated, graduates not capable of functioning in even the most menial of jobs. Now, we find the American people desperate to restore the public education system to its proper role. The stakes are no less than to make the U.S. economically competitive again. The education system is the key to the growth of the economy and the preservation of the standard of living. Koreans, Taiwanese, and other labor can perform the mass production jobs to turn out the cars, steel, and other industrial products that used to be the base of American enterprise—for much lower wages. So this country must turn out products and services made by a much higher-caliber labor force. These products and services will not be capable of being readily matched by the rest of the world—*provided* that the U.S. can rev up the school system to produce the new, higher-caliber labor force.

The argument is a powerful one that people will latch on to when their governors make it to them. There is little doubt that good politics will be to advocate radical educational policies. That is why this may well be a major and historic moment for education, for the economy, and for America's role in the world for the next half century. The stakes in educational reform are of that monumental magnitude, no less.

A Survey of the Reaction of the American People and Top Business Executives to the Report on Public Education by the Task Force on Teaching as a Profession of the Carnegie Forum on Education and Economy, conducted by Louis Harris and Associates for the Carnegie Forum on Education and Economy, June 30–July 25, 1986, among a national cross section of 1,513 adults, released August 1986.

BIRTH CONTROL AND ABORTION: CIVILIZED PLANNING FOR HUMAN LIFE OR WANTON TAKING OF HUMAN LIFE?

■ SOME COOL FACTS BEHIND A HOT ISSUE

As the twentieth century approached its last decade, the basic reproductive process that has guaranteed the survival of the human race has become a bitterly debated matter. The arguments really revolve around this central question: Is reproduction a sacrosanct process that once started should be allowed to run its natural course, or should people be allowed to decide when and whether to have children and how to engage in sex without running the risk of having them, if children are not desired at that particular time?

It is against the precepts of a number of religions and individuals to interfere with the "natural" process of conception in any way. These forces believe that conception is sacred and any interference is the equivalent of taking away a human life. Yet these preachings and tenets run smack into nearly all notions of how modern life should be controlled and organized. For example, most women who bear children aspire to successful careers. Thus, having children has to be planned carefully to accommodate both career and family. But planning in even a minimal way means taking steps not to have babies if women are to make love, a perfectly natural act in marriage. Thus, birth control methods are used in order to avoid having unwanted children or being "surprised," even if a child is eventually wanted.

The most emotionally charged scenario occurs when a woman—married or unmarried—becomes pregnant when she doesn't want to be. Then a decision must be made to bear the child or to abort the fetus. Without doubt, this is one of the most difficult decisions any human being can face.

In the latter part of the 1980s, birth control and abortion have become commonplace. Yet both evoke social divisions that split the country literally down the middle. Before reporting the polarization of attitudes, it may be well to examine the relevant facts that can be drawn from federal government data.

Of all women in the normal childbearing period, those 15 to 44 years old, 61% of those who have never been married nonetheless have had sexual intercourse. A quarter of a century ago, in the early 1960s, 52% of women who had had sex before marriage went on to marry the men with whom they had had sexual relations. But with each passing year that is happening less and less—to the point where in the latest period measured, only 21% of all women who have premarital sex go on to marry the men with whom they have had sexual relations. This means that sex among unmarried women is on the rise. In turn, the risk of unwanted pregnancy is increasing and the likely antidotes are birth control devices and the ultimate fail-safe of abortion.

In fact, four in every ten conceptions of babies in the country are not planned. In 29% of the births, the U.S. National Center for Health Statistics reports, the baby was wanted but the timing went awry—a pleasant surprise of sorts. But in 11% of the cases the baby was unwanted.

To avoid having a baby when they don't want one, fully 83% of all women who are vulnerable to unplanned pregnancies use birth control methods to avoid becoming pregnant. Only 17% take the chance of not using birth control devices. Most commonly used are the pill (43%), followed by condoms (18%), diaphragms (12%), IUDs (11%), the rhythm method

(6%), foam (4%), and assorted other methods such as withdrawal, douches and suppositories (7%).

During the 1980s the Alan Guttmacher Institute reports, roughly 3% of all women have abortions each year. Nonetheless, when asked directly about it, 28% of the adult public report that "someone close to them" has had an abortion.

As these facts amply demonstrate, the issue of birth control has virtually been settled. Vast majorities of the people support it and indeed use birth control methods themselves.

A few years back the Reagan administration made the United States the only country in the world that did not participate in world planning to try to contain the soaring birthrate, especially in developing countries. The U.S. parted company by refusing to fund birth control clinics in developing countries if those clinics recommended the use of abortion. By 81% to 15%, a big majority of Americans favor this country helping with birth control in Third World countries, including a 82%–16% majority of Catholics and a 72%–19% majority of born-again Christians. Two of every three Americans believe that overpopulation is a major cause of the food shortages that are resulting in so much starvation worldwide. Even when birth control programs also have built-in abortion programs, a sizable 61%–35% majority of Americans still favor spending U.S. dollars to help finance such efforts in developing countries, including a 56%–40% majority of Catholics and a 52%–42% majority of born-again Christians.

■ BUT HOW TO REACH THE UNEDUCATED ON BIRTH CONTROL?

Two major pieces of unfinished business in birth control are the development of a fail-safe contraceptive and an effective campaign to inform the uneducated—mainly teenagers—on the most effective means of birth control and how to obtain them.

By 76% to 20%, a majority of the American people are convinced it is highly likely that there will be a new breakthrough or invention of a more effective form of birth control during the next five years. Whether this is a well-founded expectation or just the usual American optimism that science will miraculously solve all our problems remains to be seen.

But a matter of growing public concern is the role that television plays in *not* helping to properly educate the uneducated on birth control. Fully two in every three think that TV gives an exaggerated picture of love. A plurality is convinced that television simply ignores the question of unwanted pregnancies and what the consequences of uninformed sex can be. Another two in every three people believe TV also ignores planning to prevent pregnancy and to control the size of the family. An equal number think TV does virtually nothing to spread information about sexually transmitted diseases. The reason TV is so pivotal: teenagers and others most prone to unwanted pregnancy are far more likely to look at the tube than to expose themselves to any other medium that might address the subject. At last count, NBC showed signs of being the first network to break the logjam on helping to educate the uneducated. But no network has yet accepted ads for birth control devices.

■ THE HOT ISSUE OF ABORTION

In 1973 the U.S. Supreme Court in a landmark decision made it legal for women to have abortions during the first three months of pregnancy. At the time, a 46%–42% plurality nationwide opposed legalizing abortion. After the Court acted, backing for abortion soared, so that by 1976 a wide 60%–31% majority favored it.

But in 1976 Jimmy Carter, who opposed abortion, was elected, followed by Ronald Reagan, who not only opposed abortion but could effectively campaign against it. As a result, by the mid-1980s, backing for the original 1973 Supreme Court decision had dwindled to no better than a narrow 50%–47% plurality overall, with a close 50%–47% plurality of

Catholics and a big 66%–31% majority of born-again Christians opposed. The issue that seemed settled in the mid-1970s was up for grabs again in the 1980s.

The abortion issue comes down to two central points: one is whether the national decision will be made on a rational or emotional basis. The other is whether a Supreme Court that has held fast for legalized abortion for 13 years will continue to hew to that line, despite the appointment of a Chief Justice, William Rehnquist, who is adamantly opposed to the original decision.

On an emotional basis, it is not hard to get a majority of Americans quite worked up in their opposition to abortion. By 56% to 40%, most Americans feel that to perform an abortion is the equivalent of murder, because the life of the fetus has been eliminated. By 68% to 27%, a bigger majority thinks it is against God's will to destroy the life of an unborn baby. A 61%–36% majority also holds that no one's life should be taken without the permission of the individual, and an unborn baby cannot give or refuse permission. And a 60%–37% majority believes a fetus should have rights, just like all other human beings. This is obviously powerful stuff, stimulated by the film made by the Right to Life movement, *The Silent Scream,* which among the 14% who saw it left them 9 to 1 more opposed to abortion, even though most felt it was a biased presentation.

Arrayed against these emotional charges is a whole assortment of both logical and much lower keyed arguments. For example, 72% hold that unless abortions are legal, many women will die from illegal abortions. A basic 67% to 30% feel that as long as a woman and her doctor are agreed, abortion should be permitted. Most compelling are the majorities ranging from 56% to 90% of the adult public who would opt for legalized abortions if the woman's life was endangered by the pregnancy, if the pregnancy was due to incest or rape, if there is every likelihood the child will be deformed or retarded, if the mother is an unmarried teenager whose future life might be seriously affected, if a woman's mental health would be endangered by the pregnancy, and if the woman's physical health could be endangered by the pregnancy.

OBSERVATION

The case for birth control has been sold to the American people and is well beyond major contention. For example, by a nearly unanimous 87% to 12%, most people are convinced that the best way to avoid the need for abortion is to have better contraception in the first place so that no pregnancy occurs.

Abortion is a different matter. That issue might also have been settled by now, except for two adamant White House occupants in a row who threw the weight of their office against it. What is clear about the abortion issue is that the American people are opposed to any outright ban. Indeed, by 55% to 37%, a solid majority opposes a constitutional ban on abortion. In addition, there are close to ten specific situations in which goodly majorities of the public would favor legalizing abortion. The key is whether or not people will make up their minds to be rational on the subject and to allow the decision to be a matter of *choice* for the pregnant woman and her doctor to decide. When posed in these terms, a 69%–30% majority comes down on the side of legalized abortion.

As for the U.S. Supreme Court, polling can hardly provide a clue, of course, as to whether it will maintain its position of 13 years' standing. But there are two clues. First, Justice John Jay long ago said that the courts at any given moment are a broad reflection of public opinion. Second, by 74% to 18%, a big majority of the public simply does not believe that abortion will ever be outlawed again. In other words, despite the heat and controversy, the American people, at least, think the issue has been resolved.

William F. Pratt, "Understanding U.S. Fertility: Findings from the National Survey of Family Growth, Cycle III," *Population Bulletin*, Vol. 39, No. 5 (Population Reference Bureau, Inc., Washington, D.C., 1984), and U.S. National Center for Health Statistics, *Advance Data from Vital and Health Statistics*, No. 107, as reported in the U.S. Bureau of the Census, *Statistical Abstract of the United States, 1986* (Washington, D.C., 1985), Table 99: Sexual Experience of Never-Married Women and Timing of Marriage Relative to First Sexual Intercourse for Ever-Married Women: 1982, p. 64.

U.S. National Center for Health Statistics, *Advance Data from Vital and Health Statistics*, No. 102, as reported in the U.S. Bureau of the Census, *Statistical Abstract of the United States: 1986* (Washington, D.C., 1985), Table 100: Contraceptive Use by Women, 15–44 Years Old, by Marital Status and Method of Contraception: 1982, p. 65

U.S. National Center for Health Statistics, unpublished data as reported in the U.S. Bureau of the Census, *Statistical Abstract of the United States: 1986* (Washington, D.C., 1985), Table 102: Unwanted Births of Mothers, 15–44 Years Old: 1982, p. 65.

U.S. Centers for Disease Control, Atlanta, Ga., *Abortion Surveillance*, *Annual Summary*, 1972, 1974, 1973–1980; S.K. Henshaw, ed., *Abortion Services in the United States, Each State and Metropolitan Area, 1979–1980*, The Alan Guttmacher Institute; New York, N.Y., 1983, and previously unpublished data as reported in the U.S. Bureau of the Census, *Statistical Abstract of the United States: 1986* (Washington, D.C., 1985), Table 103: Legal Abortions—Estimated Number, Rate, and Ratio, by Race: 1972 to 1982 and Table 104: Legal Abortions, by Selected Characteristics: 1973 to 1981, p. 66.

Public Attitudes about Sex Education, Family Planning, and Abortion in the United States, conducted by Louis Harris and Associates for the Planned Parenthood Federation of America, Inc., August 13–25 and September 13–17, 1985, among a national cross section of 2,510 adults, released October 1985.

CRIME: STALKING THE STREETS PEOPLE LIVE ON

■ THE PERCEIVED TREND ISN'T WHAT
   YOU READ IN THE PAPERS

There was a time of innocence, back in 1966, when no more than 3% of the American people reported a rise in crime where they lived. But with the racial violence of the late 1960s, followed by the deep and sometimes violent divisions over Vietnam, the growth of the use of illicit drugs, the crime rate rose sharply, as did public awareness of it.

Concern over crime reached an all-time peak in 1975, when 70% of all adults reported that crime was increasing where they lived. This dipped sharply to 46% in 1978, but rose again in 1981 to 68%. The feeling that crime has been increasing has declined since 1981. It went down to 59% in 1982, to 41% in 1983, then to a current 40% who say crime is increasing in their area.

Significantly, rises in the crime rate are perceived far less in white than in black or Hispanic neighborhoods. Many whites may think the color of crime is black, but blacks themselves know that they suffer more from crime than whites by a wide margin. Now, for the first time, more Hispanics (54%) report crime increasing than do blacks (45%). By region, the South at 46% is the scene of more increase in crime than any other. The big cities are no longer seen by their residents as the exclusive center of crime. Instead, that dubious honor is now shared by the suburbs. An identical

44% say that crime is increasing in both their areas, but the cities have been declining on this measure, while the suburbs have been rising steadily in the 1980s.

■ A MAJOR SADNESS OF MODERN LIVING: TO FEEL UNEASY ON THE STREETS

In the early 1970s crime became so pervasive that sizable numbers of citizens reported feeling a deep sense of unease whenever they ventured forth on the streets in the neighborhoods where they lived. In turn, this meant that for many their home was akin to a fortress under siege. This "bunker mentality" was not uncommon, especially in urban life. It reached its peak in 1975, when a majority of 55% of all adults reported feeling uneasy when they walked their own streets. But then, as with the perceived rate of crime, the number who reported feeling unease on the streets went down to 49% in 1977, and to 40% in 1978. It rose to 48% in 1981, but declined again to 41% in 1982, dropped way down to 26% in 1983, and then up two years later to 32%. But, taken over the decade, the number of Americans who reported feeling uneasy on the streets had gone down sharply from 55% to 32%, a drop of 23 points.

The groups who feel the most discomfort on the streets remain the same—women at 42%, older people at 35%, blacks at 36%, big-city dwellers at 37%, and low-income people at 40%. Again, the poor, the minorities, and the least privileged possess the most stark fear of going out on the streets at night. But there has been a decided downward trend for the past decade in the number expressing such apprehensions about going out of their houses and walking the streets. This does not make it any easier for those who still live with the sense that they are in peril. But the decline in such reported fears matches official statistics that show it is in fact getting safer to venture forth.

■ RESPECT FOR LAW ENFORCEMENT OFFICIALS ON THE RISE

Indeed, the other major development is that respect for law enforcement officials, especially at the local and state level, has risen sharply as the crime rate has declined and the public has perceived the decrease. Federal law enforcement officials weigh in at the bottom of the heap, given a positive rating of no more than 52% to 41%. Local law enforcement officials come up with a much higher 65%–34% positive rating. And state law enforcement is out in the lead, rated positively by 66% to 31%.

In a word, as people think the crime rate has declined, they have been quick to credit the law enforcement people around them for doing a better job, which the facts themselves bear out.

■ TOO MUCH MEDIA ATTENTION TO CRIME AND VIOLENCE

A substantial 71% of the public is convinced that outside the news area, television has simply devoted too much programming time to depicting violence, up from 59% who felt that way back in 1968. A big 78% to 17% of the public nationwide disapproves of the kind of violence shown on the tube.

What is more, four times as many people believe that the news media give too much attention to reporting crime than think they give too little. The network news shows are believed to be more the culprits than either local news programs or local newspapers.

OBSERVATION

Once again, the public emerges as highly sensitive and highly accurate in yet another area: what is happening to the crime rate. The reason, of course, is not hard to find. In the end, the people themselves are the victims of crime. Their own safety depends on how accurately they are able to gauge the nature of crime where they live.

But these results, contrary to so much prevailing and conventional wisdom, point up just how out of touch and perhaps how cynical are those in public life and the media who continually claim that "crime has never been worse." Such appeals to fear are not likely to win many votes these days and are not going to create a mass reaction that will rally around such bully pulpits.

Once more, the public has been underestimated by the establishment. These results do not mean that people have become recklessly unaware of the dangers of street crime— far from it. Much more than those in the sanctuaries of power, the rank and file are the ones at physical risk. What it does mean is that people are prepared to face reality, for better or for worse, and do not need to be told what they are supposed to believe. They have lived with crime and violence for a long time and have become sophisticated about its manifestations. And, most of all, perhaps far better than the establishment, they know about the kind of job being done by law enforcement officials, whom they are prepared to pay high tribute to, especially at the state and local levels.

The Harris Survey, conducted by Louis Harris and Associates, June 7–11, 1984, among a national cross section of 1,247 adults.

The Harris Survey, conducted by Louis Harris and Associates, January 1975, among a national cross section of 1,543 adults; April 1978, among a national cross section of 1,567 adults; January 1981, among a national cross section of 1,250 adults, released February 21, 1981; March 12–16, 1982, among a national cross section of 1,249 adults, released May 24, 1982; August 18–22, 1983, among a national cross section of 1,257 adults; and January 24–27, 1985, among a national cross section of 1,254 adults, released March 21, 1985.

THE UNENDING TALE OF DISCRIMINATION AGAINST WOMEN AND MINORITIES

■ ONCE UPON A TIME

The United States was founded as a mecca for political and religious refugees seeking to escape oppression in their homelands and for those who had suffered from famine and economic deprivation. Yet the new American society these refugees shaped has had real trouble shaking its own practices of discrimination. The Swedish social scientist Gunnar Myrdal long ago described it as the American dilemma: we suffer from a bad conscience over the discrimination visited upon racial minorities, but are also highly uncomfortable about taking the painful steps necessary to end that discrimination.

In addition to the way it treats minorities, the U.S. has also shown that it is capable of exercising discrimination against a majority in its midst: women, who make up 53% of the adult population. The emergence of women as a major force in the workplace brought to the surface a whole spate of assumptions about "a woman's proper place"—that is, the home—which generally could be taken to mean that women should be willing to accept something less than equal status in the larger world.

Thus, as far back as 1963, when Martin Luther King, Jr., emerged as the most forceful black leader in the country's history, a landmark *Newsweek* poll conducted by the Harris firm found that 66% of all whites felt that "blacks have less ambition than most other people" and that an even higher 71% felt that "most blacks ask for more than they are ready for." And as the modern women's rights movement was aborning in 1970 a Virginia Slims poll the Harris firm conducted revealed that most Americans did not think women were discriminated against in getting skilled-labor jobs, manual-labor work, or in being able to earn enough to support themselves independently.

This was the way it was not very long ago.

■ CONSCIOUSNESS ON THE RISE

By the latter half of the 1980s, a generation later, much has changed in the consciousness of the American people about the condition of minorities and women:

□ In the case of blacks, the number who think they are less ambitious has dropped from 66% to only 26% in just over two decades. And the number who say blacks are asking for more than they are ready for has plummeted from 71% to 40% over the same period. Indeed, by 76% to 20%, the American people overwhelmingly reject the claim that "most racial minorities get what they deserve." And by 57% to 39%, a majority now believes that "blacks suffer more in hard times and gain less in good times." Finally, by 66% to 27%, a big majority of whites agrees that "the same people who would like to keep blacks down would also like to keep other minorities down."

□ Attitudes toward women have taken a similar turnabout. The number who think women are discriminated against in getting manual-labor jobs has jumped from 41% to 57% over a 15-year period. In getting skilled-labor jobs, the number who feel women are discriminated against has risen from 42% to 54%. And the number who believe women are discriminated against in being able to earn enough to support themselves independently soared from 33% in 1970 to 58%

in 1985. Similarly, while no more than 42% favored social efforts to strengthen women's status back in 1970, by 1985 71% favored such steps. In addition, by almost 3 to 1, most feel that women often do not receive the same pay as men for doing exactly the same job. That, of course, is the "equal pay for equal work" rallying cry. And, a harbinger of the future, an almost identical 70%–27% majority believes that women often do not receive the same pay as men for doing comparable jobs demanding similar levels of skill and training. This is the "comparable pay" issue that is just surfacing in many places.

■ SO WHY ISN'T MORE BEING DONE TO CORRECT THE INEQUITIES?

One of the real anomalies of modern life is that attitudes toward discrimination against minorities and women have literally turned around but evidence of real progress in rooting out prejudice and discrimination is difficult to find. A full 20 years after the passage of the Civil Rights Act of 1964, a symposium of moderate black leaders concluded that the act has not brought about an appreciable improvement in the lot of most blacks. Indeed, the number of poor in the country, including a vastly disproportionate share of blacks, has increased rather than decreased in the 1980s. While some small improvement took place, nonetheless blacks were still getting in pay no more than 78% of what whites earn for the same work, while women were getting no more than 64% of the pay men receive for the same work, according to the U.S. Bureau of Labor Statistics.

In short, people may now be far more aware of discrimination against minorities and women, but the underlying, basic disparities have barely budged.

One suggestion that emerges over and over in surveys of public opinion is that special efforts and special programs be utilized to make certain that the status of women and minorities is advanced. This, of course, is what affirmative action is all about. In the Harris surveys on this subject the questions have been careful to point out that while special efforts would be made to enhance the opportunities for women and minorities, there would be no rigid quotas used—as the Bakke, Weber, and other Supreme Court decisions have ruled.

Attitudes about affirmative action have been among the most underreported and misreported facts about public opinion. Overall, the number who favor affirmative action programs for women and minorities has risen from 61% to 31% in 1983 to a current 75% to 21%.

Equally significant is the fact that three common objections to affirmative action are rejected by resounding majorities nationwide:

□ The claim that "once affirmative action programs for women and minorities are started, the result is bound to be reverse discrimination against men" was rejected by 47% to 38% in 1978, but is rejected by a much wider 59% to 39% today.

□ The charge that "minorities and women are *not* entitled to any special consideration" was adhered to by 73% to 20% in 1978, but has now completely turned around and is rejected by 64% to 35%.

□ The claim that "white men learn faster, are better qualified, and will continue to hold down better jobs, no matter how many affirmative action programs for women and minorities are started" is also rejected by 71% to 27%, compared with a similar rejection by 67% to 23% in 1978.

By contrast, three other arguments in behalf of affirmative action programs meet with lopsided agreement across the country:

□ By 85% to 14%, a big majority agrees with the claim that "after years of discrimination, it is only fair to set up special programs to make sure that women and minorities are given every chance to have equal opportunities in employment and education," up from a 73%–19% majority who felt that way in 1978.

☐ By 82% to 17%, another sizable majority agrees with the view that "as long as there are no rigid quotas, it makes sense to give special training and advice to women and minorities so that they can perform better on the job," up from 71%–20% majority who felt that way back in the late 1970s.

☐ Finally, by 71% to 27%, another big majority feels that "if there are no affirmative action programs helping women and minorities in employment and education, then these groups will continue to fail to get their share of jobs and higher education, thereby continuing past discrimination in the future." This is sharply up from a 45%–36% plurality who felt that way 8 years ago.

OBSERVATION

In the face of this rising tide of sentiment for affirmative action remedies to correct discrimination against women and minorities, there has been no visible response from the Reagan Justice Department. In fact, to the contrary, Attorney General Edwin Meese has tried to do away with rules that guarantee affirmative action programs in the federal government, to end 53 affirmative action programs around the country, and to file amicus curiae briefs in cases that would either slow down or reverse previous affirmative action court rulings.

When asked directly about Meese's opposition to much of the affirmative action measures now in effect, a 69%–27% majority of the public believes he is "wrong." The explosive nature of this issue, of course, lies in the fact that the official law enforcement arm of the federal government appears to be intensifying its opposition to affirmative action just as public opinion appears to be mounting sharply in support of such programs. This collision course now shapes up as a potentially major confrontation in the 1988 elections—if the obvious trend of public opinion is to work its will on government in the immediate years ahead.

U.S. Bureau of Labor Statistics, *Employment and Earnings,* monthly reports 1980–84, as reported in the U.S. Bureau of the Census, *Statistical Abstract of the United States, 1986* (Washington, D.C., 1985), Table 704: Median Weekly Earnings of Full Time Wage and Salary Workers, by Selected Characteristics: 1980 to 1984, p. 419.

U.S. Bureau of the Census, *Current Population Reports,* series P-60, No. 145, as reported in the U.S. Bureau of the Census, *Statistical Abstract of the United States, 1986* (Washington, D.C., 1985), Table 703: Number of Workers with Earnings and Median Earnings, by Occupation of Longest Job Held and Sex: 1983, p. 419.

The Harris Survey, conducted by Louis Harris and Associates, September 5–8, 1985, among a national cross section of 1,255 adults, released October 14, 1985.

THE DISABLED MAKE THEIR MOVE TO JOIN THE REST OF THE HUMAN RACE

■ HOW CAN 27 MILLION PEOPLE BE ALMOST INVISIBLE?

Just over one in every seven people 16 years of age or older are disabled. They have a disability or health problem that has prevented them from participating fully in work or school or other key experiences—either a physical disability, such as a defect in their sight or hearing, a speech impediment, a disabling emotional or mental condition, or a learning disability. In all, there are 27 million people who fall into the disabled category.

Until Louis Harris and Associates recently completed a study of a national cross section of disabled persons for the International Center for the Disabled, little definitive information existed about them. For most of the 210 years of the country's history, the disabled had been tucked away out of sight. For the one in every seven families with a disabled member, by and large it has been a private matter. The common assumption seemed to be that misfortunes that beset families, such as idiocy, alcoholism, deformities, or worse, are best borne in silence, behind closed doors with the curtains pulled tight. The curses of fate are endured, not displayed for all to see.

■ THE PRICE OF BEING A SHUT-IN

The story of the disabled is this: if you are shut in, you are very likely to be shut out.

Most of the disabled live close to the poverty line. Fully five in every ten of their families have incomes of $15,000 or less. A third of elderly disabled are in households with incomes of $7,500 or less a year. If you are disabled, you are twice as likely to live in poverty than if you are not disabled. What is more, most of the disabled seem doomed to remain in poverty, for they are woefully undereducated. Fully 40% of them have never finished high school, compared with no more than 15% among the nondisabled.

These economic insecurities, compounded by educational deficiencies, are added to by a whole set of physical and psychological impediments that result from being disabled. Pluralities of the disabled report real apprehensions over getting hurt, coming down sick, or being victimized by crime, *because* of their disability. They also have a sense of dependence because they require help just to get around. They regularly face the bleak prospect of trying to gain access to public transportation or to find someone to drive them around. They have problems gaining access to buildings and finding bathrooms they can use in them.

It is little wonder, then, that 56% of all the disabled report having real difficulty in getting around and attending cultural and sporting events. A much higher 67% of the severely disabled say they are virtually immobile, as is the case with 79% of the very severely disabled. A few comparisons tell the tale. While 78% of all adults went to a movie last year, only 36% of the disabled get out to see one. While 60% of all adults see live theater or a musical performance, no more than 23% of the disabled get to do it. It is not surprising that 57% of the disabled say flat out that their disability has shut them out from realizing their potential as human beings.

■ THE KEY IS NOT PITY BUT A CHANCE TO WORK

The decisive division between hope and no hope among the disabled is between working and not working. Those who work by and large feel they are part of the human race. Those who do not work feel left out, alone, and largely useless.

Among the disabled who are in the 16–64 age bracket, 24% hold down full-time jobs, and another 10% have part-time jobs, but 66% do not work. Yet, that is not the way the disabled would have it. Among those not working, fully 66% say they would like to hold down a job. Sadly, only a meager 4% of them are actively in the job market, having looked for work in the previous month before the survey.

The bottom line on jobs and the key to the state of mind and the hopes of the disabled is contained in these facts:

□ Among those of working age, only 33% hold down jobs, while 66% do not.

□ But if the disabled had their way, 78% would be working and only 22% say they are incapable of holding down a job.

□ The 78% of the disabled who believe they could hold down jobs if they were trained and could find work are willing to endure fewer public and private benefits. But a massive 89% of all the disabled say that those who cannot hold down jobs should be the beneficiaries of much greater governmental and private benefits so that they can live comfortably without working.

The comparison between the disabled who work and those who don't could not be more dramatic. There are four times as many disabled who work who have completed a four-year college education as those who do not work. While 44% of the disabled who work are in households with incomes of $25,000 and over, only 21% of those disabled who don't work are in such households.

Significantly, 53% of those disabled who hold down jobs say their disability has not kept them from fulfilling themselves in life, while 60% of those who do not work say their

EMPLOYMENT AND THE ATTITUDES OF THE DISABLED

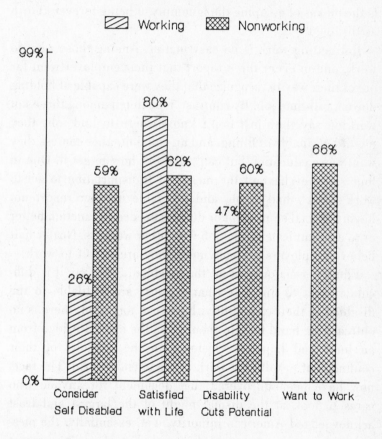

disability has locked them into never finding such fulfillment in life. Work gives hope. No work breeds despair.

Indeed, 59% of those who don't work give themselves the self-description of "disabled," while 74% of those who work now refuse to call themselves by that name. Put simply, work is the means of escaping the ignominy of being forever known as disabled.

But getting work is no easy matter. Among those who do work, one in every three report that their employer went far out of their way to recognize that they were capable of holding down a full-time job. By contrast, four in ten among those not working say they just don't know where to find jobs they might be capable of filling, and an equal number confess they want more education but can't find out how to get it. One in four say they haven't the means of transportation to get to work if they had a job, and the same number report not having special equipment or devices needed to function better or to communicate on the job with other workers. Nearly half believe employers are convinced they are not fit to work.

Finally, a majority of all the disabled, 53%, say it is difficult at best to find out what services are available to the disabled in their community. For most, too often, there is no outreaching hand to help them cross the critical bridge from an inert and hopeless existence in the shadows of their confinement to fulfilling work in the outside world. The facts now have been uncovered that document for anyone who cares to look at the dismal plight of the largest and least acknowledged American minority. Yet, essentially, the message they send is one not of despair but of hoping against hope. Back in 1963, when the Harris firm conducted landmark studies of blacks in America, a singular surprise was that blacks thought things were getting better and would get better still. Now the same hope and optimism exists among the disabled.

OBSERVATION

As clear as any message in the 1980s is that the disabled want desperately to join the human race. The vehicle for doing this is jobs, which must be accompanied by education. But, even before that, an infrastructure for the disabled must be created; society must reach out to help them. They do not want pity. They want a chance to achieve self-respect. And that will come only when they can feel independent and self-reliant. Significantly, by 45% to 42%, a plurality of the disabled now view themselves as a cohesive and disadvantaged minority, much like blacks and Hispanics. The young who are disabled feel particularly deeply about this. And fully 74% of the disabled report they have a common identity with all others who are disabled. With this common bond and a powerful determination born of their desperate and lonely plight, the disabled are beginning to feel they can overcome.

Disabled Americans' Self Perceptions: Bringing Disabled Americans into the Mainstream, conducted by Louis Harris and Associates for the International Center for the Disabled, November–December 1985, among a national cross section of 1,000 noninstitutionalized disabled persons aged 16 and over, released March 1986.

THE EMERGING WORLD OF HEALTH CARE

■ A REPORT CARD ON THE NATION'S HEALTH SYSTEM

Health is a decidedly no-nonsense subject. When you have it, there is nothing more precious. When you lose it, not much else matters. In turn, in assessing how a health care system works, an acceptable criterion for a satisfactory rating can hardly be "Well, it's working pretty well," or "I guess it's not too bad." This might be an acceptable standard for a transportation system, a garbage collection service, or even a supermarket. But not for a health care system. Anything less than high satisfaction must be taken as a signal that all is not well. By the same token, when people speak about downright dissatisfaction with health care, there is real cause for alarm.

In the mid-1980s in America, there is no major part of our health care system that has a majority of the people willing to express high satisfaction with it:

☐ *Quality of doctors.* An even 50% of the public nationwide say they are "very satisfied" with the quality of doctors available to them. But almost as many, 49%, are either "somewhat satisfied" (34%) or "dissatisfied" (15%). At best, this is a standoff. It must be kept in mind that people are rating only the doctors they go to.

☐ *Ability to see a doctor whenever needed.* On this score, only 48% are highly satisfied, while 51% express only partial satisfaction (32%) or downright dissatisfaction (19%). So even if the quality of doctors is quite good, the inability to avail oneself of that quality when you need it can be frustrating, to say the least.

□ *Availability of a specialist when you need one.* To Americans who have been raised to believe that ordinary physicians might be comforting and even helpful when you need medical aid, getting hold of a good specialist is like getting halfway to finding a cure. No more than 44% say they are very satisfied with the availability of specialists when they need one, while a higher 50% are less than well satisfied (32% somewhat satisfied and 18% dissatisfied). In short, a specialist is great *if* you can find one.

□ *Quality of hospital care.* People go to hospitals only when things get serious—as a last resort or in an emergency. Only 41% express high satisfaction with the hospitals they are familiar with and presumably where they would go themselves. By contrast, 51% are less than very satisfied with hospitals (32% somewhat satisfied and 19% dissatisfied). Most people are highly nervous about having to go to a hospital in the first place, but not a small reason for their apprehension is worry over the quality of the care they will obtain there.

□ *Availability of doctors and medical services 24 hours a day, 7 days a week.* This is no small consideration. Getting ill, especially seriously ill, unfortunately does not happen at a convenient time. A genuine cause of stress is the concern that something dreadful will happen to your health when you can't find a doctor or get ready assistance. Only 38% place high satisfaction that they can obtain such help around the clock. A much higher 59% aren't so sure, with 32% only "somewhat satisfied" they can get it, and 27% quite sure they can't get it when they need it.

□ *Amount of time spent waiting to see a doctor after you have called for an appointment.* This problem is part annoyance, especially if you have a busy schedule, and particularly since you are likely to be paying the doctor a rather hefty fee for the privilege of cooling your heels in his waiting room before getting to see him. Thus, only 29% are highly satisfied with the way appointments by doctors are kept, while 71% are less than fully satisfied, with 31% "somewhat satisfied" and a higher 40% "dissatisfied." Of course, if you are in pain or worried that you have some dread disease, the long wait to see the doctor becomes unbearable, a condition that can only contribute enormously to a stress-laden confrontation.

□ *Cost to you and your family* This is the fiscal bottom line of medical care—how much it costs you out of your own pocket, after what your insurance covers. Only a meager 26% are highly satisfied with the costs of health care these days, compared with 73% who are less than very pleased (28% somewhat satisfied and 45% dissatisfied). Here is the last straw about health care in the country. Not only do people have genuine doubts about the quality of doctors, their ability to find them when they need them, the availability of a key specialist, the quality of hospital care, and the round-the-clock availability of medical care, but the cost of it all is viewed as out of control and unbearable.

■ AN OVERALL JUDGMENT ABOUT THE AMERICAN HEALTH SYSTEM

When asked to assess the health system as a whole, by a substantial 74% to 26%, a majority reject the claim that "on the whole the health care system works pretty well, and only minor changes are necessary to make it work better." Instead, 49% say, "There are some good things in our health care system, but fundamental changes are needed to make it work better," and another 21% reach the radical conclusion that "the American health care system has so much wrong with it that we need to completely rebuild it."

Those who would defend the present health care system in the U.S. might well ponder the fact that the number of people who want to radically change it—presumably in favor of some form of state-sponsored health plan—total 21%, almost as many as the 26% who would opt essentially for the status quo.

When a cross section of physicians was asked to make their judgment on an identical question, 54% of them came down in defense of the current system, compared with only 26% of the public. Another 43% of the doctors opted for fundamental change to make things better, compared with 49% of the public. But only 3% of the physicians want radical surgery on the system, compared with 21% of the public. Clearly, most doctors want to keep the status quo, while most of the people they service want basic, if not radical, changes in the health care system.

■ HMOS: AN OPTION THAT IS GAINING FAVOR

One of the fastest-growing forms of the delivery of medical services in the United States is health maintenance organizations. From 1976 to 1984, the estimated number of HMO members in the country rose from 6 million to over 15 million, and it is projected that they will at least double again by early in the next decade.

The underlying predication of HMOs is that patients who sign up with them prepay a set amount each year, in return for which they receive an unlimited amount of care. However, the emphasis of the HMO is on preventive medicine. Physicians can spend only a limited amount of time with a patient, and participants are told that if they take better care of themselves, so that they use the HMO facilities less, their medical costs and the others' cost in the plan will not go up and may even decline.

When a cross section of HMO participants are asked to rate the health care system on the same items as the general public, they are less dissatisfied with the quality of their doctors, more satisfied with the availability of doctors when they are needed, more satisfied with the availability of specialists, most satisfied with the quality of hospital care available to them, much more pleased with the availability of round-the-clock medical services, and less dissatisfied with the waiting time when they have an appointment.

But the most dramatic evidence is that while the general public is downright unhappy with the cost of medical services, 59% of the HMO members nationwide are highly satisfied with the cost to them.

OBSERVATION

While HMOs are not the only alternative to the prevailing health care system in the U.S., obviously they are working better than the rest of the system, judging by a comparison of the relative satisfaction of the general public with their medical care experience and that of HMO members. The fact remains that by the mid-1980s the high cost of health services continued to act as a spur upon patients and those vested with the responsibilities to underwrite the system and to make it work to come up with something more than patch-and-fill solutions. The American people are patently willing to make sacrifices and even to change long-standing habits in obtaining medical care in return for cost relief. They are not willing, however, to compromise on the ultimate quality of medical care. However, if they can find alternatives that in fact increase the quality of delivery and also give them some cost relief, such options are clearly going to be big winners.

Physicians by and large still tend to be the odd people out. They still cling to the status quo, to being paid in fees instead of in salaries, to not having suggested prices set for standard medical procedures, and a host of other long-standing practices. But, for the first time, a plurality of younger physicians are now willing to accept compensation in the form of salaries rather than fees, as is the case with HMOs, and Individual Practice Associations (IPAs), an alternative based on principles similar to those of HMOs, are growing even more rapidly than group practices and HMO installations.

For a nation that has long been highly self-indulgent in its conviction that it can violate all the rules of good health and be rescued by a vast safety net of superb physician service, America now appears to be making a fundamental and deliberate shift toward opting for preventive medicine—albeit this choice is driven by the frightening extent of medical costs.

A Report Card on HMOs 1980–1984, conducted by Louis Harris and Associates for the Henry J. Kaiser Family Foundation, August–September 1984, among a national cross section of 1,004 adults, 672 physicians, a cross section of 1,004 HMO members and 230 eligible nonmembers.

Group Health Association of America, Washington, D.C., estimates of HMO enrollment growth as reported in the U.S. Bureau of the Census, *Statistical Abstract of the United States, 1986* (Washington, D.C. 1985), (Table 160: Health Maintenance Organizations (HMO)—Number and Enrollment, By Type and Size of Organization: 1976 to 1984), p 102.

SPORTS: CAN THE OPIATE OF MALE AMERICA SURVIVE THE BLIGHT OF DRUGS AND BIG MONEY?

■ A NATION OF JOCKS

An old apocryphal story told how Soviet dictator Joseph Stalin one day called in his most trusted advisers and told them to invent something that would slow down the productivity advances in the U.S. Stalin's orders were: Invent a new machine that would cut American productivity by one third. After two years, his advisers came up with a miracle machine that would absorb as much as eight hours a day of the time of the American people: television. And to make sure it would rivet the attention of male breadwinners, the new machine would be programmed with sports, especially pro football and pro baseball.

By the middle of the 1980s, following team sports has reached monumental proportions in America. Fully 81% of all adults reported they followed some organized sport, mostly live on television. But the audience for sports is largely male. Men outnumber women by 3 to 2 as sports fans. The only sports in which women fans outnumber men are horse racing (54% to 46%) and bowling (53% to 47%). Men edge out women as tennis fans by a narrow 51% to 49%. But men dominate the rest: by 60% to 40% in the case of pro football, baseball by 57% to 43%, college football by 61% to 39%, both college and pro basketball by 56% to 44%, boxing by 75% to 25%, auto racing by 68% to 32%, track and field by 65% to 35%, golf by 61% to 39%, hockey by 63% to 37%, and soccer by 57% to 43%.

The phenomenon of weekend sports widows, wives left to their own devices while husbands sit glued to the TV screen watching live sports, is entering its third generation.

The number one sport since 1969 has been pro football, a violent but spectacular sport that seems made for television, and is followed by 59% of all sports fans. Baseball, still called the national pastime, is a close second, followed by 54% of the fans. Then comes college football (followed by 47%), college basketball (32%), pro basketball (32%), tennis (29%), boxing (28%), auto racing (21%), horse racing (21%), track and field (21%), golf (20%), bowling (18%), hockey (14%), and soccer, the world's number one sport (10%).

■ IS SUCCESS BREEDING GREED IN SPORTS?

By the latter half of the 1980s, sports had become big business. The New York Mets baseball team was sold in the fall of 1986 for $85 million, after having been bought for $21 million a relatively few years earlier. The key, of course, was television, which pays huge sums for exclusive rights to put the events on live TV. For example, the National Football League is now receiving $500 million a year for TV rights, and recently signed with three networks for $2.1 billion over a five-year period. These big revenues in turn have produced instant millionaires among professional athletes with star status. A salary of a million dollars a year is no longer big news in any major pro sport.

But this has raised charges that what used to be simple fun and games for millions of fans, a wonderful escape from the daily stress of real life, now is turning into a cold-blooded business. Business priorities now seem to many to be taking the fun out of following sports and rooting for favorites.

This was never more evident than during the long strikes that have beset pro football and baseball in recent years. During the long baseball strike of 1981 an overwhelming 89%–10% majority of the fans concluded that "both the owners and the players have become so greedy they are putting the business of baseball above the game." What fans can't and won't take is the feeling that they are merely inanimate numbers of faceless TV viewers being manipulated for profit by those who are running big-time sports.

■ THE SPECTER OF DRUGS VISITS THE SPORTS ESTABLISHMENT

In many ways, the drug problem that now plagues big-time sports stems directly from the flood of money that has inundated pro football, baseball, and basketball. Many athletes are simply not prepared to handle the big money that they are being paid. Ball players spend long days on the road, yet only perform for a few hours a day at best. Boredom during nonplaying hours is high. The temptation to turn on with drugs is obviously also high. Many professional athletes are opportune targets for drug pushers.

Over the past few years, major drug cases have been revealed in nearly every major sport. Baseball had a notorious trial in Pittsburgh, which implicated such major stars as Keith Hernandez of the New York Mets and Dave Parker of the Cincinnati Reds, among others. Pro football has had its share of stars exposed as drug users, and the fatal overdose of rising star cornerback Johnny Rogers of the Cleveland Browns shook the sports world in 1986.

But the most shocking case involved Len Bias, a college basketball star for the University of Maryland, who died from a drug overdose in his dorm room in the summer of 1986 the night after he had signed a lucrative contract with the Boston Celtics and a shoe manufacturer—all worth several million dollars. The Bias case cast a pall over not only college but professional sports.

Polls are now showing that the public believes professional athletes tend to use drugs more often than people in other walks of life. A substantial 64%–28% majority of fans in a

*New York Times/*CBS News poll want drug testing of all professional athletes. By 3 to 1, the *Washington Post/*ABC News poll reports, these tests should be mandatory. What is more, by nearly 3 to 1, fans also think that professional athletes should be suspended from playing for a first-time drug offense.

But suspension is as far as fans will go. When asked if a first-time drug offender should be banned from playing, fans were opposed by 7 to 1. When asked about repeated drug offenders, only 24% of the fans said they ought to be banned from the sport.

If fans tend to be forgiving of star athletes who fall from grace over drugs, owners can be assumed to be even less inclined to toss them out of the game. As has been pointed out in the sports pages, the owners have important financial stakes in their stars. They have signed players whom their coaches tell them they need to win championships, giving them multimillion-dollar contracts, including bonuses.

Baseball commissioner Peter Ueberroth came up with a system of stiff fines and "sentences" of community service for those players who were involved in the use of illicit drugs. The fans liked this, and a plurality of 46% single out baseball as having the most intelligent approach to the drug problem. However, pro basketball is the only sport to permanently bar repeated drug users from its ranks, and has banned three players in the past two years.

OBSERVATION

The twin problems of excessive money and widespread drug usage threaten the very existence of major sports in the United States. When George Rogers, who is now a running back for the Washington Redskins, admitted after he was rookie of the year in the National Football League that he had been a repeated user of cocaine during the football season, this news could hardly have deterred future stars like Len Bias from using drugs. To the contrary, if a player can be rookie of the year and use drugs, what incentive do younger and less experienced athletes who aspire to be the George Rogerses of the future have to lay off drugs? The problem takes on especially serious proportions when we remember that athletes are viewed as role models by many young people.

And when the drug problem is coupled with the big TV money that has engulfed professional and college sports, a central question must be raised: When will cynical fans finally turn off? And if fans sour, then a decline in TV revenues is not far behind. Indeed, there is already ample evidence in some of the shrinking television ratings—for pro football, particularly—that overexposure of sports on TV is on the rise.

The ominous evidence points to the prospect that greed, excesses such as in the use of drugs, and fan turnoff could endanger the healthy fun and games that used to be known as sports in America.

———————————

*New York Times/*CBS News poll, conducted by the *New York Times* and CBS, August 18–21 1986, among a national cross section of 1,210 adults, released September 2, 1986.

*Washington Post/*ABC poll, conducted by the *Washington Post* and ABC, October 21–28 1985, among a national cross section of 1,506 adults, released October 1985.

The Harris Survey, conducted by Louis Harris and Associates, July 8–12, 1981, among 646 sports fans, released July 16, 1981; November 1–4 1985, among 1,051 sports fans, released December 12, 1985; and November 1–4 1985, 1,254 adults, released January 6, 1986.

A survey conducted by Louis Harris and Associates for *USA Today*, March 24 – April 3, 1983, among a national cross section of 1,505 adults.

Robert Raissman, "Budweiser Super Bowl?" *Advertising Age*, February 3, 1986, p. 68.

Nancy J. Perry, "A Big Winner, in Two Leagues," *Fortune*, January 5, 1987, pp. 33–34.

COMMERCIALISM AND PATRIOTISM: THEY DON'T MIX

■ **THE GREEN COVERING LADY LIBERTY WASN'T JUST PATINA**

Almost as significant as the wave of unabashed patriotic sentiment that engulfed the U.S. after the 1984 Olympics was the
remarkable feat of the organizers of those games in not only
paying for them with private funds but making an additional
$250 million to boot. This accomplishment made something
of a wunderkind of Peter Ueberroth, who headed the effort.
Indeed, a number of people saw Ueberroth as a potential U.S.
senator and even as president. In any case, it got him appointed commissioner of baseball.

Most of all, of course, the financing of the Olympics proved
to those who worship at the shrine of private initiative that
major not-for-profit ventures can be undertaken without government funds. The Olympics did it by selling to manufacturers of products and services the right to advertise that they
were the "official" Olympic camera, cereal, soft drink, snack,
or nearly anything else that was consumable. Of course, to
merit this patriotic stamp, a sponsoring company had to pay
a stiff tariff. But, for a price, such rarefied status was open to
any enterprising product line.

Not to be outdone, Chrysler president Lee Iacocca took
over the chair of the Statue of Liberty–Ellis Island Centennial
Commission. His goal was to raise $265 million wholly from
the private sector and not to spend a dime of federal monies,

even though the lady was obviously federal property. The device used was to designate special corporate sponsors of the restoration, each of whom was required to contribute a substantial sum of money. In return for this largess, the corporations were able to advertise their sponsorship and build up a reservoir of goodwill from such worthy public works. Despite a major flap over the disposition of funds for the restoration of Ellis Island, which faces the Statue of Liberty, Iacocca's efforts ended up an acclaimed success as measured by the surplus that his committee eventually produced. As with Peter Ueberroth, Iacocca's success triggered a spate of speculations about his presidential prospects.

■ SOMEHOW IT DIDN'T ALL GO DOWN AS SMOOTHLY AS THE OLYMPICS

Polling taken at the time of the big July Fourth celebration of the centennial of the statue turned up a healthy dose of skepticism and even some questioning about the symbolism of the event itself. Although America was founded as a melting pot and prominent naturalized citizens from other nations were feted at the celebration, sizable numbers of Americans have their doubts about the effects of immigration:

☐ When asked by the *New York Times,* fully 44% of a cross section of the public across the country could not name a single important contribution that immigrants had made to the U.S.

☐ By a narrow 45% to 43%, a plurality felt it was just "not practical to welcome more immigrants to the country today."

☐ By 44% to 34%, a plurality of the public held the view that recent immigrants to the U.S. had contributed more problems than positive contributions to the nation. Indeed, fully 73% of the public was able to volunteer a whole spate of such problems, such as taking jobs from American workers, causing crime, going on welfare at taxpayers' expense, and causing overpopulation.

The underlying theme of the celebration—to pay tribute to the contributions that immigrants had made to the growth and character of the country—was not appealing to many of the progeny of those immigrants. Shakespeare wrote long ago that it is the mark of most of mankind "to scorn the base degrees by which he did ascend." Denial of one's roots has occurred at other times in the history of this and other countries.

But the most unexpected reaction was over the commercialism that somehow seemed to shroud the restoration celebration:

☐ *The Harris Survey* found that a plurality (49%–43%) of the American people felt the celebration had been made "too commercial with corporations trying to get too much publicity for helping pay for restoring the Statue of Liberty." The division itself was quite close, but the important result was that what had been assumed to be a new pattern set by the Olympics two years before—to have private corporations pick up the tab in exchange for obtaining "official" sanction from the organizing committee—didn't turn out to be a popular idea after all.

☐ In fact, when asked outright if the federal government should have paid all the costs connected with the restoration, only a razor-thin 47%–46% plurality turned down the idea—even though almost no one had earlier suggested federal underwriting of the restoration project and literally millions had been spent by sponsoring companies.

☐ Coinciding with the July Fourth celebration of Lady Liberty was the Hands Across America effort to bring attention to the plight of the growing number of people living in hunger in this country. After shunning the event, at the last moment President Reagan finally endorsed it. When asked if the weekend event ought to be an all-out occasion to "speak up for America"—a euphemism born of the Olympic festival meaning to make an unabashed display of patriotism—or whether such a celebration might be "taking the country's mind off problems such as hunger and the homeless," a clear-cut 53% to 32% said they thought the latter was the case.

In fact, most of the country neither attended the Statue of Liberty bash nor watched it on TV. Most just took the long weekend off to go to the beach, relax, or have fun at some of the old-fashioned Fourth of July fireworks displays that had no connection with the New York celebration.

OBSERVATION

Given that the ungenerous prevailing view about immigration and immigrants is not new in American life, perhaps making a major national event of the restoration of the Statue of Liberty was a risky venture at best. But the straw that appears to have broken the back of the effort was what most Americans view as the rather crass commercialism attached to the fund-raising to pay for the restoration. The sight of companies buying commercial TV time and ads in newspapers in messages of self-praise was just too much for roughly half the American people to take. Indeed, the public was split right down the middle on the basic proposition of having the restoration paid for by the private sector in the first place.

The significance of the event in any case may not have been earth-shattering under the best of circumstances. The Statue of Liberty will stand now for a long time to come as a genuine and moving tribute to those refugees who found their way to

America and formed the population base of a great country. Emma Lazarus's words at the base of the statue will outlive the tag lines of the many commercials aired on TV before and during the big weekend.

And it is just possible that the whole episode will have taught those in control that, like oil and water, patriotism and commercialism are not a good mix.

New York Times poll, conducted by the *New York Times,* June 19–23 1986, among a national cross section of 1,618 adults, released June 30, 1986.

The Harris Survey, conducted by Louis Harris and Associates, June 11–16, 1986, among a national cross section of 1,250 adults, released June 30, 1986.

IS THERE ANY FUTURE FOR UNIONS IN AMERICA?

■ THE SLIDE OF UNION MEMBERSHIP

Without doubt, labor unions in the United States face a real crisis, with nothing less than their survival at stake. Union membership has not grown as the population has grown since the 1930s. In absolute numbers, the labor movement hit its peak over a decade ago. Back in the 1950s it could claim as members as many as one in every three wage earners in the country. Now that percentage has dropped to 18% and shows every sign of shrinking with each passing year.

■ WHAT LIES BEHIND THE DECLINE OF UNION POWER

With the general public as well as the unorganized—those whom unions have failed to recruit as members to maintain their 1950s share of the work force—the overall reputation of unions leaves much to be desired.

The litany of criticisms of the trade union movement is a long one:

☐ By 57% to 34% nationwide, a majority thinks that unions have become too powerful and should be restricted by law in the abuse of their power.

☐ By 54% to 28%, another clear majority thinks that many union leaders have ties with racketeers and organized crime.

☐ By an identical 54% to 28%, a majority also believe that many union leaders have abused union pension funds.

☐ By 50% to 39%, a plurality thinks that most union leaders have become arrogant and no longer represent the workers in their unions.

☐ By 57% to 32%, a majority also holds the view that most unions have forced make-work rules on employers that have cut productivity and have made the U.S. less able to compete abroad.

When union members' views on these same charges are examined, most tend to deny the claim that unions don't represent the workers and that unions have become so powerful they should be restricted under the law. However, pluralities of the rank and file of organized labor do believe the charges that featherbedding and unions are making America less competitive, that pension funds have been abused, and that too many union leaders are too close to organized crime.

■ ANOTHER SIDE

The very same survey that yielded this highly damaging set of results about unions also came up with some quite different findings:

☐ By 61% to 29%, a majority of the public nationwide believes that unions serve as a good check on the power of big business.

☐ A sizable 82% to 15% majority is convinced that in many industries unions are needed so that legitimate complaints and grievances of workers can be heard and action taken on them.

☐ By 79% to 14%, another majority thinks that most unions in the country have been good forces, working for such things as better governmental health programs, higher unemployment compensation, better social security, minimum wage laws, and other social gains.

☐ Significantly, by 56% to 38%, a majority also thinks that

if there were no unions, most employers would quickly move to exploit their employees on wages and job security.

□ And, by 68% to 28%, a clear majority is convinced that if there were no unions, many employers would hire and fire people on the basis of favoritism.

The same poll also brought to light quite unexpected results when the cross section was asked how they would regard the situation of a young person in the family if he or she was employed as an hourly worker in an industrial plant and if that same young relative was working in a white-collar office job:

□ By 73% to 16%, a big majority said they thought the young person would be better off joining a union if he or she had a job in an industrial plant.

□ By 55% to 30%, a majority also thought the young person would be better off joining a union if he or she worked in an office.

These results indicate clearly that although unions obviously have lost a great deal of clout by dint of their failure to organize many workers for over a generation, nonetheless their function is widely recognized as legitimate.

■ YET MOST WORKERS SAY "NO UNION FOR ME"

But these generalized reactions do not adequately get at the reason why unions have had so much trouble organizing new members and have not grown at all as the work force has expanded. When workers eligible to join unions are surveyed, most think they are not paid enough for the amount and quality of the work they produce and say that job security is highly important to them in their work. Unions are acknowledged as being effective both in getting higher wages and in ensuring job security. Nearly three in every four think that unions improve the wages and working conditions of workers.

However, by 54% to 38%, a majority think that unions stifle individual initiative. By a close 49% to 48%, they say that unions increase the risk that companies will go out of business. A significant 58% to 41% say that most employees today don't need unions to get fair treatment from their employers.

A bottom line is that when asked how they would vote tomorrow on joining a union, a convincing 63%–34% majority of those eligible to join unions say they would vote against such union representation.

Yet there was one other highly significant result in the in-depth survey. Substantial numbers of the same workers who would turn down a union in an up-or-down vote also say they have gone to their employer either as an individual or with some other employees to complain about matters connected with their work. Scarcely more than one in three report any real satisfaction stemming from such representations with their employers. Yet, when asked which method is more effective in getting their employer to correct their work problems, by 54% to 37%, a majority say that they would be more successful going to their employer as a group rather than as individuals. The irony of these results is that if there had been no unions in this country, it appears likely that American workers would have discovered them.

OBSERVATION

Despite the solid testimony that the function of unions is felt by sizable majorities to still be needed in America, nonetheless as unions are constituted today and with their reputation as it is, the prospect of their gaining more members in the near future appears to be slim indeed.

Perhaps the most serious charge against unions is that they hurt America's chances of competing abroad. The public is becoming aware that the U.S. can no longer compete in mass production and assembly-line operations. Asian labor, particularly, simply can outproduce this country, partly because of lower wages and partly because of higher rates of productivity.

The impact of the reality of competition has been to convince a solid 59%–38% majority that wages should go up only as productivity increases. The appeal of unions that they can get better wages appears to have been undermined by this greater realization. Thus, it seems logical that unions had better begin thinking in terms of productivity as much as they do about wages. Such approaches would appear to make more sense than relying on raising import barriers and even tariffs to keep out foreign competition. In the long term, American labor must face the challenge of how to educate and train a labor force that is much more proficient in science, math, and technology, that is capable of thinking problems through, is able to find answers to questions they do not know the answers to, and is so creative and well trained that they would be the basis for a whole new economy that could outcompete any other economy on the face of the earth. This would mean new industries with new types of work configurations, and new standards of productivity reflective of much higher worker capabilities. When just such a scenario was recently described to a cross section of the public, a 4 to 1 majority said it made sense to them.

Business Week/Harris Poll, conducted by Louis Harris and Associates, May 30–June 2, 1985, among a national cross section of 1,954 employed adults, released July 8, 1985.

FALSE HOPES, EXPLOITATION, AND POSSIBLE SALVATION: THE HEART TRANSPLANT CONTROVERSY

■ "THEY WILL FIND THE CURE BEFORE I DIE FROM IT"

Several years ago a cross section of the American people was asked what seemed to be a simple, straightforward series of questions that involved most of the big killer diseases in this society: heart disease, stroke, cancer, pulmonary diseases, pneumonia, diabetes, and liver disease. In each case, people were asked if, *in their lifetime*, a cure for each of these diseases would be discovered by medical science. Without fail, for each disease, seven in every ten people said they were quite certain a miracle cure would be found—before they die. Clearly, people were not articulating an objective judgment, but instead one of the most profound articles of faith in modern society: science will come up with an answer before the evil threat gets me.

Such optimism, of course, is the stuff that allows people to avoid stress and depression, lets them get through tough times, and gives them peace of mind. But it also makes the American people highly vulnerable to false nostrums and claims in the medical and scientific area. They start out convinced that miracle cures will happen. Thus, at least initially, they are willing to give each bit of real or alleged news of a breakthrough a credibility well beyond what it deserves.

■ HEART TRANSPLANTS: A CLASSIC CASE OF A MIRACLE CURE BEFORE ITS TIME

Certainly one of the most exciting prospects to come from medical science in recent years has been the promise that nearly any part of the human anatomy that is replaceable will in fact be capable of being transplanted or substituted for. Prosthetics promised all kinds of new parts, largely external: artificial legs, hips, joints. More dramatic was the promise of either artificial hearts or the transplantation of human hearts.

When Dr. Christiaan Barnard of South Africa conducted the world's first successful transplant of a human heart in 1967, the news was electric. In some ways, transplantation seemed even better than a miracle cure: much as with an old car, once it is all worn out, throw it away and get a brand new one! Through the years, as heart transplants progressed, new cases received instant attention. Indeed, almost invariably they attracted the modern equivalent of the front page: a big takeout on the evening network television news.

By the early 1980s, the promise of yet another breakthrough surfaced: the artificial heart transplant, pioneered by Dr. William C. DeVries. In 1982 his first patient, Dr. Barney Clark, captured the imagination of the public, but he died 112 days later. Then, in late 1984, the heart transplant issue roiled to something of a climax. Amid huge fanfare, the Humana Hospital Audubon in Louisville, Kentucky, implanted a complete artificial heart in William Schroeder. His initial remarkable recovery was then marred by a series of strokes and other difficulties, and he finally died in 1986.

The other episode was more bizarre. At California's Loma Linda University Medical Center, an animal-to-human transplant took place in a two-week-old infant born with a fatal heart defect. The heart of the infant, known only as Baby Fae, was replaced with the healthy heart of a young baboon. The baby died 20 days later.

The media attention was phenomenal and the uproar in the medical community was substantial. Bill Schroeder was a regular feature on the nightly network TV shows, talking with President Reagan, out of bed, back in bed, an instant national figure. Humana also became known nationally as the hospital chain where the artificial heart transplant took place. Humana announced that they would finance as many as twenty-five of these artificial transplants at a cost of $1 million apiece. The funeral service of Baby Fae, in which she was prayed to heaven by an overflow crowd, was also a national television event. Though many responsible medical authorities were outraged by the episode, Loma Linda was on the map, thanks to Baby Fae.

■ THE MORNING-AFTER REACTION

After sitting glued to their seats night after night to watch the twin dramas of Bill Schroeder and Baby Fae, the American people rendered a verdict of sorts about the whole event:

☐ By 64% to 33%, a majority agreed with the criticism made by a number of teaching hospital authorities that "real scientific progress is not made by making media events and spectaculars out of such experiments, but by working quietly to perfect such methods and reporting them only when it looks like they really work."

☐ By 57% to 40%, another majority concluded that "it's not right to claim big breakthroughs when it has not been proven yet that we know how to transplant baboon hearts to other baboons, let alone to human babies, and when it hasn't been proven that mechanical hearts can work in animals for extended periods of time, let alone in human beings."

☐ By 55% to 41%, a majority also agreed with the charge that "with costs so high for each heart transplant operation, it would be better to spend the money in more important ways, making medical care available to those who can least afford it."

Nonetheless, there were also some rationalizations that all the media attention was worth it:

☐ By a big 82% to 15%, a majority agreed that "by making the heart transplant cases such major events on TV and in the newspapers, it encourages financial and other support for other experiments like this," the implication being that the operations were hyped as promotional events. In this respect, the public might well have been more perceptive than the Humana or Loma Linda people have suspected.

☐ By 66% to 32%, a better than 2 to 1 majority of the public also concluded that "the recent experiments show that the time is not far off when most people with failing hearts will be able to have them replaced successfully with heart transplants or mechanical devices that will work." Here, of course, is the miracle-cure syndrome hard at work.

The net reaction of the public, however, was that there was real doubt about the legitimacy of the media spectacular that had been paraded before their eyes on nightly TV. By 60% to 35%, a solid majority of the American people held the rather firm view that "such experiments in the future should be conducted in more scientific settings without any fanfare," rather than be given "the kind of publicity and attention to cases of heart transplants and mechanical hearts" that Bill Schroeder and Baby Fae received.

OBSERVATION

Time has passed since the late 1984 spectacular of heart transplants. Humana's program was postponed because of financial troubles besetting the burgeoning Humana hospital chain, and Loma Linda has made a few sputterings about other medical events, but nothing that has approached the Baby Fae uproar.

Serious work in heart transplants no doubt is proceeding, but far more quietly and, presumably, in somewhat more scientific and more responsible settings. The penchant of the American people to expect the quick cure, especially in medical science, will continue. Nor will those who want to give a growing hospital chain major publicity or a small-time medical center that wants to become "famous" overnight stop trying to play their games. But maybe, just maybe, the media will have gained some perspective, and maybe some of those who would exploit the American people's tendency to rely on blind faith will realize that such tactics can all backfire badly. As Abe Lincoln said, "You can't fool all of the people all of the time."

The Harris Survey, conducted by Louis Harris and Associates, December 27, 1984–January 1, 1985, among a national cross section of 1,255 adults, released January 14, 1985.

THE LOVE AFFAIR OF CITY FOLK WITH FARMERS

■ WHERE HAVE ALL THE FARMERS GONE?

In the course of its history, the United States has moved from being a dominant agricultural country to the point where farmers have nearly disappeared. Back in 1950, an estimated 15.3% of the population lived on farms. Since then it has steadily shrunk: the latest estimates are that the farm population now makes up only 2.4% of the entire country.

Over the same 26-year period, the number of farms in the country has shrunk by fully 75%, with over 17 million farms going out of existence. Yet the total value added—a kind of net worth measurement used by the Department of Agriculture—of the food and fiber sector of the economy has more than doubled since 1950, from $318 to $659 billion a year. Ironically, the value added of just the farm sector, where all that food and fiber is grown, has actually declined from $20.5 to $18 billion over the same period of time.

These facts dramatically illustrate what has happened to agriculture in America. The family-sized farms have been consolidated into huge farms, run by businesses headquartered in big cities. The farmers have been mechanized off the farms. But the land has been made more productive. And agribusiness, as it is called, now accounts for 18.5% of all the employment in the country and 18% of the total domestic economy in dollars. Taken together, next to government, agribusiness is the biggest business in the entire economy.

Yet the farmers who produce this enormous output get only

a meager 3% of the total take from the food and fiber sector. The bulk of the money goes for processing the food, manufacturing it for sale in the supermarkets, transporting it to market, and in serving it in eating places. Indeed, it might fairly be concluded that rarely in history has the output of so few affected the livelihood and well-being of so many.

A serious question remains: If farmers have declined in number almost to the vanishing point, then why has there been such a storm of political protest and complaint across the farm-belt states and in Congress about how neglected the farmers have been? Why wasn't David Stockman, the unlamented former head of the Office of Management and Budget (OMB) in the earlier Reagan years, considered right when he said publicly that he had little sympathy with the farmers who were going broke? After all, he said, they took deliberate gambles on farm prosperity and they happened to lose, much as others take economic gambles and lose.

Although few in number, farmers are hard put. Over one in ten farms have been steadily going out of business every year. It is estimated that another 30% will go out of business in the next few years. The family farm looks to be headed for extinction.

But, like other endangered species, the American farmer is a popular cause. Intuitively, the nonfarmers of the country know that what farmers produce is critical to the nation's economy. And, of course, the food and fiber industry gives employment to a substantial 18% of the entire work force. So the lot of the farmer, even though by now they are a microscopic part of the population, is of high concern.

A striking 94%–5% majority of the American people feel strongly that the plight of the American farmer is serious. And the public backs this up by wanting to spend sizable amounts of tax dollars giving financial help to hard-put farmers. Put it this way: rarely have so many wanted to do so much for so few, who, in turn, provide so much to sustain so many.

■ THE PUBLIC PUTS ITS POCKETBOOK WHERE ITS SENTIMENT IS

When asked directly, a big 72%–26% majority say they favor a program of federal price supports and subsidies for farmers. They reject the oft-repeated statements that farmers must learn to live without government assistance. Their reasoning is that such subsidies and support prices are necessary because of the uncertainties of the weather and of the prices that farmers can get in the open market.

During a period when it has been popular to want to get the federal government "off the back" of business and other sectors of the economy, obviously it is not popular to take the federal government out of the lives of the farmers. Significantly, most people are quite aware that the prices farmers can get simply do not cover their cost of production and the carrying charges they have to pay on their debt.

In fact, the public is willing to go a long way toward helping farmers meet that debt. In 1985 a substantial 65%–31% majority of the country favored the federal government putting up $100 million to help farmers pay the interest on loans they now owe the government. And by 69% to 28%, another sizable majority favored allowing farmers to be paid in advance for future crops to allow them to buy their seeds for planting.

OBSERVATION

For a people who have been in no mood to see the federal budget freely expand in recent years, the American public is remarkably liberal in its willingness to spend extra governmental funds on farmers. Indeed, both major political parties are well aware of this fact. When in trouble in the 1986 off-year elections in the farm belt, the Reagan administration announced in the last fortnight before the voting that it was going to institute an old-fashioned farm subsidy program. This announcement was undoubtedly too little and too late to help in the six agricultural states of the Midwest and the South that the Republicans lost. Democrats also talk quietly about the fact that farm subsidies and price supports cannot go on indefinitely into the future.

The farm situation is a strange one. Nearly everyone is looking for an original approach to the problem, but also to find a way to contain the billions upon billions being paid out and even to cut back. It is popular for politicians to say in one breath that the farmers have to find a way to make it without federal largess, but in the next breath that if need be, they will vote to break the budget to appropriate subsidies and supports.

After 6 years, the country has about had it with Republican farm programs, which have spent many billions but have not left farmers in a better condition. Thus, on the eve of the 1986 election, a substantial 66%–21% majority of voters said they thought a Democratic-controlled Congress rather than a Republican-controlled Congress would do a better job of helping individual farmers who are in financial trouble. A comparable 63% to 21% of rural voters shared this view. Now the Democrats get their chance to come up with programs to help the farmers.

There is a farm constituency out there, of course, but it is not made up mainly of farmers. It consists of those who work in food processing and manufacturing plants, in wholesale and retail distribution outlets, and in restaurants and other eating places. They all have a high economic stake in what is done to help the farmer.

But the real secret weapon of American farmers does not lie in the voting power of those employed in agribusiness but instead stems from the love affair that the rest of the American people have for farming and people who work the earth. In a society where people live surrounded largely by concrete and buildings, dependent on an involved, complicated, and sophisticated distribution system to obtain the food necessary to live, the American people instinctively admire farmers who still have the good fortune to have fertile and ample land and the good sense and know-how to produce abundant crops to feed the people of this country and much of the rest of the world. In fact, farmers and nonfarmers join ranks by a better than 2 to 1 margin to favor the U.S. giving $175 million to starving African countries, most of which would be sent in the form of surplus U.S. food.

To most Americans, farmers still represent the best in the national character, in the work they do and in their struggle to make it through hard times. Support for them has truly become a cause of the heart.

U.S. Department of Agriculture, Economic Research Service, *Economic Indicators of the Farm Sector: Farm Sector Review,* annual, as reported in the U.S. Bureau of the Census, *Statistical Abstract of the United States: 1986* (Washington, D.C., 1985), Table 1114: Food and Fiber Sector of Domestic Economy—Employment and Value Added: 1970 to 1984, p. 633.

U.S. Department of Agriculture, Economic Research Service, *Farm Population Estimates, 1910–70* and *Farm Labor,* quarterly, through April 1981, and annual, beginning July 1982, as reported in the U.S. Bureau of the Census, *Statistical Abstract of the United States: 1986* (Washington, D.C., 1985), Table 1115: Farm Population, 1950 to 1984, and Farm Employment, by Type, 1950 to 1985, p. 633.

The Harris Survey, conducted by Louis Harris and Associates, March 2–5, 1985, among a national cross section of 1,256 adults, released March 7, 1985; October 23–25, 1985, among a national cross section of 1,252 adults, released December 5, 1985; and October 13–14, 1986, among 921 voters, released October 27, 1986.

THE HONEYMOON WITH BUSINESS IS OVER—AGAIN

■ BUSINESS HAS RARELY HAD IT SO GOOD

The first six years of the Reagan administration will be looked back on as an almost unprecedented honeymoon between the federal government and the business establishment. The most recent comparable period occurred during the halcyon years from 1920 to 1928, when Calvin Coolidge occupied the White House.

Although there have been times when the business community and the federal government have cooperated in adopting programs that expanded governmental authority, mainly what business has wanted is less federal involvement in the affairs of business. The vast majority of businessmen are convinced that they can achieve this goal far more effectively under the Republicans. Thus, by a 7 to 1 margin, businessmen are more Republican than Democratic. While most Republican presidents tend to be more friendly to business interests than Democratic occupants of the White House, not all GOP occupants of the Oval Office have been looked on as real friends by the business community. For example, Dwight Eisenhower was viewed as too moderate by many businessmen, while Richard Nixon was seen as an outsider.

But Ronald Reagan has been something else again. When he ran successfully in 1980, his main campaign theme was a firm pledge to "get government off the backs of business." In fact, this promise met with the approval of a big 69%–26% majority of the voters that year.

As he has often done in his long career, Reagan had correctly read the prevailing mood of the American people back in 1979 and 1980. Business had risen dramatically in public confidence by the end of the decade of the 1970s. For example, the number of people who gave business high marks for providing steady work for employees rose from 48% in 1972 to 69% in 1979. The number who felt that business was doing a good job of installing the most modern machinery and technology had gone up from 59% to 74% over the same period. The number who were prepared to say that business paid fair wages and salaries had risen from 48% to 57%.

Since assuming office, President Reagan has cut back on the basic regulation of business, especially in the economic area. This has been evident in the relative inactivity of such agencies as the Federal Trade Commission, the antitrust division of the Justice Department, the National Product Safety Commission, Occupational Safety and Health Administration, the Environmental Protection Administration, and countless other agencies of government. Under Democratic regimes in the past, and even under some Republican presidents, these agencies have been viewed as watchdogs of business behavior and have pursued aggressive policies of crackdowns on what they have viewed as corporate misbehavior. In the Reagan years, Vice President George Bush has headed a vigorous effort to seek out more ways of relieving rather than adding to federal regulation of business.

By any measure, business has good reason to be grateful to President Reagan. It has enjoyed years of unprecedented prosperity and has faced less harassment from government than in any other regime since the 1920s.

■ DEEP CLOUDS ON THE HORIZON

As the 1980s unfolded, business was set back temporarily by the recession of late 1981, but then made a strong comeback in the recovery of the economy in late 1983 and since. Profits and employment have remained high, inflation has sharply declined, productivity has started up again, infusion of higher technology has accelerated, and the country has enjoyed its longest sustained prosperity in modern times.

Yet there were some signs that the appetite of business for doing well may have outreached some of the bounds of propriety. Increasingly, there were reports of business executives benefiting from misuse of corporate facilities, such as company planes, lodges, expense accounts—high living that was clearly outside the law. In the case of a number of corporations, especially those in defense industries, the news that they had avoided paying any taxes for a number of years did not set well with the public, who are used to having taxes automatically deducted from their paychecks. In the environmental area, reports of literally thousands of toxic-waste dump sites has triggered concern over why business allowed these conditions to happen in the first place.

The critical question: To what extent does the public believe these excesses and vagaries are the work of only a small number of companies, that they are exceptions and not the general rule among corporations? Or does the public now feel that business greed has once more taken over and that there is a need once more to use the powers of government to curb those excesses?

■ THE TIDE IS TURNING AGAINST BUSINESS

Across the board, compared with the high-water mark achieved in 1979, which preceded the Reagan years, the ratings accorded business by the public have fallen sharply:

☐ *On providing steady work for employees,* a key basis for judging business, the rating of corporate America has dropped from 69% to 35% positive since 1979, a drop of 34 points in seven years.

☐ *On finding the money to expand business and provide more jobs,* the capital expansion function of an enterprise, business

THE PUBLIC RATES BUSINESS

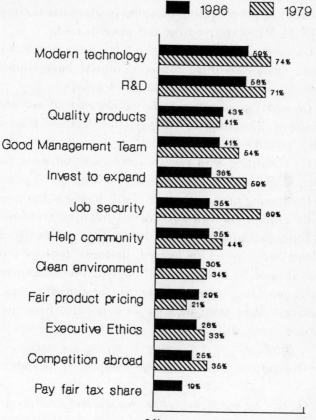

■ 1986   ▨ 1979

Modern technology	59% / 74%
R&D	58% / 71%
Quality products	43% / 41%
Good Management Team	41% / 54%
Invest to expand	36% / 59%
Job security	35% / 60%
Help community	35% / 44%
Clean environment	30% / 34%
Fair product pricing	29% / 21%
Executive Ethics	28% / 33%
Competition abroad	25% / 35%
Pay fair tax share	19%

0%   99%

Positive

has gone from 59% to 36% positive, a falloff of fully 23 points over 7 years.

☐ *On installing the most modern machinery and technology,* the number of people rating business positive has declined from 74% to 59% positive over this same period.

☐ *On hiring, developing, and retaining the best management team,* marks accorded top corporations have slipped from 54% to 41% positive, a drop of 13 points.

☐ *On carrying on research and development of new and better products,* the rating of business has declined from 71% to 58% positive since 1979.

☐ *On competing with foreign companies,* business has gone from 35% down to 25% positive, a drop of 10 points.

☐ *On keeping the environment clean,* business has gone down from a rather low 34% positive in 1980 to an even lower 30%.

☐ *On contributing to the well-being of the community where its plants and factories are located,* business' positive reputation has slipped from 44% to 35% during the Reagan years.

☐ *On providing career opportunities for minorities and women,* business went from 52% to 41% positive over the 7-year period.

On one count alone, business improved its standing:

☐ *On turning out high-quality products and services,* American business has gone up from 41% positive in 1979 to 43% now.

But two other dimensions were probed in this latest survey and both came up decisively negative:

☐ *On paying its fair share of taxes,* business receives a rating of 79% to 19% negative.

☐ *On seeing to it that its executives behave legally and ethically,* business is given marks of 70% to 28% negative.

OBSERVATION

Clearly, with only a few exceptions, the mood about business has turned negative on a massive scale. Three candidates emerge as likely triggers that are provoking this sharply negative reaction.

First is the 73%–25% negative rating accorded business on competing with foreign companies. This is a particularly galling realization for most Americans, who had long felt that the U.S. was superior in basic research and development, in creative and innovative management qualities, in a superior work force, and in employment of modern technology. Now, Americans en masse are coming to realize that in basic industries, assembly-line type of production, high-tech electronics, and other cherished American-associated product lines, the Japanese and now the Koreans are able to outproduce this country. Such realizations are fundamental and undermine confidence. They can be restored, not by erecting protective barriers to insulate American mediocrity, but instead by reorganizing corporate America to become competitive up and down the line once again.

Two other keys also seem to emerge. One is the overwhelming view that business does not pay its fair share of taxes. This objection might have begun to be rectified with the passage of the tax reform law, which added approximately $140 billion to business taxes over the next five years. But the issue is a bedrock one: it arrived at full consciousness on the American scene during Watergate, when the lesson was that there are two standards of justice—one for the privileged and another for ordinary people. Today there is a sense that business and the rich get out of paying taxes, while ordinary people pay through the nose. The other is the widespread feeling that business does not instruct its executives to behave ethically and legally. The spate of insider trading revelations on Wall Street, as well as charges in the corporate community of illegal and unethical behavior, have fed this feeling.

Taken together, these overwhelming majorities add up to an indictment of business for allowing greed to blind it to ethical behavior, to cheat on taxes, expense accounts, and other privileges, and in the process to let American industry be outcompeted by countries that obviously are deeply driven to make it. The signs now point to another period during which business will be on the defensive and under attack by populist governmental figures who will cry out for reform— an old refrain in America, but one that is no less painful to business because it has all happened before. Significantly, in the 1986 off-year elections, one Democrat from the deep South (Georgia), one from the breadbasket (North Dakota), and one from the Far West (Washington) all ran largely populist campaigns targeting business greed, in what they called a callous disregard of the public interest. All three were elected and will be heard from.

The Harris Survey, conducted by Louis Harris and Associates, January 3–7, 1986, among a national cross section of 1,254 adults.

ABC News/*Harris Survey*, conducted by Louis Harris and Associates, April 26–30, 1980, among a national cross section of 1,188 adults, released May 8, 1980.

THE TYLENOL CRISIS: A CASE OF INDUSTRIAL STATESMANSHIP

■ THE NIGHTMARE OF TYLENOL POISONING

One of the real efficiencies of the modern system of mass merchandising is that consumers in massive numbers can enjoy both the real savings in cost and in time of purchasing all sorts of products in self-service drug and food stores. The manufacturer makes the product, packages it, ships it in quantity to the wholesale warehouses, and then it is put on shelves and sold to consumers who serve themselves.

This process of retail selling, of course, is the envy of the rest of the world, and has been copied in many countries. It is essentially predicated on two basic safety tenets: first, that the manufacturers will produce and package reliable and safe products; and second, that shoppers will only pick up merchandise to examine, but not alter or damage it.

From standard packaged grocery items, this mass merchandising concept was extended to health and beauty products and then to proprietary products, such as aspirin and other pharmaceuticals not requiring prescriptions.

The worst scenario that could befall a manufacturer happened to Johnson & Johnson in October 1982, when seven people died from the use of poisoned capsules of Tylenol. Although there were suspects in the case, no indictments were ever handed down and the case remains unsolved. However, without any hesitancy, James Burke, chairman of Johnson & Johnson, ordered the withdrawal of all stocks of Tylenol from the shelves of supermarkets and a refunding of all purchases by the company at an unprecedented cost of over $100 million. Exhaustive inspections and checks indicated that the poisoning had taken place on a localized basis and not in the manufacturing process. Confidence was restored in the Tylenol brand and sales rose once again.

Early in 1986 the Tylenol nightmare struck again. This time it occurred in Bronxville, New York, where two contaminated bottles of Extra Strength Tylenol were found in two different stores, one of which resulted in the death of a woman. This time, Johnson & Johnson recalled all of its Tylenol in capsules and announced that it would not again manufacture the product to be sold in this form. In fact, J&J went a step further and pledged that since it could no longer guarantee that its capsules could be kept free from poisoning, it was going to discontinue making all medicine in capsule form, although it would still put out the same products in tablets and pills.

For any company, such a happening is the realization of the worst possible nightmare, especially when the product is a proprietary medication, which is advertised to cure or to relieve an ill, not to kill.

■ THE PUBLIC REACTION WAS DECISIVE BUT NOT PANICKED

Here is the no-nonsense response of the American people to the Tylenol crisis of early 1986:

☐ By 84% to 13%, a big majority concluded that "the latest case of putting poison into drugs like Tylenol shows that it is just about impossible to make sure that poison is not put into medicine that comes in a capsule." This dominant view, in effect, meant that any future claims by manufacturers that their products sold in capsules are tamperproof are likely to fall on deaf ears.

☐ However, when asked directly if the draconian solution of banning all manufacture of drugs in capsule form should be adopted by the government, the public split down the middle: 48% in favor and 49% opposed.

☐ A clear-cut 62%–35% majority, however, did opt for the alternative that medicines that can be tampered with should be taken off the shelves and sold in pharmacies from behind the counter, as with prescription drugs. This solution, of course, would set back the merchandising of proprietary drugs to the days when they were hand-dispensed by pharmacists in drugstores. But for safety's sake, people are willing to live with such an alternative.

■ A MODEL OF WHAT CORPORATE BEHAVIOR SHOULD BE

Although both Tylenol episodes cost the company literally hundreds of millions of dollars, ultimately Johnson & Johnson gained because by overwhelming margins the decisive action of Chairman Burke met with firm approval and even admiration from the consuming public:

☐ By 91% to 7%, a nearly unanimous majority agreed that "in the way they have handled this case, as in the way they handled the deaths of seven people in Chicago a few years ago, the maker of Tylenol, Johnson & Johnson, has behaved in a completely responsible and admirable way."

☐ By an almost identical 91% to 8%, another huge majority agreed that "Johnson & Johnson was right to announce that because they could not guarantee that its capsules could be kept free from poisoning, they were going to discontinue making all medicine in capsules in the future, including Tylenol, although they would still put out the same products in tablets and pills."

The impact of this decision on Tylenol sales could have been devastating. The survey revealed that 66% of all the households had used Tylenol in the previous year, and of those, 57% reported using the product in capsules. That could have meant cutting off close to 40% of the entire public who had been customers of Tylenol. Yet, when asked if Tylenol was not made in a capsule but instead were available only in pill or liquid form, an even higher 78% said they would buy or use the product.

By making its drastic decision, Johnson & Johnson management risked losing almost an entire market for its most successful product. However, in the end, the willingness of the company to risk so much in order to restore confidence in its product and its corporate good name meant that the future of both the product and the company was assured.

OBSERVATION

The Tylenol cases stand out as classic examples of industrial statesmanship. In both instances, instead of issuing pious statements insisting that nothing was really wrong and that the contaminated bottles were isolated cases tampered with by cranks, the Johnson & Johnson management stepped in and made the difficult and lonely decision to lose huge amounts of money by withdrawing stock already manufactured and on store shelves and by offering to refund money to people who had bought the product in the same form as the contaminated samples. It also took the bigger risk that people would not buy the product if it did not come in the convenient capsule form, which many consumers correctly felt was easier to swallow but also incorrectly assumed contained a stronger dosage.

It is a tribute to both American consumers and the management of Johnson & Johnson that Chairman Burke made decisions that were clearly right and that the public reacted to reward those tough decisions. If more of American business were distinguished by such tough and principled decision-making, perhaps it could begin to turn around its deteriorating position. But for every Johnson & Johnson, unfortunately, there are other companies that in similar crises stepped up, blinked, ducked, and hoped the moment would soon be forgotten—which, of course, never really happens.

The Harris Survey, conducted by Louis Harris and Associates, February 22–March 3, 1986, among a national cross section of 1,305 adults, released March 13, 1986.

JOBS OR A CLEAN ENVIRONMENT: NOT A HARD CHOICE AT ALL

■ SOME THINK IT'S "IN" TO WRITE OFF THE ENVIRONMENTAL MOVEMENT

Most hard-bitten politicians have a distinct inclination to give public lip service to cleaning up the environment. But in private, they tend to be skeptical of the need for tough environmental legislation, especially if it costs a lot of money, and of the environmental movement in general. Part of the reason for this is money, the kind that fuels politics. Today, there is at least as much political money available from those who want to slow down environmental cleanup as from any other source. And the people devoted to environmental reform have had terrible trouble communicating with most politicians. The politicians think environmentalists are impractical, while the environmentalists tend to think politicians are predatory.

But there is also a key issue at stake here. Those opposed to environmental measures inevitably put the question this way: "You can take your pick: if you want to keep your jobs, then you have to slow down environmental cleanup, and if you want to end pollution, make up your mind it will cost you jobs. And anybody in politics knows you don't advocate anything that costs people their jobs without paying a pretty price." So being pro-environment has been described as being antigrowth, anti-big PAC money, and not very smart politically. Thus, recurrently along the banks of the Potomac —no matter what the polls, election returns, or letters from constituents show—the environmental cause somehow seems to slip out of sight and is proclaimed either dead or half dead.

But every time it is written off, the cause of cleaning up pollution and waste in America comes back with a vengeance.

■ ENVIRONMENTAL ISSUES THAT WON'T GO AWAY

During the 1980s, poll after poll has come up with similar results. Whenever the public is asked about environmental issues, the returns point almost always nearly unanimously in one direction: deep worry and concern about the ecological state of the country.

Here's a sampling from 1986 polling, but it might just as easily have been 1985 or 1981 responses, because it never seems to change much:

☐ By 93% to 6%, a big majority of the public is convinced that pollution of lakes and rivers by toxic substances from factories is a serious problem facing the country. Water pollution has been seen for many years as the most pressing environmental issue.

☐ By 92% to 6%, another massive majority believes that disposal of hazardous wastes is a serious problem. The suspicion has spread across the country that no one can any longer safely assume that any community or home site is free from the potential ravages of toxic wastes dumped there years ago.

☐ By 86% to 13%, another sizable majority holds the view that contamination of drinking water is a serious problem. Reports such as recent estimates that as much as 40% of our potable water may be affected no longer surprise the American people.

☐ By 79% to 19%, a majority also feels that pollution by radioactive wastes from nuclear power plants is a serious problem. The question of nuclear waste disposal sites has yet to be settled definitively, and in 1986 became a hot issue in

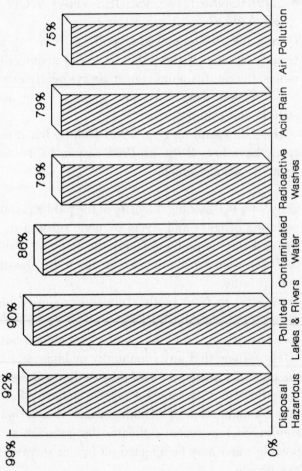

ENVIRONMENTAL PROBLEMS
VIEWED AS SERIOUS

Disposal Hazardous	92%
Polluted Lakes & Rivers	90%
Contaminated Water	86%
Radioactive Washes	79%
Acid Rain	79%
Air Pollution	75%

both Nevada and Washington, which initially had been selected as places to dump such waste.

□ By 79% to 17%, another majority believes that pollution from acid rain is a serious problem facing the country. It took five years for the establishment in the nation's capital to recognize acid rain as a problem worthy of federal attention.

□ By 75% to 22%, a majority also is convinced that air pollution by coal-burning electric power plants is a serious problem. This issue has risen in importance of late, as confidence in nuclear power generation went down after the Chernobyl disaster.

The striking mark of these polling results, as has been the case time after time over the years, is that they are not even close. Overwhelming majorities express deep worry and concern about the perceived decline in the quality of the environment.

■ UNFINISHED ENVIRONMENTAL BUSINESS

Ongoing tests in the Northeast and lately in the Southeast continue to reaffirm the increase of acid rain in the waters of those parts of the country. Still a major unresolved matter between the U.S. and Canada is how to control the spread of acid rain.

An important question is just who should bear the cost for cleaning up the effects of acid rain. When this question is put to the public, no more than half believe it should be borne by consumers, presumably either in higher taxes or in higher utility rates, since much of the pollution emanates from coal- and oil-burning power plants. The clear candidates are the electric utilities themselves. In formulating the questions to be asked, representatives of the power industry charged Harris polltakers a few years back not to ask if the electrical utilities should pay, but instead to ask about the *shareowners* of such utilities. When asked this way, a big 73%–23% majority feels it is eminently fair for the shareowners of electric utilities to pay for the cleanup of acid rain.

But a preliminary piece of business before cleanup is how to estimate the extent of hazardous waste desposits in as many as 8,000 locations across the country. In 1986 the Congress passed the five-year "superfund" appropriation of $10 billion, which will be used to clean up toxic-waste dumps, and President Reagan signed it just before the off-year elections.

Another major unresolved issue is who should bear the liability for payment when someone is injured by proximity to a toxic waste landfill. When the public was asked directly about this, a clear 58% majority said the companies who have used the landfill should pay.

■ THE CONFRONTATIONAL ISSUE OF THE CLEAN WATER ACT

Although President Reagan had earlier signed the toxic-waste superfund bill, after the 1986 elections he vetoed the extension of the Clean Water Act that had also passed the Congress virtually unanimously. Indeed, polls have repeatedly shown that voters want even stricter enforcement of the antipollution laws now in effect to clean up the lakes and streams of the country. The last such poll yielded an 85%–7% majority who wanted the Clean Air Act made even stricter.

The Clean Water Act case graphically illustrates the real power and appeal of the environmental cause:

☐ When asked point-blank if factories should be required to install the best possible antipollution systems available, even if this meant that *fewer* jobs would be available, a decisive 65%–27% majority answered that the requirement nonetheless must be abided by.

☐ The next question dealt with the ultimate trade-off at the heart of the entire environmental issue. Here is what was asked: "Do you think a factory whose pollution is clearly dangerous to human health should be granted an exception from this requirement for any reason—such as that jobs will be lost, the factory will have to shut down, or the company will lose money—*or* should a factory whose pollution is clearly dangerous to human health be strictly required to install the best antipollution systems available?" The result was an overwhelming 81%–15% majority who answered that no exception should be granted.

OBSERVATION

When it comes down to choosing between health and jobs, obviously the American people will opt by a wide margin for health. When it comes down to preventive safety vs jobs, the same result will occur. When it comes down to stricter environmental controls vs jobs, people will once again opt for environmental controls.

When people are asked if they are willing to pay $75 more in taxes in order to achieve tougher enforcement of antipollution laws, they are willing to pay by better than a 2 to 1 margin. When a careful and conservative analysis is made of just what political clout can be generated by the opposing sides on the environmental issue, the anti-environmental cause can muster 6% of the electorate who will vote for their point of view on a single-issue basis. By contrast, the pro-environmental forces can rally a larger 10%. This means that in any contest where the environmental issue is front and center, the pro-environmentalists can win a victory for their cause by a 56%–44% margin.

In the 1986 elections, the environmentalists did have singular success in passing special amendments at the state level and in electing their candidates and defeating those opponents they had targeted. The environmental movement showed more political clout than ever before. Nonetheless, it would be vastly premature to conclude that in the real world of politics as it is played on Capitol Hill between midnight and dawn, environmental matters can now take their place among the major issues of concern. Conventional wisdom just doesn't die that easily.

The Harris Survey, conducted by Louis Harris and Associates, May 5–8, 1986, among a national cross section of 1,254 adults, released May 19, 1986.

A Survey of American Attitudes Toward Water Pollution, conducted by Louis Harris and Associates for the Natural Resources Council of America, June–November 1982, among a national cross section of 1,253 adults, unreleased.

Remarks of Louis Harris at the "Environment 2000" conference held in New York, May 12, 1986.

WHEN REVEREND JERRY FALWELL WENT TO SOUTH AFRICA, ARCHBISHOP TUTU ROSE IN STATURE

■ A TALE OF TWO MEN OF THE CLOTH

Back in August of 1985 Reverend Jerry Falwell, the evangelical preacher who rose to national prominence as the head of the Moral Majority and an associate of President Reagan, visited South Africa. When he returned to the U.S., Falwell denounced the congressional drive to adopt sanctions against South Africa, and he urged that American business "reinvest" in that country rather than divest its capital. He also urged Americans to buy more South African gold coins instead of having their sale banned in the U.S.

Reverend Falwell did not stop there. He also denounced Nobel Prize–winning Bishop Desmond Tutu, who has since become Anglican archbishop for South Africa, as a "phony" in his claim to represent the blacks of that country.

For his part, Bishop Tutu has become more and more outspoken against both the system of apartheid in South Africa and the ruling Afrikaner government. Conservative criticism of Tutu recently has reached the point where some South African whites have called for him to be tried for treason.

Both the Reverend Falwell and Archbishop Tutu have been important figures in their respective countries. Both have achieved notoriety for their outspoken pronouncements on social conditions. Falwell has been an important voice of the New Right, vigorously condemning legalized abortion, homosexual rights, and sex education in the schools. To many, he is both a symbol and an architect of the white Moral Majority movement to change the social agenda of America.

By contrast, Tutu has become both an outspoken critic of the system of apartheid in his own country and also, by virtue of his ascendancy to the top position within his church in South Africa, a symbol of the fierce opposition of the Anglican Church to all that apartheid stands for, a stance that is in sharp contrast to the position of, say, the Thatcher government in Great Britain.

Falwell and Tutu, a white and a black, an American and a South African, yet both leading, members of the clergy, could not be more different in philosophy, style, and stance. In effect, they met in a symbolic confrontation before the court of public opinion.

■ THE AMERICAN PEOPLE ASSESS REVEREND FALWELL'S PRONOUNCEMENTS ON SOUTH AFRICA

The reaction of Americans to Reverend Falwell's stand on South Africa was sharp and decisive:

□ A 67%–30% majority of the country nationwide disagreed with him on opposing sanctions against South Africa, on having American business pursue a policy of reinvesting there instead of disinvesting, and on urging the American people to buy South African gold coins instead of prohibiting their sale in the U.S. Even among followers of Falwell's Moral Majority, a 53%–41% majority opposed his suggested policies toward South Africa.

□ The reaction to Falwell's criticism of Bishop Tutu as a "phony" was even more decisive. By 76% to 17%, the national cross section thought Falwell was wrong to make such a characterization of the South African clergyman. White

Moral Majority followers reacted negatively to Falwell's remark by a big 67% to 24%.

■ REVEREND FALWELL AND ARCHBISHOP TUTU AS RELIGIOUS LEADERS

Finally, the cross section was asked to make a separate assessment of Falwell and Tutu as religious leaders:

☐ A substantial 58%–32% majority nationwide gave Archbishop Tutu positive marks as "a religious leader who is a real moral force in his country and the world." Even among the white Moral Majority group, he received a 48%–39% positive rating. Among blacks, a 77%–21% majority gave him high marks.

☐ By contrast, the Reverend Falwell was accorded a negative rating of 70% to 26% by the same cross section of the American people as "a religious leader who is a real moral force in his country and the world." Among blacks, Falwell's rating was 73% to 24% negative, while among white Moral Majority followers it was 57% to 40% negative.

OBSERVATION

There is little doubt that in this high-noon confrontation between two quite different church leaders, Archbishop Desmond Tutu won decisively over Reverend Jerry Falwell. Falwell's visit to South Africa had been preceded by his visit to the Philippines just prior to the departure of Ferdinand Marcos. Falwell made statements during and following his visit there in praise of Marcos. Since the South Africa and Philippines episodes, the Reverend Falwell has been less visible in this country. He has backed Vice President Bush for the 1988 presidential nomination, but has said that he is not opposed to having his fellow evangelical preacher Reverend Pat Robertson run for the Republican nomination. It also has been reported that Falwell has had to cut back staff and some of the operations of his church establishment, a sign that all may not be going as well for him these days.

Archbishop Tutu has been installed as head of the Anglican Church in South Africa and has become even more outspoken against apartheid and the policies of the Botha government. He has also been highly critical of President Reagan's opposition to U.S. sanctions against South Africa, which now are in force. Tutu continues to be the target of charges of treason by conservative white elements, but these threats do not appear to have deterred him in his outspoken course.

The Harris Survey, conducted by Louis Harris and Associates, September 5–8, 1985, among a national cross section of 1,255 adults, released September 12, 1985.

CONFIDENCE IN INSTITUTIONS: THEY HAD A GREAT FALL AND NEVER GOT PUT TOGETHER AGAIN

■ THE HALCYON DAYS OF 1966

There was a time, about two long decades ago, when most people running the establishment in the United States were held in high regard. Not that the early 1960s were without their traumas and challenges. The assassination of President John F. Kennedy wiped out a figure who had come to symbolize the hope of an entire generation. And the surge of blacks for equality, led by Martin Luther King, Jr., and capped by the 1963 March on Washington, had dramatically pointed up centuries-old racial inequities in the country.

Nonetheless, 1966 was still the time when the country was closing ranks behind Lyndon Johnson, whom people wanted to succeed because they missed the martyred Kennedy so sorely. It was also a time of relative prosperity without inflation. And although the seeds of conflict over the Vietnam war that were to tear the country apart had been planted, the bloody losses abroad and the divisions at home had not yet taken hold. The phenomenon of double-digit unemployment side by side with inflation had not yet been experienced and Watergate was far into the future.

The reason for dwelling on 1966 is pure artifact, for that was the year that the Harris firm stumbled onto a measurement of confidence in the institutions of the country that has become something of a national norm and an enigma ever since. *Newsweek* magazine wanted to find out what the public thought of business. One way to do that was to discover the level of confidence people had in business and then compare that with what they thought of the country's other major institutions.

What made 1966 special was that never again in the next 20 years would the establishment be held in such esteem. It is difficult to imagine that Lyndon Johnson, of all people, presided over the last era of innocence. But even during the peaks of Reagan's popularity, the confidence ratings accorded our institutions have never approximated those of the mid-1960s.

■ THE TOP TIER OF LEADERSHIP

From 1966 on, three institutions have been held in relatively high regard by this country: higher education, medicine, and the military. Indeed, at last count, doctors are still high up, with 33% of the people giving them high confidence marks. However, this is far below the 73% high-water mark recorded back in 1966. Leaders of medicine are beset with reputations for charging too-high fees and not being available when needed. But they are still closer to God than most other types in the judgment of the people.

University presidents are given high confidence marks by 34%, but this is well below their peak of 61% recorded two decades ago. They fell from grace during the turbulent Vietnam years when campuses became battlegrounds of protest and administrators appeared to be not in control much of the time. There are signs that they are coming back into grace.

The military weigh in at 36% high confidence, but this is also down sharply from the 61% high recorded for them back in 1966. The really low point for the military came in the immediate post-Vietnam era, when defense spending was almost totally out of favor. Resentment against military leaders came from opposite extremes: from the hawks who blamed them for not winning Vietnam, on one side, and from the

CONFIDENCE IN INSTITUTIONS

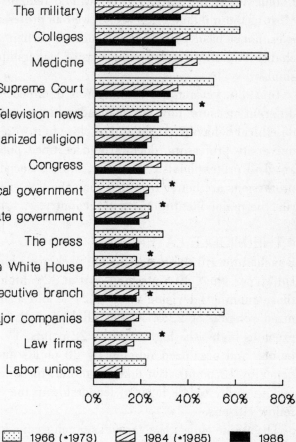

The military	
Colleges	
Medicine	
The Supreme Court	
Television news	*
Organized religion	
Congress	
Local government	*
State government	*
The press	
The White House	*
Executive branch	*
Major companies	
Law firms	*
Labor unions	

0%   20%   40%   60%   80%

▫ 1966 (*1973)   ▨ 1984 (*1985)   ■ 1986

doves, who blamed them for getting the country into an immoral war. The military has since recovered, although the extent of the damage done by Colonel North and Ambassador Poindexter in the Iranian arms scandal remains to be seen. Most of the military brass are viewed as professionals, however, not as basic policymakers. Indeed, perhaps it is not just chance that all three top categories of leadership are professionals.

In 1986, yet another ranking was obtained on a slightly different measure: how various leadership groups stacked up on ethical behavior. At the top or close to it were college and university professors, doctors, and certified public accountants, all professionals. Obviously, those associated with the professions are better regarded than the line executives who run the major institutions of the country.

■ THE MIDDLE LAYER

Bunched toward the middle of the pack are a host of leadership types: the U.S. Supreme Court at 32% high confidence, those running television news at 27%, and leaders of organized religion at 22%. Again, all have fallen below their previous highs: the high court by 22 points, TV news by 18 points, and organized religion by 20 points and the presidency by 12 points. But taken together, these five currently make up the middle layer of leadership in the eyes of their fellow citizens.

The White House has varied as much as any institution on the list. The high was actually not Lyndon Johnson's rating in 1966, but instead Ronald Reagan's in 1984, after his huge reelection victory. The lows were shared by Jimmy Carter at 11% in 1976 and Richard Nixon at 18% in 1973, when he resigned from office. Ronald Reagan has dropped from his 42% high confidence in 1984 to 19% in 1986, following the Iranian arms disclosures. The rise of the evangelical preachers has not raised the level of confidence in religious leaders.

TV news people have never regained the level of respect they earned during Watergate.

■ THE BACK OF THE PACK

Finally, a sizable group of eight types of leaders bring up the rear. Business leaders come up with a confidence rating of 16%, far below their 1966 mark of 55%. Back in 1984 they were a bit higher, at 19%, but they have never really regained their earlier status. Those who run the press evoke high confidence among 19%, down from their high of no better than 30% at the time of Watergate. (Print media has never scored well.) The executive branch of the federal government, as distinct from the White House, evokes no better than 18% high confidence, down from 41% two decades ago—the notion that they are an entrenched bureaucracy took over and remains the dominant public impression. Two other levels of government do not fare any better: those running state government have a score of 19% high confidence, and local government leaders stand at 21%. Over the years neither has ever achieved as much as 30% in high confidence.

Lower still are three other groups of institutional leaders. Leaders of Congress are currently at 21% high confidence, well down from their high of 42% back in 1966, but much higher nonetheless than their low of 9% in 1976. One of the reasons Congress comes up so low is that individual members like to position themselves against their own institution, saying in effect that they vote right but that the rest let the country down. Thus, individual members of Congress achieve a 59% positive rating. Labor union leaders achieve no more than a high confidence level of 11%, but this is higher than their all-time low of 8% registered in 1982. Their high was 22%, back in 1966.

Close to the bottom are lawyers, with a high confidence rating of only 14%. Lawyers' high-water mark over the years was recorded at only 24% in 1973, just as the Watergate disclosures were hatching. In the aftermath of Watergate, lawyers dropped to 16% and then went into a gradual slide to their current all-time low. Ironically, lawyers may well be making more money overall than those in any other profession, and they may be at the peak of their power. But not only are they the exception among the professions in being ranked so poorly, but they are also the target of public outrage over liability insurance rates. It is no happenstance that lawyers and insurance agents ranked at the bottom of the heap on the 1986 measure of ethical standards.

OBSERVATION

More significant than the standing of any one profession or leadership group is that all fell so far below the marks achieved in the 1960s and have not regained their prestige since. The sole exception was Ronald Reagan, who brought confidence in the White House to a higher level than ever before recorded in 1984. However, the latest readings indicate that he could well end his last two years back at normal levels for most presidents.

It is fair to conclude from these results that the country somehow does not any longer produce leaders of heroic stature. Certainly there is a sense that mediocrity has been too amply rewarded in far too many institutions in the U.S. over the past two decades. In business, new professional types have largely replaced the old dramatic, charismatic tycoons and geniuses of the past. The mark of this new business leadership—and that of other institutions run along similar patterns—is that they carry out their tasks, often with much competence, but in much quieter and less visible fashion. The Lee Iacoccas are the exceptions and do not seem to have made much difference in the level of respect accorded businessmen.

Regardless of the rationales that might be conjured up to explain the phenomenon, one thing is certain: the American people are ready for competent and inspirational leadership in nearly all fields. It is not an understatement to say that they are aching to respond to real leaders again, not because they are less devoted to an open society, but because the existing leadership has been so lacking in coming up with adequate solutions to current dilemmas.

The Harris Survey, conducted by Louis Harris and Associates in 1966—no sample size recorded; September 13–22, 1973, among a national cross section of 1,594 adults, released December 6, 1973; February 23–March 4, 1976, among a national cross section of 1,512 adults, released March 22, 1976; November 9–14, 1984, among a national cross section of 1,247 adults, released December 17, 1984; July 12–15, 1985, among a national cross section of 1,252 adults, released September 2, 1985; November 1–4, 1985, among a national cross section of 1,254 adults, released December 16, 1985; November 26–December 2, 1986, among a national cross section of 1,250 adults, released December 15, 1986.

AS PIETY AND IDEOLOGY FADE, EXCITING THOUGH PAINFUL NEW OPPORTUNITIES EMERGE

■ THE WHITE MORAL MAJORITY BECOMES AN IDEOLOGICAL MINORITY

Ronald Reagan was the first president in modern times who appeared to be committed to the new ideology of the right: a church-based coalition determined to bring a new moral order to politics, then to government, then into such private institutions as the press and TV and, finally, into the daily lives of the people themselves.

The coterie of issues that drew the ideological right together ranged from foreign policy objectives such as a huge buildup of arms to face the worldwide menace of communism, a liberation of Central America from the clutches of Castro in Cuba and the Sandinista government in Nicaragua, ridding Africa of communist incursions as in Angola and Ethiopia (even if this meant embracing the government of South Africa), to domestic priorities such as outlawing abortion, defeating the Equal Rights Amendment, doing away with sex education in the schools and access to birth control for teenagers, introducing prayer into the schools, banning evolution from the school curriculum, allowing parents to take their children out of school to educate them in accordance with a new moral dictum, outlawing pornography, opposing all efforts to control the sale and ownership of guns, barring homosexuals from any jobs in the public sector and especially in the schools, and ending all busing to achieve racial balance.

In short, if consummated, the revolution of the white Moral Majority would have dismantled the last vestiges of John Dewey's permissive philosophy and the liberal governmental programs that stemmed from the notion that government should be a vehicle for redistributing wealth.

As the Reagan era entered its sixth year and approached its finale in 1989, it was evident that the New Right had failed in its bid to take over mainstream opinion. Indeed, both politically and socially, what Reverend Jerry Falwell had called the Moral Majority appeared to be well on its way to becoming a major target of wrath for a sizable majority of the American people and a distinct political liability to those who embraced its cause.

In fact, Falwell himself had fallen considerably from grace. At one time he talked openly about his access to the Reagan White House and was courted by powerful politicians, such as Senator Jesse Helms, and the number of his flock and his minions grew apace. There seemed to be no area of social life or governmental activity that escaped Falwell's sweeping pledge to radically change the American landscape. He was only one of dozens of evangelical preachers who built huge television followings that at their peak came to fully 20% of the entire adult population and a quarter of all whites.

Yet somehow, as the Reagan years began to wind down, the cause had achieved few of its objectives, was rapidly losing its political clout, and showed signs of coming apart at the seams. Indicative of its demise were Falwell's trips in 1985 to the Philippines, where he applauded the regime of Ferdinand Marcos shortly before it fell, and to South Africa, where he championed the Botha government, called for reinvestment instead of disinvestment by U.S. companies, and denounced as a "phony" Archbishop Desmond Tutu, the black Anglican leader in that country. The American people rejected Falwell's stance on the Philippines by 4 to 1, his advice on reinvestment in South Africa by 2 to 1, and his criticism

of Tutu by nearly 5 to 1. The bottom line: the public disagreed, by 70–26%, that as a religious leader Falwell is a real
moral force in this country. By contrast, the same cross section rated Nobel Laureate Archbishop Tutu by close to 2 to
1 as a real moral force. Indeed, Falwell no longer calls his
followers the Moral Majority and was last reported as being
forced to make heavy cutbacks in his own church operations.
His endorsement of Vice President George Bush has been
increasingly viewed as a liability. And the candidacy of Reverend Pat Robertson, another of the evangelical preachers,
for the Republican presidential nomination in 1988 has appeared likely to isolate the religious New Right even further
from the mainstream of power in the United States.

But it would be a mistake to identify this rejection of the
religious Right as simply a rejection of the personalities of
some or most of its leaders. Far more significant is the basic
failure of the movement to convince the American public of
the soundness of its positions. The plain facts were that on
most of its major tenets, the Moral Majority simply did not
reflect the views of the vast majority.

Indeed, the evidence all points to what some of Reagan's
more pragmatic aides had been quick to realize after coming
to power in 1981. They knew that if President Reagan made
issues such as outlawing abortion and sex education in the
schools and other major items of the religious right's social
agenda the main business of the country, he would tear apart
the fabric of the nation, would fragment his coalition, and
would divert the national focus from urgent economic and
foreign policy matters. Except for his appointments to the
federal judiciary, President Reagan has steered clear of confrontations over the social agenda of the New Right. As the
second term unfolded, Attorney General Edwin Meese became the point man for pushing abandonment of affirmative
action, outlawing of pornography, slowing down or ending
busing for racial purposes, and some of the other major social

issues. But it was doubtful that Meese's efforts would yield much of a crop. More promising was what the new Chief Justice, William Rehnquist, and some of his other highly conservative colleagues on the high court might do to reverse some of the more liberal landmark decisions of the Warren Court. But that would not be clear for years after the Reagan presidency.

What is certain now is that many of the major positions of the religious right are meeting with outright rejection from the American people. In turn, this means that those occupying the seats of power, especially those who either win or lose elections by accepting or opposing such stands of the New Right, will increasingly encounter that rejection by the people. And the more strident the evangelical preachers become and the more they themselves enter the political arena instead of depending on popular surrogates such as Ronald Reagan, the more and the faster their cause will come a cropper.

Here is a roll call of how the American people react to major planks in the social agenda of the New Right:

☐ By 8 to 1, an overwhelming majority rejects the call for an end to sex education in the schools. To the contrary, even among followers of Reverend Falwell and the others, solid majorities of mothers of teenagers desperately want help from the schools, the churches, from *any* source, to help them educate their daughters to avoid pregnancy.

☐ By close to 6 to 1, a majority favors the use of birth control pills, devices, and other methods as a practical necessity in a society where large families are not socially or economically desirable.

☐ By nearly 2 to 1, a majority also opposes a constitutional amendment to ban abortion. While the 1973 U.S. Supreme Court decision in *Roe* v. *Wade* had lost some support, nonetheless the list of situations in which majorities feel abortion should be legal has grown apace, ranging from pregnancy resulting from rape or incest to possible physical or mental impairment of the mother from pregnancy, to probability of producing a deformed or retarded child.

☐ By 3 to 1, most feel that women do not get equal pay for equal work, and by almost that margin, majorities also support the principle of comparable pay for women in jobs requiring skills equal to those of jobs held by men. These, of course, are prime objectives of the National Organization for Women (NOW) and the women's movement. Indeed, although it is currently dormant, the Equal Rights Amendment (ERA) is favored by a 2 to 1 margin nationwide.

☐ Backing for affirmative action, defined as special efforts to enhance opportunities for women and minorities, but without rigid quotas, has grown from 71%–20% to 82%–17% during the Reagan years, despite the adamant opposition of the New Right to all such programs.

☐ A better than 2 to 1 majority of both whites and blacks whose children have been bused to schools in order to achieve racial balance say that the busing and subsequent integration in the schools worked out well for their kids.

☐ By close to 3 to 1, a majority would favor the registration of all handguns in the country and a comparable majority support keeping the federal statute that prohibits the sale of handguns to a citizen of another state.

☐ By better than 2 to 1, a majority is opposed to banning magazines that show nudity, and majorities also oppose banning theaters from showing X-rated movies and the sale or rental of such video cassettes for home viewing.

☐ Over the past decade, there has been a decline in both public apprehension about crime on the streets and the actual crime rates reported in official federal crime reports. There has not been the panic and widespread outrage at the failure of the apparatus of law enforcement that New Right spokesmen regularly claim. On the contrary, respect for law enforcement, particularly at the local level, has grown apace, because people think the police are primarily responsible for their feeling safer on the streets.

☐ By a decisive 80% to 17%, a big majority nationwide rejects the notion that AIDS victims, many of whom are homosexuals, should be isolated and in effect treated as lepers. On the contrary, close to nine in ten support having all hospitals admit AIDS victims for treatment and having the government provide funds for free blood tests to all who are concerned about contracting AIDS, and seven in ten firmly believe that information about those who test positive for the AIDS virus should be kept totally confidential in the absence of the carrier's permission. The Reverend Pat Robertson will have trouble mobilizing the country behind a platform that attempts to use the genuine fear about AIDS as a device for choosing up sides for or against homosexuals.

☐ By a massive 85% to 13%, a big majority believes that a terminally ill patient being sustained with a life-support system has the right to tell the doctor to pull the plug on the support system so that the patient can die. This support has risen by 24 points in the past dozen years. In fact, by any measure, the right to die when in terrible pain or terminally ill has arrived as an important front-and-center issue. Its urgency is underscored by the fact that a major part of the big increases in Medicare expenses are due to care for the terminally ill. Indeed, the issue is so powerful and commanding that unless they alter their position, the Right to Life movement could be in deeper trouble over the right-to-die issue than they have been on the abortion question.

The litany of rejection of many of the most fervent causes of the religious right is a long one and can be cited in many additional polling results. Opportunity for their cause is now dwindling, and the more they press, the more likely it is that they will trigger a fierce backlash from a solid majority of the American people. In short, the Moral Majority cause has failed to become the wave of the future as we approach the last decade of the twentieth century.

Of course, it must be acknowledged that the phenomenon of religious input in politics neither is new in American life nor in this latest period has been confined to those who supported the candidacy of Ronald Reagan and the Republicans. President Jimmy Carter made much of his born-again status and of morality in general in his campaign for the presidency in 1976. Later, when the bottom dropped out of public support for his presidency and more than seven in ten people felt he was not competent to be president, there was widespread disenchantment with what many called the pious and self-righteous overtones of his manner.

After 10 years of piety and ideology, the American people have about had it with the approaches of political religious types. To be sure, the clergy of many faiths will continue to speak their mind on key issues, and public figures will continue to seek religious inspiration. But the prospect of men of the cloth taking over civil leadership seems to be rapidly passing.

■ THE ERA OF THE ESTABLISHMENT'S POWER ALSO WAS PASSING

Without doubt, most heads of the labor movement were shut out of power during the Reagan years. Less noticed was the fact that labor's clout with the Democrats also had slipped. The reasons were not hard to find: union membership had declined not only in absolute numbers but also, more dramatically, as a percentage of the work force, from 33% to 18% over a generation. The irony was that workers' feeling that they needed collective representation to deal with employers had not diminished at all, suggesting that if there had never been unions, workers would have invented them. Nonetheless, big labor lost much power during the Reagan years.

By contrast, the influence of business, especially big business, reached a peak under the Reagan regime. Indeed, business hardly had to press this administration to hear its case. Reagan went into office pledging "to get the federal government off the back of business." Agencies that had been the bane of business under previous regimes were hardly heard from after 1981. Yet, after a five-year honeymoon for business, equaled only by the Coolidge years in the 1920s, by 1986 the pendulum had swung back. Business was being taken to task by the public once again. On the bedrock function of providing steady work for employees, the number of Americans who gave business positive marks plummeted from 69% in 1979 to 35% in 1986. The three dimensions that appeared to trigger the new disenchantment with business could be found in the 4 to 1 majority who gave business negative marks on competing with foreign companies, the eight in every ten who did not feel business had been paying its fair share of taxes, and the close to 3 to 1 majority who felt that business executives had not by and large behaved in a legal or ethical manner. Perceived greed and lack of ethics, along with a failure to measure up to the challenge from foreign competition has put corporate America back in the public's doghouse.

As a result of the decline of both big labor and big business, and the Reagan administration's deliberate withdrawal from the federal role in influencing private sector initiatives, yet another time-honored tradition appeared to be passing. During most of the twentieth century, Democratic and Republican administrations alike could enlist the support of business and labor leaders in handling economic or even national problems. Together the three institutions could exercise enough wisdom and clout to come up with answers. If the problem was agricultural, the tried-and-true formula was to enlist the counsel and participation of leaders of farm groups as well.

All of these groups—business, labor, farmers—are in fact

probably more active politically than ever before, mainly through the mechanism of political action committees (PACs), which have grown enormously as contributors to election campaigns. Yet it appears that the policy of asking leaders of key groups to make common cause to help solve national problems may well be passing. The reason: there is considerable doubt that they can deliver their own constituencies. Or, put another way, just because leaders of business, labor, farmers, or other groups unite in pledging that a policy ought to be adopted for the common good may not guarantee that public opinion will follow. On the contrary, it would not be surprising to find that the rank and file of the people would be singularly unimpressed by such an approach.

The decline in confidence in nearly all major institutions has been precipitous. Compared with the benchmark year of 1966, high confidence in business leaders has declined from 55% to 17%. Those with a great deal of confidence in labor leaders has gone down from 22% to 13%. High confidence in the White House has slipped from 42% to 30%. The same pattern has eroded the standing of doctors, lawyers, local and state officials, the U.S. Supreme Court, the military, college presidents, leaders of the clergy, those who run TV news, and those who run the press.

The plain truth seems to be that solutions bearing the imprimatur of the establishment are for the most part likely to fall flat on the public. The price of cynicism and disillusionment has been so great that endorsement by those running major institutions is no longer a strong testimonial at all.

This means that in the period ahead, problems must be approached far more on their merits than ever before, with a candor from leaders in the public and private sector that usually has not been forthcoming. But problems have a way of shaping up without waiting for the kind of staging that leadership may think appropriate.

Indeed, the country is now faced with a series of problems

that simply will not be postponed and are not susceptible to quick and easy answers. After a decade of much rhetoric, ideology, and pledges to let the private sector do the job, the central concern appears to be: not who does what, but instead when real problems will be attacked and workable solutions will be forthcoming.

■ WOULDN'T IT BE NICE IF IT WERE ALL SIMPLE

By the last quarter of the twentieth century the web of American society had been spun in such intricate patterns that any master spider who had designed it would hardly have recognized what had been wrought.

In the end, any people and any country must latch on to and hold dear some reasonably clear values in order to survive. Ideas are important, if for no reason other than that they give people something to live by, find solace in, fight wars for, even die for, and, above all, take part in fulfilling. The trouble is that the ideas people live by and the grinding reality of day-to-day survival often have little in common. So when the real problems have to be dealt with, the answers that make sense may or may not fit those cherished ideas.

As we approach the 1990s and the new century a decade beyond, America seems to be on the threshold of just such a series of tough challenges, in which it appears that the fulfillment of certain ideas or dreams can only take place if new and sometimes radical approaches become the order of the day.

For example, as a nation, probably the most golden of all American dreams is that parents can make up for what they never achieved by ensuring that their children get the best education, which in turn will open doors to the good life. In short, education is the key to making it—*big*. Yet, by 1986, the American people were beginning to realize that the entire educational system had to be overhauled radically if it was just to do the job it once did, let alone to successfully meet the challenge from abroad by turning out a better-trained and more capable work force than any other on the face of the earth. The engine that might fulfill the golden dream obviously needs an overhaul.

Another example is the great unfinished business of our national health and medical system. For generations, Americans have been raised to believe that doctors are nearer to God, that miracle cures will save their lives, and that nearly every disease, even those stemming from neglect or abuse of one's body can be cured by the safety net called modern medicine. Suddenly it became evident that just to ensure delivery of adequate basic health services, leaving aside all the miracles, a whole series of radical changes had to be made in the health care system.

Many other issues are raising similar dilemmas. Can an environmental cleanup really take place without making compromises to allow for economic growth? Are people prepared to allow their genetic structures to be plumbed to allow for unprecedented approaches to disease prevention, but at the risk of revealing their secret health vulnerabilities and even their fitness to be a parent? In the face of a Medicare system that could bankrupt the country with the cost of extending the lives of the hopelessly ill, is the country prepared to grant the terminally ill the right to die? And in light of the fact that by every measure there will be serious labor shortages in the U.S. in the 1990s, is the nation prepared to allow the elderly, the disabled, the disadvantaged poor and minorities, and women to make their full contribution to the mainstream of American society? Or, if not, is the country then prepared to pay the piper to the tune of increasing the national debt by billions upon billions? Another issue: Is the country prepared to radically overhaul an agricultural system that produces an overabundance of food in a world where millions of Americans are hungry and other millions abroad are starving, and under which the farmers themselves are going broke? Finally, is the nation prepared to go through the painful throes of seriously retraining its current work force, which may be just as uncompetitive as the industries that employ it?

These problems are not easy to solve, nor are they going away soon. On the contrary, what marks them all is that they seem to be becoming exacerbated rather than settling down. The common thread that runs through them all is that in order to make substantial progress in solving any of them, some important vested interests are undoubtedly going to be violated.

Equally important is the country's need to find the mix of leadership in the power centers of the public and private sectors that will be sensitive and attuned to the problems crying out for solution, and be capable of wielding the power while having the know-how to do the job.

But the best bet for the days ahead is that the emphasis will be far less on ringing words and inspirational qualities and far more on getting things done, tending to the vast array of unfinished business that faces the country and the world. Intelligent pragmatism—strongly tempered by a sense of a larger community, firmly rooted in the center of the political spectrum but unafraid of the truly radical programs needed to overhaul out-of-date and even decadent institutions—appears to be the new order of the new day.

PART THREE

THE NATION AND THE WORLD

GREAT PRESIDENTS
NEVER DIE . . .

Historians might have assessments of past American presidents that will withstand the scrutiny of their fellow scholars. But the people have their own way of remembering presidents and giving them their places in history, irrespective of what the historians might write. That custom probably has not changed down through the ages.

America in the late 1980s is no exception. The people have distinct and decisive views about recent presidents and those past. A special few are part of a folklore that will not go away.

■ WHO ARE AMERICA'S GREATEST PRESIDENTS?

When asked directly, over the past 10 years, three former occupants of the White House are singled out above all the rest. John F. Kennedy held the number one spot, cited by 52% a decade ago, and still holds it with an even higher 56% today. For all the books, articles, and political talk that have claimed to take a critical look at JFK without sentiment and with so-called objectivity, deep admiration for him continues unabated.

In second place is Abraham Lincoln, mentioned by 48%, hardly changed from the 49% who put him there a decade ago. In third place is Franklin D. Roosevelt, singled out for greatness by 41%, slightly down from 45% 10 years ago. When people think of great presidents, Kennedy, Lincoln, and Roosevelt come to mind. Significantly, two of them were shot and the other died in office. All three had memorable funerals that deeply moved the nation.

Next come four other presidents: Harry S. Truman, mentioned by 26%, down from 37% a decade ago; George Washington, mentioned by 25%, no change; Ronald Reagan, volunteered by 21%; and Dwight Eisenhower, named by 16%, down from 24% 10 years ago.

Then come two recent and highly controversial presidents: Richard M. Nixon, cited by 11%, up from 9% a decade back; and Jimmy Carter, mentioned by 9%. They are followed by Thomas Jefferson at 7%, Theodore Roosevelt at 7%, Lyndon Johnson at 5%, and Woodrow Wilson and Herbert Hoover at 1% each.

■ AN IN-DEPTH LOOK AT THE LAST NINE PRESIDENTS

When the public is asked to choose from *just* the past nine presidents—going back to Roosevelt—Kennedy and FDR have consistently dominated on most dimensions ever since 1972, when the first measures were taken.

☐ On which president "most inspired confidence in the White House," Kennedy leads with 39%, followed by Roosevelt at 15% and Ronald Reagan at 13%.

☐ On which chief executive "was the most appealing personality," JFK wins again, cited by 57%, followed by Reagan at 15%.

☐ On who "could be most trusted in a crisis," Kennedy again came out on top, mentioned by 32%, followed by Reagan at 15%, and Roosevelt at 12%.

☐ On who "was best able to get things done," JFK also wins with 26%, followed by FDR at 21%.

□ On who "was best on domestic affairs," Kennedy wins with 25%, followed by FDR at 20%.

□ On who "set the highest moral standards," JFK once again finishes on top with 26%, followed by Carter at 16%.

□ On who "likely will be viewed as the best president by history, Kennedy wins top honors with 29%, followed by Roosevelt at 28%.

□ On who "was best in foreign affairs," JFK leads with 23%, followed by Richard Nixon at 22%.

Finally, two negative attributes were also tested:

□ On which president "set the lowest moral standards," Nixon wins hands down, cited by 41%.

□ On who "was least able to get things done," Jimmy Carter wins this dubious honor easily, singled out by 43%, followed by Gerald Ford at 14%, and Nixon at 10%.

OBSERVATION

Kennedy's showing remains dominant and impressive, even having more appeal among those under 30 than any other president. Roosevelt is felt to be a giant in history and the memory of him simply does not fade. Reagan was showing strongly until the Iran arms scandal surfaced. What his staying power will be beyond 1988 remains to be seen. His strongest impression is as a personality, and he does less well on performance, especially in the foreign policy area. By contrast, other recent presidents tend to do rather poorly, with the exception of Nixon on foreign policy, an area he has led on more years than not since he resigned from the presidency in 1974. But the Watergate memory does not fade, either.

The Founding Fathers above all did not want a king. The

office of president is the most exalted position allowed under our system. The people clearly have their heroes and will not give them up easily. They hang pictures of Kennedy, Lincoln, and Roosevelt in their homes, tell their children about them, save and pass down magazines that marked their inaugurals and their deaths. The memory of a certain few presidents is an important anchor for literally millions of Americans.

The Gallup Opinion Poll, conducted by the Gallup Organization, July 7–10, 1985, among a national cross section of 1,540 adults, released July 18, 1985

The Harris Survey, conducted by Louis Harris and Associates, April 1–3, 1985, among a national cross section of 1,254 adults, released April 15, 1985; February 20–24, 1987, among a national cross section of 1,250 adults, unreleased.

THE POLITICAL LEGACY OF RONALD REAGAN I: REPUBLICAN HOPES FOR REALIGNMENT

■ AT LAST A REPUBLICAN TO MATCH FDR

In 1980 Ronald Reagan did what Barry Goldwater utterly failed to do in 1964: he became the first outspoken, full-fledged ideological conservative to occupy the White House since the 1920s. Eisenhower, Nixon, and Ford had been conservative on many issues. But they all had one characteristic in common that Ronald Reagan did not share: none of them had the daring to assault the federal government as the last haven for help in solving social ills. All tacitly assumed that the basic thrust of the New Deal would remain intact. None dared to make the federal government an object of attack, as the root of most of the evil.

Early on in his administration, Ronald Reagan dared to take on twin evils: the "evil empire" of the Soviet Union and the dead hand of government in the private sector. He vowed to give the Soviets more than their match in military buildup. And he vowed before and after the 1980 election that he would get government off the back of business. A big 66%–28% majority of the voters agreed with him before the election, and an even larger 73%–25% majority endorsed his ringing reiteration of this pledge in his first inaugural address.

Reagan was swept to landslide victories over Jimmy Carter in 1980 and, by an even wider margin, over Walter Mondale in 1984. In 1980 his coattails were long enough to give the

Republicans control of the U.S. Senate for the first time since Dwight Eisenhower carried in a GOP majority in the election of 1952. At last, the Republicans had a charismatic leader in the White House, who stood in bright contrast to the lackluster succession of recent presidents—Lyndon Johnson, Richard Nixon, Gerald Ford, and Jimmy Carter. FDR had been able to inspire the country. Even Truman had, in his down-home way. Ike had real magnetism about him. Kennedy was the embodiment of the hope of youth, who took on larger-than-life proportions when his life was cruelly and prematurely terminated. Then, from 1963 through 1980, there entered the White House a procession of presidents who had little capacity to communicate, to inspire.

Ronald Reagan changed all that in a hurry. Once again, the people had a president whose ringing words were great to listen to and aroused latent hopes. One might not go along with all the right-wing rhetoric, but the polemics were softened by this "aw, shucks" nice guy's genuine appeals to home, family, and country.

■ THE CONSERVATIVE CHANCE OF A LIFETIME

For conservatives who had suffered through the long period following the Goldwater debacle of 1964, Reagan's victory was a dream become reality. Not only did Reagan adhere to the New Right dogma, but he appointed to office genuine conservatives who openly pledged to repeal the liberal social agenda. He embraced the nostrums of the Moral Majority, on the one hand, and the new theories of George Gilder and supply-siders endorsing big tax cuts and economic growth, on the other. Federal spending was not a real problem because a stimulated economy would yield record revenues to the U.S. Treasury off a lower tax base.

By the beginning of 1986 there was a promising roster of developments that pointed to a realignment that could result in long-term Republican majority rule in the country:

☐ By 1988 the GOP will have controlled the White House for 16 of the past 20 years;

☐ Republicans had controlled the U.S. Senate for 6 years, the longest period of time in 60 years;

☐ The popular-vote percentages for the Republicans in the House races had risen steadily, and the gap between Democrats and Republicans was narrowing.

☐ The number of voters who identified with the Republicans had grown right after the 1984 election to 31%, compared with only 36% who identified with the Democrats.

☐ The national Republican party had blunted the Democrats' traditional hold on blue-collar workers, union members, and white Catholics in the big cities of the North, and now seemed capable of winning the South consistently in presidential elections. By any measure, the old New Deal coalition appeared to have been broken, and the groups that formed it seemed destined to become a distinct minority in the American electorate.

☐ The fastest-growing parts of the country—the Sunbelt, the Southwest, and the West—were far more inclined toward the GOP than other regions.

Taken together, many New Right politicians, some political scientists, and even some polltakers concluded that the time was ripe for a new Republican majority in the country—a majority that would be firmly anchored to the right, for the conservative sweep had only begun to take hold.

■ WAITING FOR THE RIGHT-WING DAWN

The recession of 1981 and 1982 put a temporary crimp in the speed of this realignment. The 1982 elections proved that the popularity of the president and the new tide of conservatism were not so strong that either could withstand a deep and punishing recession. The Democrats made a net gain of 8 seats at the statehouse level and, most of all, won a 26-seat gain in the House of Representatives. President Reagan's positive job rating plummeted to 41% from a high of 52% earlier that year. Significantly, however, the Republicans held on to their control of the U.S. Senate. Realignment did not take place during the first term, but, incredibly, the chances of it happening survived a full-fledged recession.

By 1984 the economy had recovered, the president's popularity was soaring once again, and the Democrats kept alive the Carter tradition by nominating Walter Mondale as their standard-bearer. In addition, when, early on, Mondale became the handpicked candidate of organized labor, this allowed Reagan, the most pro-business occupant of the White House since Coolidge, to target him early as the candidate of special interests—poetic irony, indeed. Finally, Mondale came out for a tax increase, without specifying that it would be dedicated to deficit reduction, and Reagan was able to lambaste him mercilessly as the last of the big-time spenders. After coopting the Olympics as almost his own patriotic celebration, Ronald Reagan blew Mondale away in the big landslide of November 1984. Significantly, once again the Republicans kept control of the U.S. Senate.

The question after 1984 was whether the GOP could capitalize on the enormous popularity of Ronald Reagan and the momentum from his big reelection victory to navigate that last mile toward becoming the majority party. Somehow despite all of Reagan's success, and the weakened and demoralized state of the Democratic party, the Republican realignment had not quite made it.

■ A BIG-ISSUE WINDFALL FOR THE GOP

In the summer of 1985, however, there was new hope of fueling a GOP majority, some signs that the big Reagan sweep of 1984 might have created a new Republican dominance on the issues:

□ On domestic economic issues, the Republicans held commanding leads across the board. They were preferred to the Democrats by 57% to 34% for ability to cut federal spending, by 53% to 36% for ability to handle the federal deficit, by 55% to 33% for ability to control inflation, and by 52% to 38% for ability to keep the economy prosperous. The long bout with inflation and the fact that under the Republicans rises in the cost of living had been brought down from double-digit levels to the 3%–4% range gave visible proof of the GOP's claim that it could deliver on bread-and-butter issues. Inflation looked to be the bedrock issue of the 1980s for the Republicans, just as the unemployment spawned in the 1930s had been for the Democrats. Indeed, when people were asked who could best cut the rate of unemployment in the summer of 1985, the Republicans emerged in a 45%–45% standoff against the Democrats, proof that the party of FDR had finally lost its golden issue of 50 years' standing. Above all, the Republicans seemed to be literate on economic issues, while the Democrats either were by and large tongue-tied or were able only to echo a long-gone New Deal past.

□ On foreign policy and defense matters, Republicans also had the edge, although not by the same decisive margins as in the domestic economic area. On ability to control the nuclear arms race, the GOP held a slender 44%–43% lead, and on working for peace, was ahead by a 45%–43% margin. The big spread occurred over building up national defense, where the Republicans won hands down by 60% to 29%. Backing for the Reagan defense effort was fueled by pride that America was once more standing tall in the world. However, some of the edge was taken off this big lead on the national security issue by responses on defense spending: Democrats were believed to be more able to control defense spending than Republicans by a wide 58% to 31%.

OBSERVATION

Significantly, out of eight key issues dealing with the economy at home and war and peace abroad, the Republicans under Reagan led in six, were behind on only one and were tied on one (unemployment). This was the kind of issue advantage the Democrats had enjoyed for nearly 50 years.

The key question: Would this issue advantage provide the leverage needed to push the Republicans over the top to make it the majority party in terms of the voters' party affiliation, which would mean continued control of the White House in 1988, control of the U.S. Senate for another decade, gains at the governorship level, and—the ultimate prize—control of the House of Representatives? To achieve all that would be to have brought about a true Republican realignment, a magical moment for the conservative cause.

Hopes quickened in conservative hearts when the President's approval rating soared to a nearly consistent mark of over 60% throughout 1985 and into 1986, the highest in history for a second-term president. The test would come in the 1986 off-year election. Normally, a second-term president is well advised not to venture forth in support of the election of his fellow party members, since the "out" party almost always makes substantial gains. But Ronald Reagan was no ordinary president. And, despite having twice as many Senate seats up for reelection as the Democrats, Republicans trumpeted far and wide that a victory under such circumstances in 1986 would be proof positive that realignment had finally arrived. Many Democratic leaders privately expected the worst as 1986 hove into view.

In 1985 the Republicans made extensive plans for 1986. They would ignore the governorship and House races, by and large, and concentrate on the U.S. Senate. The 1986 election would be the worst they would have to face—1988 and 1990 would give them a far better chance of breaking even and thus holding on to the prized upper chamber of the Congress. They knew that they would have to find a way to get out the young people, who now were more Republican than Democratic. That would mean a massive get-out-the-vote campaign. They knew that heavy TV saturation would cost a record sum of campaign money. They made up their minds that they would mount the most effective off-year election drive in the history of modern politics. They were ready to go for broke. And Ronald Reagan, ignoring all of political history, was ready to take to the hustings, and go for broke with them.

The Harris Survey, conducted by Louis Harris and Associates, August 14–18, 1980, among a national cross section of 1,514 adults, released September 1, 1980; December 3–6, 1980, among a national cross section of 1,200, released December 18, 1980; January 8–12, 1982, among a national cross section of 1,256 adults, released January 25, 1982; August 26–30, 1982, among a national cross section of 1,253, released September 13, 1982; April 5–8, 1986, among a national cross section of 1,254 adults, released May 5, 1986; October 13–14, 1986, among 921 voters, released October 27, 1986.

THE POLITICAL LEGACY OF RONALD REAGAN II: THE LANDMARK 1986 OFF-YEAR ELECTION

■ BRIGHT PROMISES FOR A MONUMENTAL TASK

Out of the 34 U.S. Senate seats at stake in the 1986 election, 22 were occupied by Republicans who had been elected in a string of upset victories in 1980. They had retired from public life such staunch Democratic liberals as George McGovern of South Dakota, Gaylord Nelson of Wisconsin, Birch Bayh of Indiana, John Culver of Iowa, and Frank Church of Idaho. They had written a new chapter in modern politics by capitalizing on the negative 30-second TV spot. The basic campaign strategy consisted of having organizations such as the National Conservative Political Action Committee (NCPAC) run TV ads making scurrilous claims against incumbent liberal Democrats. The candidates and even the Republican party would disavow any sponsorship of or responsibility for the TV ads. The object of the attack was thereby forced to defend himself or herself against a shadowy adversary who was neither the opponent nor the opposition party.

The negative campaigns and Ronald Reagan's coattails worked in 1980, and the GOP swept into control of the U.S. Senate. The shift was a major one: from a 55–45 Democratic control to a 53–47 Republican dominance.

But in 1986 the shoe was on the other foot. The election was the Republicans' to lose. Now they had to fight to keep the seats they had picked up in 1980. The Senate class of

1980 was not known for its brilliance; it had not produced outstanding leadership. Even White House staffers joked about how some of its members likely would never have made it on their own, but had simply ridden in on the Reagan tide and NCPAC's clever ads. Several were virtually unknown back home. The main trouble in 1986 was that, with no Ronald Reagan on the ballot, they had to run on their own this time.

■ THE TACTICAL BATTLE LINES ARE DRAWN

For their part, the Democrats were desperate to win back control of the Senate. Six years was the longest in six decades that Democrats had been the minority party in the upper chamber. Losing committee chairmanships and the perks of power were bitter experiences. But the Democrats were also gun-shy about Ronald Reagan and defensive and fuzzy on the issues. They knew that the public mind-set on the domestic economy, defense, and even war and peace was against them. So they decided to run on local issues, state by state, or simply as more attractive personalities than the Republicans.

They also opted for heavy TV exposure of their pretty faces, on the one hand, or emulating the negative tactics of their GOP opponents, on the other. Traditionally, the Democrats had always figured they had to depend on rallying the faithful in person during the campaign and then dragging them to the polls on Election Day—a strategy that rested, however, on the assumption that a solid Democratic majority was always there, waiting to be tapped. By contrast, the Republicans' largely media-centered campaigns were designed to reach defecting Democrats, precisely because there were *not* masses of GOP voters out there waiting to be reached. By 1986, however, the Democrats had decided that they had to ape the Republicans even in campaign tactics, of which the TV spots were the essence. This meant raising record sums of money, which in turn meant that a candidate had to spend more time in fund-raising meetings than in visiting voters. And the impossibility of matching Republican financial resources meant that Democrats had to get even more mileage out of less TV money.

Obviously, the Democrats found themselves in a highly defensive posture in this campaign for control of the Senate. Short of money, issues, and campaign know-how, lacking a leader like Ronald Reagan to rally around, each candidate in the end had little more than his or her resilience and resourcefulness to fall back on. Most Democrats running for the U.S. Senate against Republican incumbents in 1986 were faced with a lonely journey and a formidable task, indeed. Many however, found that their desperation, their sense of abandonment, eventually gave them the feeling that they had little to lose and liberated them to find the way to win.

The Republicans early on decided on a strategy that almost all successful athletic coaches live and die by: Go with what got you there in the first place. They were banking on the ever-popular Ronald Reagan to raise money, and indeed the GOP edge in funding in the Senate campaign was at least 5 to 1. They were also counting on the president to get their vote out, especially among the young who had turned Republican under Reagan, but who had a history of being no-shows on Election Day, especially in off-year elections. A record $10 million would be spent in special get-out-the-vote campaigns.

Finally, they counted heavily on the same type of negative TV campaign that they had used in 1980. Spots would feature Jane Fonda, the original "Hanoi dove" from the Vietnam war days, as a prominent booster of Democratic opponents. In South Dakota, Fonda was even pictured as a backer of Democrat Tom Daschle, and at the same time as being against eating red meat, a major product of that agricultural state.

Strictly on the basis of personality, the Democrats running for the Senate in 1986 were by and large a more attractive lot than their Republican counterparts. In fact, in that same

South Dakota race, incumbent Republican Senator Jim Abd-
nor, who suffers from a lisp, began a commercial by admitting
he was no great shakes as a talker, but claimed that he more
than made up for that fault with homespun, old-shoe sincer-
ity.

■ AS USUAL, CONVENTIONAL WISDOM HAD IT ALL FIGURED OUT

The pundits who left Washington in September for the states
that would determine the control of the Senate made a major
prediction that quickly became the standard party line on the
1986 election. They claimed that this was to be an *issueless*
election. It was also going to be the most negative campaign
in modern times, with both sides gearing up to see which
could outdo the other in negative 30-second spots. Reporters
joked about how they never saw the candidates anymore, but
instead reviewed their commercials as they were readied for
air time. In effect, they reported, the races were no more than
personality contests, spiced with local issues at best. No matter who finally won control of the Senate, the 1986 election
would have been much sound and fury, signifying virtually
nothing.

Even after the election, when the Democrats had won a
significant victory in the Senate races, the pundits insisted
that it had been a largely localized affair with little national
significance.

This conventional reading of the 1986 elections must be
classified as nothing but patent nonsense.

Basically, the media had many of the right signals but read
them wrong. So did most of the pollsters who were taking
surveys state by state. Here is what happened: When polltakers and reporters asked voters about the issues, they found
that the issues were not decisive. When they went to the
young people who had voted for Reagan in 1984, they found
them still more Republican than Democratic. When they went

to the followers of evangelical preachers, they found them also still heavily Republican. And when they went to conservatives they found them continuing to be solidly Republican. So they concluded that nothing much had changed. It would be a status quo election, with the Republicans probably keeping control of the Senate by a close 51–49 majority, though it would not be an upset even if the Democrats gained control by a single vote.

■ THE REAL STORY OF THE 1986 ELECTION

The Democrats did not win in 1986 so much as the Republicans lost. But the fashion in which the GOP lost control of the U.S. Senate and the consequences of that loss have a significance that reaches far beyond 1986.

In effect, 1986 was the last thrust of a conservative Republican Party's attempt to become the majority party in America. The issues failed to work for the GOP. Their most popular president, Ronald Reagan, failed either to bring out the Republican vote or to convert Democrats to the GOP cause as he did in 1980 and in 1984. Negative Republican campaign ads backfired. The most massive expenditure of money in an off-year election for get-out-the-vote drives and for TV saturation proved to be a wasted effort. Perhaps the greatest irony is that precisely where the Republicans nationally paid little attention and spent very little money, in the races for governor, they had their only successes, with a net gain of eight governorships. At their postelection celebration in Parsippany, New Jersey, GOP governors twitted Republican National Chairman Frank Fahrenkopf for not having discovered their merit as candidates until after the election.

■ BREAKING THE REPUBLICAN LOCK ON KEY ISSUES

In the history of the U.S., the sure mark of a fundamental political change is that the key issues begin to work for the new majority party. Between 1985 and 1986 the enormous issue advantage the Republicans had enjoyed slipped away.

Only a year before, out of eight key issues surrounding the domestic economy and war and peace, the Republican position was preferred by wide margins on six, the Democrats led on one and the parties were tied on the other. By Election Day in 1986 those Republican leads were just about wiped out. The Democrats had moved ahead on four of the issues, the Republicans led on three, and one was a tie.

Here is how the two parties fared in the pivotal area of the domestic economy:

☐ On cutting federal spending, the GOP edge went from 57% to 34% down to 46% to 39%. A 24-point lead shrunk to a 7-point edge in only 14 months' time. Despite the claims of Representative Jack Kemp and the supply-siders that the public really did not vote protests against excessive federal spending, the Republicans' inability to bring down the levels of federal spending was taking its toll.

☐ Most striking was the shift in opinion on which party in control of Congress could best handle the problem of the federal deficit. The 1985 Republican lead of 53% to 36% shrank to a 42% to 42% stand-off. Six years of the Reagan administration had produced a deficit greater than that of all the previous presidencies combined. Now there was every sign that the Republicans' long-standing reputation for fiscal responsibility was being seriously eroded. Predictably, unless the Reagan administration did something in its final two years to materially cut the deficit, it was conceivable that the Democrats could have that issue working for them in 1988. This was nothing short of an incredible turn of events. Significantly, along with maintaining prosperity and working for peace in the world, finding a way to cut federal deficits had become a major public concern.

☐ On cutting the rate of unemployment, the 1985 45%–45%

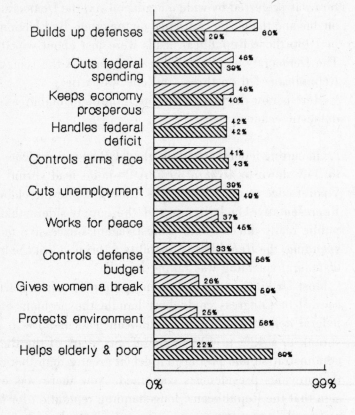

WHICH PARTY FARES BETTER ON THE ISSUES?

Issue	Republican	Democratic
Builds up defenses	60%	29%
Cuts federal spending	46%	39%
Keeps economy prosperous	46%	40%
Handles federal deficit	42%	42%
Controls arms race	41%	43%
Cuts unemployment	39%	49%
Works for peace	37%	45%
Controls defense budget	33%	56%
Gives women a break	26%	59%
Protects environment	25%	58%
Helps elderly & poor	22%	69%

0%   99%

Republican party   Democratic party

standoff between the Democrats and Republicans turned into a 49%–39% Democratic lead by Election Day, 1986. This was a sure sign of what was happening. Just as it was critical for the Republicans to dominate the Democrats on spending, the federal budget, inflation, and economic growth, it was also necessary for the GOP to keep the old Democratic issue of unemployment neutralized. Now their old bread-and-butter issue was working again for the Democrats.

☐ On keeping the economy prosperous, pivotal for any incumbent administration, the 1985 GOP lead of 52% to 38% dwindled to a bare 46%–41% edge by Election Day in 1986. Partly, the many pockets of economic trouble in the agricultural breadbasket, in energy-producing areas like Texas and Louisiana, and in the industrial areas of the South and Midwest were now taking the bloom off the general sense of economic well-being. And overall economic growth had slowed to a crawl, with most economists wondering how much longer the recovery could be sustained.

Clearly, the Republicans could no longer count on the economic issues working for them. At best they enjoyed only a marginal advantage, and that might be disappearing.

In addition, even before the Iran arms affair broke, the Republicans had lost their edge on defense and foreign policy issues:

☐ On working for peace in the world, the 1985 Republican lead of 45% to 43% gave way to a Democratic edge of 45% to 37%.

☐ On controlling the nuclear arms race, the narrow GOP margin of 44% to 43% in 1985 became a Democratic lead of 43% to 41% in 1986.

☐ The Republicans still led by 60% to 29%, on building up the national defense, but the Democrats also held a big 56%–33% lead on controlling defense spending.

But the decisive development on the issues in 1986 was not so much that the Democrats made marginal gains and even gained a slight lead on the Republicans, but rather that the Republican lock on economic and foreign policy issues had been broken. Without a built-in advantage on the issues, a realignment that would make the GOP the majority political coalition now seemed all but impossible to attain.

To add to Republican woes in 1986, four issues that had appeared not to be dominant now seemed to be working heavily for the Democrats: *protecting the environment,* where they led by 58% to 25%; *giving women a better break,* where they were far ahead of the Republicans, by 59% to 26%; *helping the elderly and the poor,* where the Democrats dominated, by 69% to 22%; and *helping farmers who are in financial trouble,* where the Democrats were preferred, by 66% to 21%. Given the lack of Republican dominance on the central issues of the economy and war and peace, these Democratic advantages in turn could gain new significance in 1988.

■ THE NEW REPUBLICAN COALITION WAS ALSO BROKEN

In the 1986 election the Democrats won the popular vote in the contest for the House by 52% to 48%, for the Senate by 50% to 48%, and for the governorships by 52% to 48%. Obviously, all these races were close, yet the Republicans, who had swept the presidency by close to 60% to 40% in 1984, lost them all.

Even more significant is the fact that the GOP lost control despite its continued hold on the three groups that were supposed to lead it into the new era of dominance. In the House races they swept the votes of white evangelical followers by 54% to 38%, of conservatives by 57% to 35%, and of the 18–29-year-old group by 49% to 44%.

The failure of the votes of the religious right, the conservatives, and the middle-aged to secure a win for the Republicans can be found in the emergence of quite a different roster of key groups in 1986. Two groups of former Democrats who had defected to Reagan in 1984 were pivotal: white Catholics, who went 55% to 45% for the Democrats after going solidly for Reagan in 1984, by 58% to 40%; and union members, who had backed Mondale by only 51% to 46% in 1984, but snapped back to the Democratic column in 1986 by a decisive 63% to 37%. The gender gap also surfaced again, with men going Republican by 51% to 49%, but women going Democratic by a wider 54% to 46%.

But without doubt the decisive factor in the 1986 election was the politically moderate vote, which had gone 58% to 39% for Reagan in 1984 but which went an almost equally decisive 58% to 42% for the Democrats in 1986. This loss of the center is crucial to understanding the full significance of the 1986 elections, for it means that as long as the Republicans are identified with the New Right and out-and-out conservatism, they will invite rejection by the political mainstream. By 1986 the conservative tilt of the GOP had worn out its welcome. The Republicans basically failed in the critical off-year election in their attempt to move the center of gravity of the electorate to the right.

This failure became evident when voters were asked to state their political philosophy. In November 1986 conservatives made up no more than 39% of the electorate, behind moderates at 40%, and liberals at 16%. Conservatives had risen only from 31% to 39% since 1976, while moderates had remained constant over the 10-year period and liberals had dropped 2%.

■ LOW TURNOUT HURT REPUBLICAN CHANCES

One of the quirks of the 1986 election that misled polltakers, politicians, and journalists alike was the impact of voter turnout. In the last two thirds of the twentieth century, since 1932, it's been a given that the higher the turnout, the better the Democrats' chances; and by the same token, the lower the turnout, the better the Republicans' prospects. The reason for this is that lower-income groups and minorities, who are more heavily Democratic, also tend to turn out to vote in much smaller numbers.

In 1986, as in 1954 and 1958, during the Eisenhower years, this traditional pattern was reversed. The lower the turnout, the less chance the GOP had of winning, and the better the Democrats' chances of regaining control of the Senate. When a cross section of adults 18 and over were polled on the eve of the election, it was found that the race stood at a dead heat: 44% to 44%. But when those most likely to vote were broken out, the Democrats showed a narrow but clear 48% to 43% lead. Among nonvoters, the Republicans were ahead by 45% to 41%.

The reasons for this departure in turnout patterns were twofold: first, Ronald Reagan, like Dwight Eisenhower before him, was an extraordinarily popular Republican president, who was even more so with nonvoters than with voters. Nonvoters tend to think of politics in much more personalized terms than voters, who are more issue-oriented. For example, in the Senate races, 33% of black nonvoters said they would vote Republican, compared with no more than 7% of black voters. The second and key reason, however, lies in what happened to the vote by age groups. People under 30 held Republican by 53% to 47%, while those 65 and over went Democratic by 62% to 38%. In other words, the older the voter, the more Democratic the vote.

The real significance of this age difference is turnout. As in previous off-year elections, the young turned out dismally —at an estimated rate of 17%, compared with a 37% turnout among the electorate as a whole. By contrast, 48% of the 65 and over age group is estimated to have turned out, well above the national average. The failure of the Republicans to get out the vote of the young proved costly, indeed.

■ VOTERS PAID LITTLE HEED TO THEIR POPULAR PRESIDENT

It's almost an ironclad rule that last-term presidents who venture forth in an off-year election to ask for votes for the candidates of their party court rejection. Although he was enormously popular at the time of the election, President Reagan proved to have virtually no impact on the outcome, unless it was negative. In all but two states where he campaigned for a Republican Senate nominee, his candidates lost. This was the case in Florida, Georgia, North Carolina, Maryland, Louisiana, South Dakota, North Dakota, Colorado, Nevada, and California. His candidates did win in Idaho and in Missouri.

California and Nevada were the most embarrassing defeats. In Nevada, Reagan's closest political friend, Senator Paul Laxalt, had vacated his seat. Partly not to dampen Laxalt's chances as a Republican presidential nominee in 1988 and partly because of plain bad counsel, the president went back to Nevada repeatedly. In the end, Democratic Representative Harry Reid was elected over Representative Jim Santini, a former Democratic turned Republican, by a clear 51%–45% margin. In California, his home state, the president virtually put his own political standing on the line to go all out in behalf of Representative Ed Zschau, who lost to Democratic Senator Alan Cranston by a close 51% to 49%.

───────────

OBSERVATION

History will likely look back on 1986 as the year that broke the Republican conservatives' hold on the electorate. Some claim that the GOP's net gain of eight governorships offset the Democratic gains in the Senate. That is a misreading of the role of gubernatorial elections in national elections. First, there is usually a tendency for the "out" party to gain statehouses while losing the presidency and the U.S. Senate. A

72%–20% majority of the public now actively believes that one party should not dominate officeholding from top to bottom, but instead welcomes ticket-splitting as a way to make sure that one set of politicians they don't entirely trust keeps an eye on the other set they don't entirely trust. Second, back in 1982, the Democrats picked up a net of seven governorships, but no one seriously took that as a sign that the Democrats were making a big comeback. Indeed, if the Democrats were to win back the presidency in 1988, it would not be surprising to see the GOP garner a clear majority of the governorships, in another instance of the electorate's commanding desire for checks and balances.

But 1986 was distinguished by still other significant developments. One that went largely overlooked was that many of the successful Democratic candidates for the Senate ended up taking tough and controversial stands on key national issues, even though their media advisers and the national party leadership may have warned them not to. For example, in North Carolina, Terry Sanford stood squarely behind abortion rights, even though the other senator from the state, Jesse Helms, had made his anti-abortion crusade a cornerstone of his political career. Wyche Fowler campaigned through conservative rural south Georgia blasting special business interests, as did Brock Adams in Washington, Tom Daschle in South Dakota, and Kent Conrad in North Dakota. All were elected. When negative attacks drove them to assert themselves in their personal campaigning, apart from their TV commercials, a majority of the Democrats who ended up being elected to the Senate spoke out in sharp criticism of the national administration and of Republican policies. Without realizing it, they were capitalizing on the underlying shift in the issues.

In some ways, the ultimate irony of 1986 was that in pursuing their tack of running a negative television campaign, the Republicans probably did more to sour the voters' attitude and to cut their turnout than anything else, in effect undermining their $10 million effort to get out the vote.

In short, in 1986, the Republicans and President Reagan waged one of the most heavily financed off-year campaigns in history and failed dismally. The defeat shattered conservative Republican dreams for a realignment for a long time to come.

A centrist stance is now likely to dominate the nation's politics, as it has for most of American history. The day when ideology drove mainstream politics appears to be finished. In fact, a major problem facing the Republican party is whether it can dismantle the right-wing infrastructure that has had a disproportionate influence in that party for the past decade and can find a way to rebuild itself from a base of moderates. As the important 1986 election determined, the immediate future of American politics is likely to be controlled by which-ever party can put together a successful centrist coalition.

The Harris Survey, conducted by Louis Harris and Associates, April 1–3, 1985, among a national cross section of 1,254 adults, released May 9, 1985; July 25–28, 1985, among 1,254 adults, released August 29, 1985; October 13–14, 1986, among 921 voters, released October 27, 1986; October 13–14, 1986, among 904 adults, released October 31, 1986; October 29–November 1, 1986, among 1,207 voters, released November 3, 1986; September–early November 1986, among 3,895 Congress voters, released November 10, 1986.

New York Times/CBS Poll exit polls conducted by the *New York Times* and CBS among 8,997 voters leaving polling places around the nation November 4, 1986.

ABC News Poll exit polls conducted by ABC News among 17,611 voters leaving polling places around the nation November 4, 1986.

SURE SIGNS THAT THE SURGE OF THE CONSERVATIVE RIGHT IS FADING

■ TOUCHSTONES

Perhaps the two pillars of the conservative movement in recent years have been a deep aversion to the use of government power to promote social programs and to regulate business, and strong opposition to busing school children for racial balance.

The two issues come together, obviously, when busing is enforced or justified in terms of advancing social justice and equality. In effect, busing pupils to achieve racial balance is a firm application of governmental power. But the roots of the antigovernment sentiment that has fueled the conservative revolt in the country are more likely to be found in the skepticism that has abounded over "the dead hand of government" in business and other parts of the private sector. Senseless bureaucratic regulation by government has been widely believed to be a major deterrent to economic growth, to increased productivity, to America's becoming more competitive abroad, and to technological advances. The public, however, has always drawn a sharp distinction between regulation of business in strictly economic areas, to which it has been strongly opposed throughout the Reagan years, and regulation of health and safety measures, on which the public has been about 7 to 1 in favor of stricter government enforcement.

The busing issue raises the hidden question of race, which has been a major theme in the nation's history, especially over the past quarter of a century. The cry for racial equality and an end to discrimination has been an important factor in the periodic swings from left to right in the United States. Stemming from to the days of slavery, racial injustice has sharply divided the country. There is little doubt that major forces in the New Right have regularly laid the ills of society at the doorsteps of those who press for racial equality. In 1986 Senator Jesse Helms proudly campaigned in North Carolina on his opposition to making Martin Luther King, Jr.'s birthday a national holiday. And shortly after Evan Mecham was elected governor of Arizona in 1986, he announced that one of his first acts on assuming office would be to abolish the celebration of King's birthday as a holiday in that state.

Some on the right believe that raising the race issue is good politics. Given that blacks constitute no more than 12% of the population and about 10% of the vote, and that whites are opposed to busing by almost six in ten, their cold-blooded assumption is that trading the nearly unanimous opposition of blacks for the support of a majority of the whites makes sense as a winning formula in national and state elections. The other side of the coin, voiced by many moderate and liberal Democrats as well as by two Republican governors, Thomas Kean of New Jersey and James Martin of North Carolina, is that it is both unconstitutional and bad politics to exploit race and implicitly to advocate segregation. Kean is one Republican who won reelection with 60% of the black vote in his state. In the recent Senate races in the South, the black vote was the determining factor in Democrat wins in Georgia, Alabama, Louisiana, and North Carolina. And the Hispanic vote made the difference in Democratic Senator Robert Graham's triumph in Florida.

But conventional wisdom has held that public opinion is

VIEWS ON GOVERNMENT POWER: A TURNAROUND

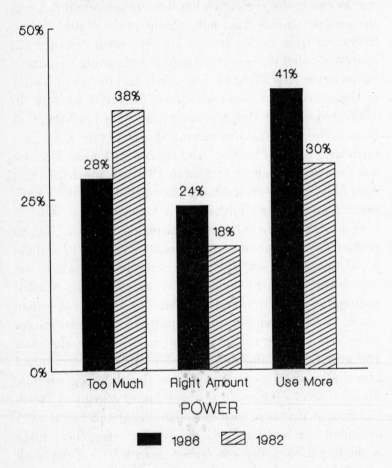

50%

41%

38%

30%

28%

25%

24%

18%

0%

Too Much Right Amount Use More

POWER

■ 1986 ▨ 1982

against making government any bigger, on the one hand, and against school busing for racial balance, on the other. Now there is solid evidence of rapid movement away from the conservative position on both issues.

■ GROWING SUPPORT FOR MORE VIGOROUS USE OF GOVERNMENT POWER

Back in 1982, early in the Reagan years, the thrust of public opinion on the use of federal power seemed to be clear. When polled on the subject, no more than 30% of the American people thought that "the federal government should use its powers more vigorously to promote the well-being of all segments of the people." Another 18% adhered to the view that "the federal government is using about the right amount of power for meeting today's needs." But the largest segment, 38%, identified with the view that "the federal government has too much power."

This, of course, was very much President Reagan's view of the matter, which he pursued with vigor in his public pronouncements and in the steps he took within the government to deregulate business.

Now there is solid evidence that the American people have had a profound change of heart. By mid-1986, the number advocating the position that "the federal government has too much power" has dropped a full 10 points, from 38% to 28%. The number opting to maintain the status quo has risen from 18% to 24%. But the biggest change has occurred in the number who believe that "the federal government should use its powers more vigorously to promote the well-being of all segments of the people," with a jump from 30% to 41%, or 11 points in the past four years.

As significant as the overall numbers is the makeup of the groups who have moved most decisively behind advocacy of more federal power: women, up 19 points; people 18 to 24 years of age, up 13 points; those with some college, up 16 points; white-collar workers, up 13 points; those who live in the Northeast, up 15 points; those who live in the north central region, up 16 points; and residents of the suburbs, up 16 points. The young suburbanites have tended to be more Republican in recent years. In fact, the suburbs can be called the very hub of current Republican strength. If these important segments of the Reagan coalition are now beginning to favor greater federal activism, the ultra-conservative cause would appear to be in deep trouble.

■ A SOMEWHAT DIFFERENT TUNE ON BUSING

Over just the past five years, the number of parents who report that their children are or have been bused to school to achieve racial balance has increased from 19% to 32%. Among blacks, 48% now say that their children are or have been bused for racial reasons, compared with 40% back in 1981. Among white families, 31% say that their kids are or have been bused for racial reasons, compared with only 17% in 1981.

A serious question, then, is just what impact this increased experience with busing has had on attitudes toward it. If it is a matter of "forced busing," the term used by many opponents of the court-ordered process, one might expect the number who report their children having a bad time with busing to have gone up sharply.

Just the opposite has happened. The number of parents whose children have been bused for racial balance who say that the experience has been "very satisfactory" has risen dramatically, from 54% in 1981 to 71% in late 1986. Significantly, the number of whites who say that it has been highly satisfactory has gone from 48% to 73%.

Moreover, in the past, those whose children went through the busing experience were perhaps surprised by how well it

ATTITUDES ON BUSING
TO ACHIEVE
RACIAL BALANCE

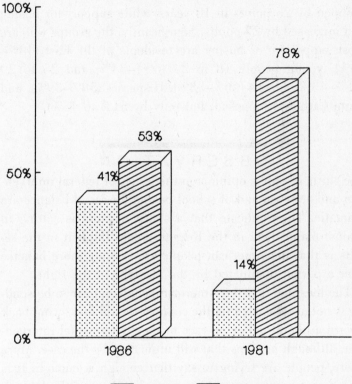

worked out, but when asked categorically whether they favored busing children to achieve racial balance, overwhelming majorities opposed it by 78% to 14% in 1976.

By late 1986 there seemed to have been a major shift in attitude. The public still opposed busing, but by a much narrower 53% to 41%. This meant that opposition had dropped by 25 points in 10 years, while support for busing had increased by 27 points. Significantly, the groups who are most supportive of busing are residents of the East (48%–46%), young people 18 to 24 (60%–34%) and 25 to 29 (51%–43%), blacks (66%–33%), Hispanics (58%–39%), and white Catholics (opposed, but only by 51% to 43%).

OBSERVATION

The shifts in public opinion on the issues of federal intervention and activism and of school busing for racial balance are dramatic. They indicate that a sharp reaction is setting in against major dicta in the Reagan credo. Implicit in the results is that the American people are seeking more balance after a period dominated by the ideology of the right.

The message that the American people appear to be sending is not necessarily that the country should now swing back toward a liberal policy on race or on governmental intervention, although perhaps that will ultimately be the case. More likely, people are trying to say that enough is enough. It is now time to move toward more moderation, to think more about the human condition, to care more about the less fortunate, the less privileged, those who have suffered most from neglect during the Reagan years. Additional evidence on that score is found in the late 1986 result showing that the number of Americans who think the hunger problem in the U.S. is "very serious" has jumped from 36% in 1984 to 55% in 1986, a rise of 19 points in two years.

These results suggest a return to a period of greater national conscience, perhaps a reaction to the "make it big while you can" attitude that seemed to characterize most of the 1980s in America. If this becomes a dominant concern, the politics of the late 1980s and 1990s would be radically different from those of the 1970s and the 1980s up to now.

Changing Public Attitudes on Governments and Taxes: 1986, conducted by the Gallup Organization for the Advisory Commission on Intergovernmental Relations, May 17–18, 1986, among a national cross section of 1,004 adults, released September 1986.

The Harris Survey, conducted by Louis Harris and Associates, November 26–December 2, 1986, among a national cross section of 1,250 adults, released December 22, 1986, and January 5, 1987.

THE AMERICAN PEOPLE STILL CAN'T BELIEVE WHAT THEY THINK HAPPENED IN THE IRAN ARMS AFFAIR

■ THE CONSEQUENCES OF LETTING REAGAN BE REAGAN

Only seven short years ago, in 1980, challenger Ronald Reagan promised that if he was elected to the White House, he would "stand tall for America" and that "this country would never again have to crawl begging the likes of the Ayatollah Khomeini." At the end of 1986, a sizable 64%–29% majority of the American people said they agreed with the view that "it is very upsetting that after all the tough talk from President Reagan that he would never make deals with the Ayatollah Khomeini of Iran and terrorist leaders, he ended up secretly making a deal with, and shipping arms to, Iran."

The distinguished *Washington Post* reporter and biographer of Ronald Reagan, Lou Cannon, put it in terms that summed up much of the dismay and amazement of the American people: "The betrayal seemed greater because the betrayer was Reagan, who had spent 50 years insinuating himself into the national consciousness as a believable character who was America's best version of itself. Reagan was identified with baseball, football, and Hollywood. He was 'The Gipper' who gave his life for Notre Dame and country, a governor who stood up to rioting students, a president who restored the nation's patriotic identity and celebrated heroism. Then the symbolmaster threw it all away in an escapade so preposterous in its premises and implications that Hollywood would never have accepted the script. The president who had promised that America would 'never again' bow to dictators or yield to terrorism was revealed as doing secret business with the representatives of the Ayatollah Ruhollah Khomeini. Suddenly, superimposed on the blaze of light with which Ronald Reagan had illuminated the Statue of Liberty was a remembered image of a burning American flag in Teheran."

Immediately after the revelation of the secret shipment of arms to Iran, the number of Americans convinced that Ronald Reagan could continue to inspire confidence in the White House dropped from 66% to 43%, a fall of 23 points—more than for any other president in modern times. The more he talked about the matter, the more people doubted that he was leveling with them about it. Fully 79% were convinced that "he deliberately left a lot out to avoid further criticism." From the beginning, three in every four simply did not believe that the arms shipments had nothing whatsoever to do with the release of American hostages held in Lebanon by pro-Iranian terrorists.

The fallout proliferated over a wide area and worried the American people the more they thought about it. Three quarters of the people were convinced that Reagan was wrong in not telling the intelligence committees of Congress about the secret arms deal and guessed that the reason the operation was carried out from the White House instead of the CIA was precisely so that Congress would not have to be told.

There is deep distress about what the entire Iran arms affair has done to relations with allies of the U.S. in Europe, Israel, and the moderate Arab nations of the Middle East. A sizable 77% believe that the government was wrong in telling our allies not to ship arms to Lybia and Syria and Iran while

PUBLIC REACTION TO U.S.-IRAN ARMS SHIPMENTS

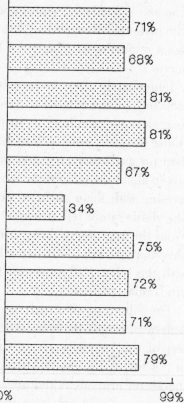

Let down that Reagan dealt with Khomeini	71%
Arms were ransom for hostages	68%
Iran is enemy of U.S.	81%
Reagan decision to send arms was wrong	81%
Worst mistake Reagan has made	67%
Reagan can inspire confidence in White House	34%
Wrong not to tell Congress	75%
Hurt relations with allies	72%
Terrorists encouraged to seize Americans	71%
Reagan deliberately misled public	79%

0%   99%

we were secretly selling arms to Iran. Two in every three people think that moderate Arab states no longer have reason to trust the U.S.

The public is convinced that any semblance of a firm American policy on terrorism and terrorists has been undermined for the indefinite future. A big 82% of the public is now convinced that terrorists have been emboldened to take American hostages in order to get ample booty as ransom for their release. Reagan's rating on sending arms to Iran is a staggering 84%–12% negative. On his handling of terrorism, his rating has plummeted from a high of 61%–37% positive after the bombing of Libya to 57%–41% negative after the disclosures. Moreover, as a result of this episode, the American people have reassessed previous acts of the president. The 52% to 42% who had reacted positively to his performance at Reykjavik reversed itself to a 52%–41% negative rating after they learned about the Iran arms deal. When the White House insisted that Lieutenant Colonel Oliver North could divert funds for the use of the Contras in Nicaragua without orders from someone higher up, seven in ten people steadfastly refused to believe it.

What has hurt the most is that the president was making deals in secret with Iran while at the same time he was publicly talking tough about the U.S. standing up to terrorists. A nearly unanimous 91% of the American people are hostile to the present government of Iran and will never believe that it was right to try to make contact with moderates in that government. A substantial 67% think that the Iran arms affair is the president's most serious mistake, and no less than 81% think it was a serious mistake.

Most serious is the total erosion of confidence in Ronald Reagan's capacity to lead in matters of foreign policy. On his handling of foreign policy, his rating in late February had dropped to 65%–32% negative, a complete turnaround from the 53%–44% positive of the previous April—a net loss of 42 points in his positive margin.

OBSERVATION

As this is written, the Tower Commission has issued its report on how the Reagan administration committed the serious blunders of policy that allowed the shipment of arms to Iran in the hope of gaining release of the hostages. Donald Regan, the former chief of staff, has been forced to resign, and the highly respected Howard Baker, former Senate majority leader, has succeeded him. There is much talk of a brave new beginning. The new White House staff will bear little resemblance to the old. The president's admission of guilt will ensure some forgiveness by the American people.

Yet the scar tissue from the entire Iranian arms episode will take up much of the time of Reagan's team to mend. It is not likely that this president will ever again be able to generate a sense of real faith and trust in foreign policy matters. He can get backing on foreign policy, but only on an issue-by-issue basis. It is unlikely that he will be able to take his case to the people in disregard of Congress, as he could before the Iran arms affair disclosures.

A sense of sadness and even tragedy has descended over the American people in their reactions to the episode. They are deeply unhappy at having yet another presidency end in doubts and shadowy suspicions. Their sadness over Ronald Reagan is special, for he had an inordinate capacity to evoke a spirited identification with the higher purposes of the nation. He revived patriotic fervor and a good feeling of purity about country. The gnawing doubt that he did dishonor to the nation in a bizarre arms deal with a sworn enemy who has been the epitome of evil to us hurts deeply. This wound will not heal easily or quickly, and the scar it leaves will remain beyond the time of Ronald Reagan in the White House. The people may try to understand, and perhaps even to forgive, but they are not likely to forget. And they will ask over and over again: Why did he ever do that?

The Harris Survey, conducted by Louis Harris and Associates, Inc., November 23–28, 1986, among a national cross section of 1,252 adults, released December 1, 1986; November 26–December 2, 1986, among a national cross section of 1,250 adults, released December 5, 1986; February 20–24, 1987, among a national cross section of 1,250 adults, unreleased.

Lou Cannon, "Why the Band Has Stopped Playing for Ronald Reagan," "Outlook: Commentary and Opinion," Washington Post, December 21, 1986.

THE OTHER FAILED REAGAN FOREIGN POLICY: LIBERATING NICARAGUA WITH THE CONTRAS

■ IN THE POST-IRAN-AFFAIR U.S. THERE WILL BE A FOREIGN POLICY

After the Irans arms episode, it is doubtful that the American people will soon invest very much blind faith in Ronald Reagan on matters of foreign policy. Indeed, his overall rating on foreign policy flipped from 53%–44% positive before the Iranian arms-deal revelations to a rather consistent and depressing 56%–41% negative, a net fall of 12 points. People have firmly concluded that whatever other redeeming attributes Ronald Reagan may possess, trustworthy leadership in foreign policy is not among them.

Yet well before Ronald Reagan made the incredible blunder of thinking he could get away with doing business with the Ayatollah Khomeini, the American people had made some tough foreign policy decisions of their own, few of them to the President's liking.

■ THE GREAT COMMUNICATOR NEVER COMMUNICATED CLEARLY ON CENTRAL AMERICA

The purest foreign policy stand taken by Ronald Reagan has been on Central America. His position has been based on the absolute conviction that this hemisphere is not safe for democracy as long as there are communist regimes in the Caribbean and in Central America. This means that Castro must be gotten rid of, even though little has been suggested on how that might be done. The rest of the Caribbean must be secured against communism, which justified the invasion of Grenada. In Central America, the communist insurrection against the government of El Salvador must still be thwarted. Most of all, in Reagan's view, the pro-communist Sandinista government in Nicaragua must be overthrown.

■ THE KILLING OF THE AMERICAN NUNS IN EL SALVADOR

Early on in the administration, the central focus was El Salvador, where the military government was fighting guerrilla forces in the countryside. Although the administration claimed that the war there was a classic anticommunist struggle, Catholic clergy and others in El Salvador disagreed. They accused that country's defense department of conducting a reign of terror through right-wing death squads who engaged in widespread assassinations and atrocities in violation of human rights.

In many ways, the decisive event that colored all that was to follow in El Salvador occurred in 1983, when three American Catholic nuns were murdered by Salvadoran army officers. The event had an immediate and electrifying impact in the United States. A 59%–35% majority of the American people condemned all U.S. intervention in El Salvador. An even bigger 77%–17% majority said they wanted all aid to El Salvador to depend on how much that country restored the human rights of its citizens, did away with the death squads, and set up a fair system of justice. The U.S., it seemed, was on the side of the oppressors of the people. The urgency of the communist threat somehow got lost in the violence visited upon the El Salvadoran people in the name of anticommunism.

■ THE NEW RALLYING CRY: OVERTHROW THE SANDINISTAS

With the election of the more moderate José Napoleón Duarte as president of El Salvador, U.S. attention turned sharply toward Nicaragua, where the Sandinista government not only was making more pro-Soviet statements, but was described by the administration as a major Soviet beachhead in Central America. The Reagan White House made a concerted effort to announce support for the Contra rebels who intended to overthrow the government in Managua.

Right from the outset, aid to the Contras was an unpopular cause, with a 66%–23% majority opposing such U.S. assistance as far back as 1983. In 1984, opposition to helping the Contras was 68% to 25%, in 1985 had risen to 73% to 23%, and in 1986 had dropped to 62% to 33%. Even after the Congress appropriated $100 million in aid to the Contras in 1986, by 60% to 30% the public still did not want military or nonmilitary supplies sent to them. By the same token, President Reagan's rating on his handling of the situation in Central America went from 59%–34% negative in 1983 to 65%–30% negative in 1984, to 63%–32% in 1985, and to 64%–29% in 1986 after the disclosure of the diversion of Iranian arms funds to the Contras.

■ A THEATER OF THE BIZARRE

From the beginning, Reagan policies on Nicaragua seemed dogged by a series of bizarre developments. Early on, the CIA got caught mining the harbors of Nicaragua, an act that met with a rejection of 56% to 38% by the American people. Then, in 1986, an American soldier of fortune, Eugene Hasenfus, was shot down in a military cargo plane that was carrying arms from a secret base in El Salvador to the Contras in Nicaragua. A 61%–25% majority of the public back home was convinced that Hasenfus was indeed a CIA agent, as claimed by the Sandinistas, who convicted and then released him.

Strangest of all were the apparent activities of Lieutenant Colonel Oliver North, who was apparently running his own covert war in Nicaragua, with private financing, private mercenaries, and a private chain of command—all out of the basement of the White House, under the auspices of the National Security Council. Finally, the administration itself announced that it had good reason to suspect that Lieutenant Colonel North had siphoned off funds from the Iranian arms deal and diverted some of the money to the Contra cause. Seven out of ten Americans roundly condemned what they suspected North of doing.

■ A CASE THAT NEVER WENT DOWN

Underlying it all was the fact that for all his persuasive powers, his televised speeches on the subject, his appearances before Congress, his press conferences, Ronald Reagan simply had never made a convincing case for U.S. intervention in Nicaragua. When told that Nicaragua was only 800 miles from the U.S. border, by 2 to 1 people chorused that Cuba was only 90 miles away but the President had not suggested another Bay of Pigs invasion. Basically, most Americans felt that the return of the Panama Canal was a signal that Central America was not of vital strategic importance to national interests.

Of course, the real fear of the American people about Reagan's Nicaraguan policy is that one day he will send in American troops to overthrow the Sandinista government, all in the name of keeping the communists out of the hemisphere. By 63% to 30%, a big majority is adamantly opposed to the use of any U.S. military force in Nicaragua, even as a last resort.

OBSERVATION

If President Reagan were to announce one morning, as he did about Grenada, that the U.S. had invaded Nicaragua in order to keep the communists from a major takeover in the Western Hemisphere, he would unleash a storm of protest from the American people, Congress, and the establishment. While few have doubts about the leftist and pro-Soviet ties of the Sandinistas, the portrayal of Nicaragua as a threat to the security of the United States is a notion that just will not go down.

Sophisticated observers know perfectly well that just as the U.S. would not set up a major military base on the borders of the Soviet Union because it would cause an immediate crisis of major proportions, so the Russians are not about to do the same on the borders of this country, for precisely the same reason.

The less sophisticated rank and file of the American people take a more visceral approach: they see no justification for risking the lives of American fighting men in Nicaragua. The memory of the loss of over two hundred marines in Lebanon still rankles, as do the unpopular wars in Vietnam and Korea. The Grenada invasion, in retrospect, no longer evokes majority support, as it did when it was staged.

The last straw, of course, was the apparent diversion of funds from Iran arms deals to the Contras, in direct violation of the Boland Amendment. It is now unlikely that the Contra cause will receive the support of Congress. Indeed, if President Reagan were to send the marines to Managua, it is possible that the 100th Congress would be the first in history to refuse to declare an act of war when a president requested it. It has reached the point where the people would demand nothing less from their elected representatives.

The Harris Survey, conducted by Louis Harris and Associates, August 18–22, 1983, among a national cross section of 1,257 adults, released September 8, 1983; December 8–12, 1983, among a national cross section of 1,249 adults, released December 16, 1983; May 10–13, 1984, among 1,108 voters, released May 17, 1984; March 2–5, 1985, among a national cross section of 1,256 adults, released March 18, 1985; April 4–8, 1986, among a national cross section of 1,254 adults, released April 14, 1986; October 29–November 1, 1986, among a national cross section of 1,207, released November 17, 1986; November 26–December 2, 1986, among a national cross section of 1,250 adults, released December 5, 1986.

APARTHEID IN SOUTH AFRICA IS APPALLING, BUT U.S. DISINVESTMENT COULD HURT THE BLACKS THERE

■ THE EVIL OF APARTHEID

Most Americans are genuinely disturbed by the system of apartheid in South Africa. They find it totally unacceptable that a small minority of whites cannot only rule a country with a big black and "colored" majority but completely disenfranchise the blacks by stripping them of all freedoms.

Little wonder, then, that a nearly unanimous 87%–7% majority of Americans condemn apartheid and all that it stands for. When prominent whites and blacks took to demonstrating outside the consular and diplomatic offices of South Africa and then went to jail for it, a 63%–28% majority of Americans agreed with their tactics. At a time when the Reagan administration was not leading any efforts in behalf of racial justice, the anti-apartheid campaign in America met a most receptive popular response.

Rejected out of hand by a 67%–28% majority is the claim that "the whites in South Africa have a right to run their government, and it's about time the U.S. stood up for the rights of white people abroad." Indeed, a 2 to 1 majority of Americans believe that "it is immoral for the U.S. to support a government such as South Africa that oppresses a majority of its citizens."

■ WHY MOST AMERICANS WANT TO DO SOMETHING TO DISMANTLE APARTHEID IN SOUTH AFRICA

When Americans' anger is aroused, their response as a people is, "Let's do something about it." Yet, while they are often moved or outraged by events abroad, people here are often at a loss as to what ought to be done. It all seems so remote; the culture and the language are foreign. Americans care, but they don't see a real role for themselves in the resolution of many of the internal problems of other nations.

But apartheid in South Africa seems to be a different case. It has deeply touched the conscience and emotions of many Americans for two reasons. First, because English is spoken in South Africa, the American public can bear live witness to events as they unfold. Second, tensions and confrontations between blacks and whites are matters that face Americans as well, and one of real personal interest. What most Americans see happening in South Africa on their television sets, even with heavy censorship, genuinely means something to them.

In short, literally millions of Americans identify with South Africa and its racial problems. They are appalled by the policies of the government, and deeply want them to change. Most believe it is blatant racism that must be rooted out. Even though South Africa is not formally tied to the United States, there is an intimacy between the two countries. Thus, people reason, if the United States would never tolerate apartheid, why should South Africa? Therefore, most conclude, something should be done about it.

Thus, by an overwhelming 78% to 16%, a majority of Americans want the U.S. and other Western nations to "put pressure on the South African government to give blacks in that country more freedom and participation in government." Support for this sentiment has gone up 10 points since 1985. An even bigger 80%–16% majority takes the view that "unless pressure to abandon apartheid is applied to the white government in South Africa, then the confrontation between the races there will grow more serious and a bloodbath could easily take place."

■ YET AN AMERICAN PULLOUT FROM SOUTH AFRICA IS UNPOPULAR

But when they are presented with some possible approaches to putting pressure on South Africa, the American people balk:

☐ By 60% to 35%, a sizable majority say they are opposed to ending "all trade with South Africa."
☐ By 60% to 36%, an almost identical majority is opposed to forcing "all U.S. businesses now in South Africa to close their operations."
☐ By a narrow 48% to 47%, a plurality also opposes "barring new loans from U.S. banks to South Africa."
☐ Only by a relatively close 52% to 42% does a majority support "preventing all new U.S. business investment in South Africa."

OBSERVATION

These objections to pulling out American businesses in South Africa and to closing down trade with that country should not be taken as a sign of weakness on the part of the American people. Nor should they be taken as an endorsement of the policies of President Reagan, who vetoed a bill for sanctions against the Pretoria regime. (The bill was passed over his veto and now is U.S. policy.) A solid 60%–36% majority of the public gives the administration negative marks on the way it has handled South Africa. In other words, people think the Reagan policies have been far too easy on the South African government.

What sorely perplexes the American people is how in the

world this country is going to play a major role in changing apartheid policies in South Africa, if the American government and private companies in effect withdraw all economic involvement in that country. Such steps are seen as abandoning the field of action, rather than applying maximum leverage to produce change. Oddly, the American people view South Africa almost as a wayward state in the American union, somewhat in the way Mississippi used to be seen. You just don't walk away from the fray if you really care about the fate of the blacks and the basic injustice being perpetrated there.

They want in the worst way to punish the apartheid government and force the officials to change the system or be kicked out of office. But they don't know how to do it—except to say that pulling out probably will not help the blacks. On South Africa, as can be readily seen, there is much puzzlement and a new American dilemma.

The difference between South Africa and Central America is striking. In regard to South Africa, most Americans feel that the gross racial injustice there must be righted. They want the U.S. to use as much leverage as possible to correct the wrong. But for Central America, the case that a wrong should be righted has not been made. The public is not convinced that the communist threat in Nicaragua is pervasive, and the apprehension is that the Reagan policies there will get the country into a costly and mindless war. The prospect of going to war in Nicaragua is believed to be real, and the people don't want it. There is no such prospect of sending U.S. troops to South Africa.

The Harris Survey, conducted by Louis Harris and Associates, July 18–23, 1986, among a national cross section of 1,253 adults, released July 28, 1986.

Business Week/Harris Poll, conducted by Louis Harris and Associates for *Business Week*, January 24–27, 1985, among a national cross section of 1,254 adults, released February 11, 1985.

THE PHILIPPINES AND CORY AQUINO: COMPASSION FOR OTHERS DEFEATS GREED AND DESPOTISM

■ WHAT A DIFFERENCE A MURDER MADE

Many older Americans remember the tragic drama of the Philippines in World War II, when the island country, long a possession of the U.S., was invaded and overrun by the Japanese. The Bataan death march of American prisoners and the subsequent liberation by General Douglas MacArthur, followed by the return of the country to the Philippine people, are all stirring remembrances of American valor in battle and generosity and decency in foreign policy.

In recent years, however, most Americans had more or less lost touch with what was going on in that country. There was a general awareness that the U.S. had important naval bases in the country. Many also vaguely knew that the long-standing ruler of that country, Ferdinand Marcos, was a staunch U.S. ally and a fierce anticommunist, but also that he had a reputation for regularly repressing political opposition. The Carter administration had raised serious questions about human rights violations under Marcos, as had Amnesty International, the human rights activist organization. Still, in the late 1970s, over six in ten Americans were favorably inclined toward the Philippines as a nation, viewing the country as either an ally or a friend.

All this dramatically changed in 1983, when opposition leader Benigno ("Ninoy") Aquino, long in exile in the U.S., returned to Manila on a commercial airline flight and was shot in cold blood on the tarmac as he left the plane. The effect of the Aquino murder on the people of the Philippines was stunning. Literally hundreds of thousands of Filipinos poured into the streets in grief and protest, chanting, "Ninoy, Ninoy," while opposition leaders accused the Marcos regime of the murder. For his part, Marcos claimed that Aquino was murdered by a communist sympathizer, a charge that didn't wash in either the Philippines or the United States. Indeed, by 57% to 20%, a majority of the American people was convinced that Marcos had plotted and carried out the liquidation of his most serious political rival.

■ THE ANTI-MARCOS OUTPOURING CONTINUES TO MOUNT

In dying, Ninoy Aquino had ignited both the Philippine and American people. A substantial 77%–12% majority in the U.S. was convinced that the nightly television news presentations of the huge street demonstrations against Marcos showed that the Filipinos were "fed up with his brutal, dictatorial regime."

Even more significant, by 78% to 15%, an overwhelming majority of Americans also felt that the U.S. should make known its disapproval of the way Marcos had repressed his political opposition and had violated human rights, because "too often such dictators embarrass us with the rest of the world when they are our allies." In addition, by a closer 48% to 42%, the American public disputed the claim of Marcos and his friends in this country that "because we need our military bases in the Philippines, which are so important to our Pacific defenses, we should do nothing that will cause Marcos to be overthrown."

■ THE LINE OF DEFENSE FOR MARCOS IS DRAWN IN MANILA AND IN WASHINGTON

However, Marcos was far from down and not remotely ready to be toppled from power. And one strand of American public opinion was capitalized on strongly by his defenders. A substantial 65%–27% majority went along with the argument that "Marcos is staunchly anti-communist, and we need all the allies we can find who are against the Soviets and are on our side." Here, then, was the now-familiar criterion that had guided the Reagan policy in many parts of the world, from Nicaragua to South Africa, from Angola to Chile: the dominant consideration must be to preserve anticommunist control, and to ignore the internal conduct of the U.S.-backed government.

True to this dictum, the Reagan White House defended Marcos, strongly implying that it was dangerous to tinker with his government because the opposition could turn out to be communist-led. Marcos was interviewed in a spate of TV appearances for American consumption, in which he made essentially the same point.

■ BUT OPPOSITION TO MARCOS SIMPLY WOULD NOT DIE

In the Philippines, the opposition continued to encourage street rallies, and the leader who emerged from the demonstrations was Aquino's wife, American-educated Corazon Aquino, who quickly became known to the masses as "Cory." Significantly, too, the powerful Catholic Church hierarchy and some elements of the military became more critical of Marcos. A pivotal event was the finding of the independent commission appointed to investigate the death of Aquino: a majority of its members found that a military conspiracy led by General Fabian Ver, Marcos' personal aide and, by the time of its report, chief of staff, was responsible for the assassination. But Marcos defended Ver, and the general was never indicted.

However, the price Marcos had to pay was to call an election early in 1986. Dramatically, the election pitted Marcos against Corazon Aquino, and American television covered the race almost as though it were a domestic campaign, with top anchormen reporting live from Manila on election night. A pivotal circumstance was that all the goings-on were in English, which made good TV copy in the U.S. and therefore Americans could follow the television coverage as if the events were taking place in the U.S. itself.

The key question in the election was just how honest a count the opposition forces would get. Indeed, when the votes were tallied the official government count declared Ferdinand Marcos the winner. Initially, President Reagan indicated that he would abide by the count. The absolute anticommunist rationale looked as though it would prevail.

However, in neither the United States nor the Philippines did people believe that Marcos had in fact won the election:

☐ By an overwhelming 85% to 5%, the vast majority of Americans was convinced that "if the count had been honest, Mrs. Aquino probably would have won a majority of the popular vote in the Philippines election."

☐ Sizable majorities of Americans also felt that the U.S. should not accept the "official" election results, but instead should refuse to send more economic aid to the country "as long as Marcos remained president," that Washington should work behind the scenes to encourage pro-reform elements in the Philippine army to break with Marcos, that the Reagan administration should use its leverage to persuade Marcos to resign.

☐ Significantly, the American people had concluded that Marcos must now go, no matter what he claimed happened in the vote count. Lost in the shuffle were the arguments that Marcos must stay because the opposition "could turn out to be communist-led" and that he would ensure continuation of U.S. use of key military bases in the country. Indeed, by 62% to 26%, a big majority now rejected the claim that the military bases were so important to our Pacific defenses that nothing should be done that might dispose of Marcos. Instead, a big 80%–12% majority went along with the view that "regardless of what the final vote in the election actually was, Marcos and his people committed so much fraud, intimidation, and murder during the election that he has lost nearly all his credibility as a leader the U.S. can work with." An 81%–12% majority in the U.S. also concluded that "with the Philippine Catholic Church, middle class, and important parts of the military against Marcos, it is now clear that he can no longer rule that country."

□ The bottom line: a 70%–21% majority of Americans concluded that "because she probably actually won the vote, Mrs. Aquino should take over the presidency of the Philippines." An identical majority also felt that she was "backed by most of the educated, responsible leadership of the Philippines, and is the kind of effective, attractive, democratic leader that can keep the Philippines in noncommunist hands."

With the help of strong persuasion from the United States, Ferdinand Marcos resigned as president and Corazon Aquino took over as head of state in the Philippines.

■ AMERICANS HAIL THE NEW CHIEF OF THE PHILIPPINES

For most Americans, the ascendancy of Corazon Aquino to the presidency of the Philippines was a highly gratifying development. A leader perceived to be corrupt, dictatorial, with little regard for human rights, albeit of undoubted loyalty to the United States and staunch anticommunist convictions, had been rightfully deposed, 85% agreed.

But even more gratifying was the prospect of what President Aquino would deliver. Here the hopes were high, indeed:

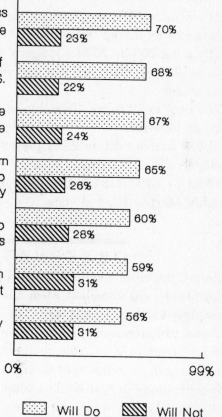

CONFIDENCE IN AQUINO'S AGENDA

Help poor and less privileged people — 70% Will Do, 23% Will Not

Reliable ally of U.S. — 68% Will Do, 22% Will Not

Effective head of state — 67% Will Do, 24% Will Not

Change country from dictatorship to progressive democracy — 65% Will Do, 26% Will Not

Stand up to communist guerrillas — 60% Will Do, 28% Will Not

Root out corruption in government — 59% Will Do, 31% Will Not

Reform the military — 56% Will Do, 31% Will Not

0% 99%

☐ Will Do   ☒ Will Not

☐ A sizable 65%–26% majority of Americans expected that she would change the Philippines from a right-wing dictatorship to a progressive democracy.

☐ By 59% to 31%, they were positive about her chances of rooting out corruption in government.

☐ By 56% to 31%, they thought she had a reasonably good chance of reforming the military.

☐ By a big 70% to 23%, a majority also was convinced that she would help the many poor and underprivileged people of her country.

☐ By 60% to 28%, they thought she would stand up to communist guerrillas.

☐ By a sizable 68% to 22%, they thought she would be a reliable ally of the United States.

☐ And by 67% to 24%, they thought she would become a highly effective head of state.

OBSERVATION

Clearly, optimism about President Aquino among the American people was abundant when she assumed office, and it remains that way to this day. The problems she faces, of course, are monumental, whether in combating the hunger and deprivation of a sizable number of her people, in coming to grips with the communist insurgency, in resisting attempts by the military to oust her in a coup, in obtaining the necessary capital infusion from foreign sources to rebuild the Philippine economy, or in outmaneuvering both the residual political supporters of Marcos and even those in her own entourage who harbor their own political ambitions.

In addition, while it is vital for her to maintain abundant support in the United States, in the end President Aquino will succeed or fail by what she does in the Philippines and for its people. For a person not particularly prepared to deal with the Byzantine political infrastructure of her country, the task must surely be difficult.

But, for all these caveats, the fact remains that in what has happened in the Philippines, the American people have discovered a prototype of the kind of allies they hope the U.S. will find and even help develop in the future. Compassion and decency, along with regard for human rights, is a combination that many Americans hope can become to a far greater extent the basis of U.S. foreign policy than the almost total reliance of the Reagan administration on making arms the currency of power and anticommunism, no matter what the consequences to the people of the countries in question. What is more, they believe that such progressive leadership can be far more effectively anticommunist. Corazon Aquino, *Time* magazine's person of the year, is the epitome of all this, say the American people in overwhelming numbers.

The Harris Survey, conducted by Louis Harris and Associates, October 5–9, 1983, among a national cross section of 1,246, released October 20, 1983; February 22–March 3, 1986, among a national cross section of 1,305 adults, released March 10, 1986.

MAYBE REAGAN CAN RESTORE HIS PRESIDENCY BY MAKING A BIG NUCLEAR ARMS AGREEMENT WITH GORBACHEV—BUT CAN HE DO IT?

■ MAKING PEACE WITH THE ENEMY

It does not seem unfair to characterize Ronald Reagan's essential approach to the Soviet Union as equating its communist government with an "evil empire" incarnate. In any case, however, it must be conceded that it is far better to reach accords with even an evil empire that possesses a full arsenal of nuclear weapons, than to drift toward confrontation and unthinkable nuclear war. But the only way to negotiate successfully with the Soviets, in the Reagan view, is to be sure that the U.S. is every bit their equal militarily and has the power to outstrip them in that regard with a system such as the Strategic Defense Initiative. Then and only then, it is reasoned, can peace be achieved through strength. Yet it is possible to heavily reduce nuclear weaponry and even to do away with all nuclear weapons eventually, according to what the President presumably said to Gorbachev at the 1986 summit meeting in Iceland.

■ NO DOUBT AT ALL ABOUT WHO IS THE ENEMY

After six years of Ronald Reagan's tutelage, it is certainly the case that the American people have no trouble identifying the

Soviet Union as the enemy, the evil empire incarnate. Back in 1979, before Reagan was elected, 3% viewed the Soviet Union as a close ally, 21% as a friendly power if not an ally, 38% as an unfriendly nation if not an enemy, and 27% as an out-and-out enemy. By 1983 the number who viewed the Soviets as close allies had dropped to 1%, as friendly if not an ally down to 4%, as unfriendly but not an enemy down to 30%, and as an enemy up 36 points, to 63%.

In short, under Reagan, the number of Americans holding hostile views of the Soviet Union has gone from 65% to 93%. This was a record high for hostility, second only to the 97% who felt hostile toward Iran in 1980 before the hostages were released, 73% of whom identified the Ayatollah as an enemy.

▪ IS THE U.S. STRONG ENOUGH MILITARILY TO MAKE PEACE WITH THE SOVIETS?

There is little doubt that under Ronald Reagan the armed might of the United States has vastly increased. According to the U.S. Arms Control and Disarmament Agency, U.S. defense spending increased 51% between 1980 and 1983, compared with a rise of 29% in the Soviet Union. However, on a per capita basis, the Soviets were spending, in current dollars, $947, as compared with a slightly lower $926 in the U.S. But even back in 1980 the Soviets were ahead: $755 per capita, as compared with $632 in the U.S.

In 1979 only 14% of the American people thought this country was stronger militarily than the Soviets, 40% weaker, and 42% at parity. At last count, a higher 24% think the U.S. is stronger militarily, a much lower 18% say weaker, and a much higher 54% say about as strong. Thus, it is fair to conclude that under Ronald Reagan, people believe that the United States has attained a position of military parity with the Soviet Union. What is more, by 50% to 46% a narrow plurality prefers military parity to superiority.

Presumably, then, according to the American people, this

country is in a position to sit down and negotiate a nuclear arms deal with the Soviet Union—at least by the standards laid down by President Reagan.

■ THE AMERICAN PEOPLE ARE EAGER FOR NEARLY ANY EQUITABLE ARMS AGREEMENT

Despite their deeply suspicious and downright hostile attitude toward the Soviet Union, the American people nonetheless see nothing inconsistent in coming to agreements with the Soviets on controlling arms:

□ By 80% to 16%, they would favor an agreement to ban all underground nuclear testing.

□ By 82% to 16%, they would support outlawing the use of weapons in outer space.

□ By 84% to 13%, another big majority would favor reducing the number of nuclear warheads and missiles on both side by 50% over a 5-year period.

□ By 82% to 15%, a majority would support greater exchange of students, scholars, and cultural groups with the Soviet Union.

□ By 68% to 27%, a majority would back a joint mission in space with the Russians.

These views and variations of them have been held consistently, almost without change, over the past 20 years. The American people are obviously convinced that one way to relieve the tensions that could lead to an outbreak of nuclear war is to find small or large areas of agreement between the two powers.

This commitment to hewing out agreements runs so deep that even in a crisis the American people will not be deterred from it. An example of this was the Soviet arrest of Nicholas Daniloff, the *U.S. News and World Report*'s Moscow correspondent, on spy charges after the United States had incarcerated Soviet physicist Gennadi Zakharov for espionage in New York. There were real worries that the Daniloff affair would torpedo any chance of agreement at the Reykjavik summit. As much as Americans wanted Daniloff released, a 56%–37% majority rejected putting off the summit and refusing to negotiate if the American reporter was not released. Daniloff was released just before the summit in an arrangement that a 3 to 2 majority called a swap and endorsed, even though it was not officially acknowledged as such by the White House.

■ LESS SWEEPING AGREEMENTS WOULD MEET WITH ENTHUSIASTIC SUPPORT TOO

At Reykjavik, Gorbachev announced radical proposals for arms control, much to the surprise of the Americans. Just what President Reagan's response was has never been made quite clear. The Soviets claim he put forth a proposal for phasing out all kinds of nuclear weapons over a 5- or 10-year period, including all cruise, bomber, and other capabilities. At one point the president told U.S. senators that this is what he proposed, but he later retracted that and said that he had only meant phasing out long-range and intermediate-range missile installations.

Reports from the ongoing Geneva talks indicate that far more modest proposals have been the subject of discussion. Yet, when their viability is tested with the American people, once again big majorities favor every one of them put forth:

□ By 92% to 5%, a big majority favor "working on methods to make sure that each side is living up to old agreements," a matter Reagan supporters have often complained about.
□ By 86% to 10%, another sizable majority opts for "setting up nuclear risk reduction centers in Washington and Moscow to reduce the chances of an accidental nuclear war."
□ By 83% to 14%, a big majority also backs "both countries agreeing to limit the size of nuclear tests."

☐ By 79% to 19%, most Americans also favor the "outlawing of chemical weapons and warfare."

☐ By 76% to 19%, a majority would favor "finding ways to avoid accidental outbreaks of war, such as allowing inspection by air of each side's military maneuvers."

☐ By 73% to 21%, another majority would support "increasing the flow of people-to-people exchanges between the two countries."

☐ By 67% to 29%, a majority would opt for the "reduction of long-range nuclear weapons."

☐ By 65% to 29%, a majority would favor the "reduction of intermediate-range nuclear weapons."

☐ By 54% to 36%, a smaller majority would back the "reduction of the number of NATO and Warsaw Pact troops stationed in Central Europe."

■ YET PEOPLE ARE PESSIMISTIC ABOUT REACHING ANY

Just before the summit meeting in Iceland broke up, hopes for an agreement soared among members of the U.S. delegation. However, when the meetings broke up without any agreement, Secretary of State George Shultz expressed deep disappointment, although later that week the president successfully put a much more optimistic face on the outcome. In retrospect, however, the summit is looked back on by 51% to 44% in a negative light.

When asked to estimate the likelihood of a major arms control agreement with the Soviets during the remainder of his term, a 55%–44% majority is pessimistic. And when asked if the world is a safer place now because of Ronald Reagan's defense and foreign policies, a 55%–41% majority is inclined to think that the risk of war is as high as ever.

Therefore, it is not surprising that the president's rating on his handling of nuclear arms reduction negotiations with the

Russians stands at no better than 55%–42% negative, just about the same as his overall record on foreign relations.

OBSERVATION

It is evident that most Americans have paid close heed to what their president has told them about the Soviets and about nuclear arms negotiations over the past 6 years. On any reasonable proposal for negotiations, the public has been highly responsive. On a whole roster of proposals that presumably would be vetted by the relatively hard-line Reagan arms control professionals, the public parts company with the administration and would like to see agreement reached on them. The public would go along with any of the prospective agreements that reportedly were discussed at Geneva.

In the end, the American people are both instinctively and rationally convinced that agreements between the U.S. and the USSR would relieve tensions, while disagreements might escalate to confrontations. The SALT II agreement, which President Carter reached with the Soviets, was never ratified by the Senate and was only mildly endorsed by the public. Yet, when the Reagan administration announced it was abandoning compliance with the treaty in late 1986, a 49%–35% plurality responded that the move was a mistake. The reason: by 72% to 21%, a big majority agrees with the view that "at a time when it's possible for the U.S. and Russia to blow each other up with nuclear weapons, it is important to keep any previous agreement that might help control the nuclear arms race."

Somehow, after all is said and done, something seems to be missing in the Reagan formula for arms reduction negotiations, in the view of the American people. If there is a flaw, they suspect that it lies in the difficulty of imagining the Soviets agreeing to nuclear arms cuts only because they must do so to keep the U.S. from achieving superiority in the absence of any agreement.

The Russians have stated quite bluntly that major agreements can be reached if the U.S. would agree to only conduct research on outer-space defense systems that could intercept Soviet nuclear missiles but would not be used offensively. Of the 58% who approved of the president's proposed Strategic Defense Initiative (SDI), popularly known as Star Wars, a majority (65%–29%) of Americans favor conducting the research even if it violates the 1972 Antiballistic Missile Treaty between the two nations. But a 53%–37% majority also agrees with the president that he should not trade away Star Wars development in order to achieve a major breakthrough on nuclear arms reduction.

Ironically, if the President decided to do just that, chances are that the American people would hail him for achieving an arms agreement. As this is written, hopes have risen that agreement on intermediate missiles is in the offing. Such a first accord with the Soviets reached by Reagan would contribute much toward at least partially restoring public confidence in his stewardship.

The Harris Survey, conducted by Louis Harris and Associates, September 9–14, 1983, among a national cross section of 1,255 adults, released September 26, 1983; July 2–7, 1984, among a national cross section of 1,259 adults, released July 23, 1984; November 26–29, 1984, among a national cross section of 1,255 adults, released December 6, 1984; June 11–16, 1986, among a national cross section of 1,250 adults, released June 23, 1986; September 6–7, 1986, among a national cross section of 802 adults, released September 10, 1986; September 15–16, 1986, among a national cross section of 1,255 adults, released October 6, 1986.

Business Week/Harris Poll, conducted by Louis Harris and Associates for *Business Week,* October 23–27, 1985, among a national cross section of 1,252 adults, released November 11, 1985.

ABC News/Harris Survey, conducted by Louis Harris and Associates for ABC News, January 17–22, 1979, among a national cross section of 1,498 adults, released February 5, 1979.

The Los Angeles Times Poll, conducted by the *Los Angeles Times,* November 1–7, 1985, among a national cross section of 2,041 adults, released November 19, 1985.

U.S. Arms Control and Disarmament Agency, *World Military Expenditures and Arms Transfers,* annual, as reported in the U.S. Bureau of the Census, *Statistical Abstract of the United States: 1986* (Washington, D.C., 1985), Table 552: Worldwide Military Expenditures: 1973–1983, p. 336.

AFTER SIX YEARS OF BIG-TIME SPENDING ON DEFENSE, THE PUBLIC SAYS ENOUGH IS ENOUGH

■ THE VORACIOUS APPETITE FOR DEFENSE SPENDING

If conservatives in the 1980s have had a higher priority than the pledge to get government off the back of business, it has been to increase federal spending on defense. The conviction that the Soviets were spending more per capita to gain military superiority has haunted conservatives such as Jesse Helms. The answer: Go all out in the commitment to beef up the defense establishment, to the point where the entire communist world together would not dare to challenge American military power.

The conservatives got what they were looking for in the way of funding, as perhaps never before in American history. Compared with $169 billion available for defense in 1980, by the end of 1986, $398 billion was available, an increase of 235% that averages out to $46 billion a year. Taking inflation into account, the rate of defense spending was at a level equal to or surpassing what it was at the height of the Vietnam war. But the 1980s were not a time of war. Compared with the levels of defense spending in the 1970s, the rate by 1986 had risen 439%.

To a degree, however, the ultraconservatives had read the public mandate correctly. Back in 1971, at the bitter end of the highly unpopular Vietnam war, no more than 10% of the American people wanted to increase defense spending, while

SUPPORT FOR DEFENSE SPENDING DECREASES

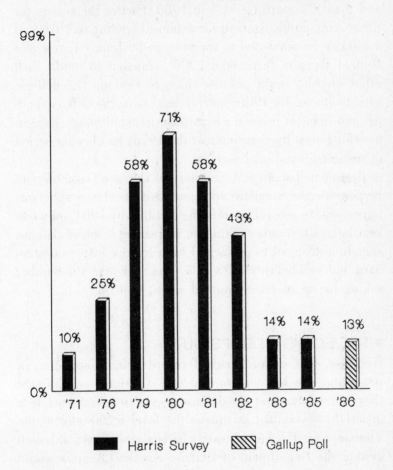

99% ┤

71%

58%   58%

43%

25%

10%   14% 14%   13%

0% └ '71 '76 '79 '80 '81 '82 '83 '85 '86

■ Harris Survey   ▨ Gallup Poll

over four times that number, 44%, wanted to decrease it. Slowly, through the 1970s, support for increasing military outlays grew: to 25% in 1976, 36% in 1978, 58% in 1979, and then to a startling 71% in 1980. Part of the reason for the soaring public demand for defense spending in 1979 and 1980 can be attributed to the attempt by Jimmy Carter and Ronald Reagan during the 1980 campaign to outdo each other on who could promise more to beef up the defense establishment. By 1980, sharply increasing the defense budget had in effect become a bipartisan issue, although Reagan benefited most by charging that the 1970s had been a period of neglect for national security.

President Reagan and Secretary of Defense Caspar Weinberger saw the mandate and poured it on. The public was impressed, as was reflected in the fact that by 1981, only one year later, the number opting for increasing levels of defense spending dropped to 58%, still high by any historical standard, but well below 1980's 71%. The next year, the number asking for an increase dropped again, to 43%.

■ THE BOTTOM DROPS OUT

By 1983, in the third year of record defense spending in peacetime, the bottom dropped out. The number who said they wanted funding for defense to go up plummeted to a miserly 14%, almost as low as the level at the end of the Vietnam war. The law of gravity had asserted itself, although neither the Department of Defense nor the Congress would get that message until the 1986 budget debates. For the first time since Reagan entered the White House, there was an actual real decline in defense appropriations, after inflation. Roughly half the public now was chomping at the bit for cuts in federal funds for defense.

Was this a fickle change of heart by a volatile public, as so many observers are fond of saying when they cannot explain a change in attitude, or was there good cause for the radical drop in support for defense spending?

The reasons were clear-cut. During the early Reagan years the thrust on budget matters had been to cut domestic social programs sharply and to increase defense spending just as dramatically. This was an obvious drastic shift in federal priorities. By 1983 the American people had had about enough of cutting back on social programs.

In addition, the defense establishment itself had lost its sacred cow status and had begun to be tainted by overtones of profligate waste, greedy profits for defense contractors, and even scandal. Off the record, some military people admitted that funding had accelerated so rapidly that it was difficult to spend it with any efficiency.

■ DOMESTIC SOCIAL SPENDING PREFERRED TO DEFENSE SPENDING

Back in 1981, when asked to choose between social programs and defense, the public by and large opted to cut social programs and to increase military outlays. But this began to change as the defense budget grew at $46 billion a year. By the middle of the decade the situation had completely turned around:

☐ In the case of three perennial social hardies, it was no contest at all. By 76% to 14%, people wanted cuts in defense before cuts in Social Security. They opted 74% to 18% to cut defense before Medicaid and, by an almost identical 73% to 18%, before cutting Medicare.

☐ Federal health and nutrition programs were preferred to defense programs as a budget priority by 67% to 25%. Veterans' health benefits scored even higher, finishing ahead of defense by 71% to 19%, and funds for cleanup of toxic-waste dumps won by 69% to 30%.

☐ But the list of priorities that now outranked defense got longer and longer. Federal aid to education won out over defense by 69% to 23%, federal farm price supports by 72% to 26%, federal aid and loans to college students by 56% to 38%, federal civilian retirement benefits by 60% to 31%, and federal aid to the cities by 51% to 40%.

□ On only one item did defense spending now finish ahead: when pitted against a pay increase for federal employees, defense spending won, but only by a narrow 52% to 41%.

Clearly, the bloom was off defense spending as far as the American people were concerned. Congress finally got the word in 1986, and it finally became unlikely that defense spending would anytime soon again enjoy its special position of the late 1970s and early 1980s.

■ MAYBE EVEN A BIG RIP-OFF?

By mid-1985, the public had just about had it with the familiar arguments for heavy increases in defense spending put forth annually by Secretary of Defense Weinberger:

□ By 53% to 42%, a majority rejected the claim that "Secretary of Defense Weinberger is right when he says the U.S. still has to increase its defense spending to close the gap of superiority the Russians have over us in defense."

□ By 51% to 45%, a majority also turned down the argument that "the Russians are rapidly increasing their defense spending, so we must increase our spending on defense to keep up with them."

□ By 55% to 41%, a majority also rejected the claim that "if we don't increase the pay of military personnel by sizable amounts, our defense will become even weaker."

But the real feelings of the public emerged in force when people were asked about the growing number of problems that were surfacing in the defense program:

□ By 87% to 10%, a big majority agreed with the criticism that "there is too much waste in defense spending."

☐ By 86% to 12%, a majority also agreed with the sentiment that "too often, companies building defense weapons end up spending much more than they were budgeted for."

☐ By 82% to 14%, another big majority expressed outrage at the charge that "companies that have big defense contracts put in false expenses and rip off the American taxpayers."

☐ And by 70% to 22%, another lopsided majority went along with the charge that "in too many cases, the military comes up with new weapons systems that turn out to be impractical or just don't work right."

OBSERVATION

Clearly, the demand for greater spending on defense that rose steadily from the ashes of Vietnam during the 1970s peaked in 1980, then declined into the middle of the 1980s.

Part of the reason for the decline was that the Reagan administration had done such a good job of restoring funding levels for defense that many believed the task had been accomplished. By the same token, a larger number had reached the conclusion that under the stewardship of Secretary Weinberger, the Defense Department had become bloated, wasteful, and even downright irresponsible. Greedy top officials of leading defense contractors, such as General Dynamics, were found to be living high on the hog on defense expenditures. Major corporations with heavy defense involvement, such as General Electric, were reported as not paying any taxes to the federal government, under a special tax rollover provision in the tax code. Systems such as the MX and the Sergeant Yorks, after having billions spend on them, just didn't seem to work.

The American people had come to feel that they had been deceived and misled by false trumpets of "the Russians are coming." They had been fully prepared to spend huge sums on greater defense budgets, but they felt that the trust they had put in the defense establishment had not been well placed. Interestingly enough, the military itself was not the butt of public criticism. Instead, the vitriol was reserved for the civilian side of the Pentagon.

It must be pointed out that in the event of a genuine national crisis the American people could be quickly persuaded to spend more on defense. But for the immediate future, the safest prediction is that when Secretary Weinberger tries to justify another defense budget increase, he is likely to get his head handed to him by the new chairman of the Senate Armed Services Committee, Senator Sam Nunn of Georgia. Nunn has promised not to put up with any more business-as-usual by Weinberger. If he handles it well, the defense spending issue could help catapult Nunn into a prominent position to seek the Democratic nomination for president in 1988, much as an unknown Missouri senator named Harry Truman used similar defense contract inquiries four decades earlier to earn a place on the ticket with Franklin D. Roosevelt.

The Gallup Poll, conducted by the Gallup Organization, March 7–10, 1986, among a national cross section of 1,004 adults, released April 13, 1986.

Business Week/Harris Poll, conducted by Louis Harris and Associates, October 23–27, 1985, among a national cross section of 1,252 adults, released November 11, 1985.

The Harris Survey, conducted by Louis Harris and Associates, January 12–15, 1984, among a national cross section of 1,251 adults, released January 26, 1984; June 28–30, 1985, among a national cross section of 1,292 adults, released July 18 and 22, 1985; January 3–7, 1986, among a national cross section of 1,254 adults, released January 27, 1986.

U.S. Office of Management and Budget, *The Budget of the United States Government,* fiscal 1987 budget.

HAS THE BRIGHT PROMISE
OF THE SPACE PROGRAM
FADED?

■ A SYMBOL OF THE UNDAUNTED
   HUMAN SPIRIT

Throughout the 1960s, an enduring development that gave America faith in both itself and the future of mankind was the crash program to successfully conquer space. It has almost been forgotten that the U.S. space effort was a catch-up operation all the way, ever since the rude shock of the Soviet's successful launch of Sputnik, the world's first artificial earth satellite, in 1957, well ahead of any comparable U.S. effort. The Soviets had much more thrust power; they launched the first inhabited capsule with a dog in it, and then in 1961 made Cosmonaut Yuri Gagarin the first human to orbit the earth.

After the U.S. had put Astronaut John Glenn into orbit three times around the earth, President John F. Kennedy made a pledge that this country would be the first to land a man on the moon. This was not simply competitiveness. The Soviet success had stung many parts of the American consciousness. It made Americans question the adequacy of the American school system and our basic competence and progress in science and technology, in terms of both pure and applied research. The space program became a major symbol of our dedication the pursuit of excellence.

■ A DREAM THAT SEEMED TO BLOW UP RIGHT BEFORE YOUR EYES

After the 1969 moon landing, the space program focused most of its efforts on the shuttle program, whose purpose was both to enhance the growing application of satellites in space to commercial purposes and to satisfy the military's need for development of space vehicles and operations. The missions seemed less dramatic, and there were some who questioned whether in a time of budget crunches, sustaining the National Aeronautics and Space Administration (NASA) program was worth spending billions.

Yet when public opinion was tested in 1981, a substantial 63%–33% majority said that the space program was worth the money and should be continued. The original impetus remained essentially undimmed, even though people did not watch the launches and follow the shuttle flights as they did when Walter Cronkite was chronicling the exciting space voyages of the 1960s.

Then on a cold morning in Florida on January 28, 1986, after several delays, the *Challenger* was launched, apparently successfully at first, but suddenly blew apart in sight of those on the ground and millions more watching on television. Among those aboard was a civilian, Christa McAuliffe, the first schoolteacher to travel in space.

A nearly unanimous 92% of the American people reported that they had been personally upset at the tragedy, with 63% saying they were deeply upset, as though they had lost a member of their own family. A 78% majority felt that there should be no further shuttle flights "until they find out what went wrong." A 66%–29% majority thought a hard look should be taken to "see if more flights can be taken which don't require risking human life." A 54%–41% majority opted for concentrating on orbiting unmanned craft such as *Voyager,* which were capable of conducting "important experiments and learning important facts without risking human life." Significantly, however, a 56%–41% majority rejected abandoning the practice of putting civilians on board space flights.

When asked if they, as civilians, were selected to go up on a space shuttle, whether they would go on a flight, a 56%–43% majority said they now would not. However, the division was essentially along gender lines: a 60%–37% majority of men said they would still go, while a higher 72%–26% majority of women said they would not.

But the most important result came when the cross section was asked again if they thought the space program was worth all the billions spent on it. Immediately after the disaster, a 63%–32% majority said that the program was worth it all. Support was shaken, but, in the end, held nearly identical with what it had been back in 1981. The question that remained was whether the inevitable inquiry would alter that immediate judgment of the American people.

THE LONG INQUIRY AND A "GO" OR "NO GO" ■ FOR THE SPACE PROGRAM

A blue-ribbon commission headed by former Secretary of State William Rogers held public and private hearings, trying to find out not only just what caused the blowup but also how the failure could be corrected, and what the future of the entire shuttle and space program should be.

The Rogers Commission report was critical of many of the procedures that had been followed, but it did conclude that NASA was making the necessary corrections and was now capable of getting the space program back on track, and that the program should be continued. A 72%–16% majority of the public was willing to go along with that basic finding.

However, as with the Warren Commission's investigation into the assassination of President Kennedy, the public had doubts about just how forthcoming the final report was. By 51% to 40%, a majority expressed doubt that the "full story

REACTION TO CHALLENGER TRAGEDY

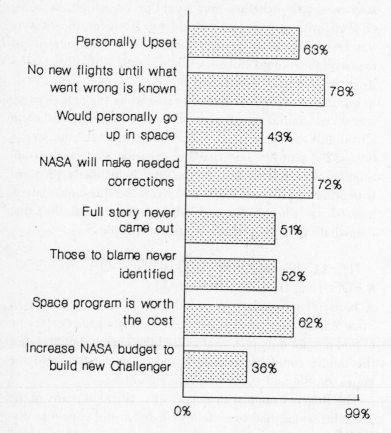

Personally Upset	63%
No new flights until what went wrong is known	78%
Would personally go up in space	43%
NASA will make needed corrections	72%
Full story never came out	51%
Those to blame never identified	52%
Space program is worth the cost	62%
Increase NASA budget to build new Challenger	36%

0%   99%

of what happened in the disaster of the *Challenger* has come out." By 52% to 25%, another majority did not feel that "those to blame for the *Challenger* disaster have been identified and have been fired or their companies fired." This meant that the delicate balance the Rogers Commission sought, between assigning responsibility and preserving the basic infrastructure and effectiveness of NASA, had not quite gone down with the American people themselves.

From the beginning of the Rogers inquiry, a key consideration for the future of the national space effort lay in the substantial $2.8 billion it would cost to build another shuttle, if that part of the program was to be continued. The question was whether or not this could be done without a sizable increase in the total NASA budget, at a time when such rises in spending for any program were almost impossible.

The Reagan administration fudged on this issue. It advocated no change in the NASA budget—in effect, a freeze —but, at the same time, recommended that a new shuttle be built for $2.8 billion, saying that funding could be found without increasing the budget.

In the end, by 60% to 36%, the public went along with the president's recommendation and opted to freeze the NASA budget, even though seven in ten were doubtful that the monies for the new shuttle could be found in the current budget. At the same time, a 62%–35% majority still said the shuttle program was worth the billions that would have to be spent on it.

OBSERVATION

Basically, the American people do not want the space program to be either terminated or cut back to a point where it will lose its effectiveness. But they are not prepared to break the federal budget to build a shuttle that blows up in space.

In other words, the American people's confidence in NASA

was deeply shaken by the *Challenger* disaster, to the point where they are not sure they want to put additional precious funds into the program. At the same time, they are not willing to see the dream that became part of the fabric of American life abandoned. If NASA can really put its act together, they seem to be saying, then the faith of today can be turned into tangible dollar support later on.

The Harris Survey, conducted by Louis Harris and Associates, May 6–10, 1981, among a national cross section of 1,250 adults, released June 1, 1981; January 31–February 3, 1986, among a national cross section of 1,255 adults, released February 6, 1986; February 22–March 3, 1986, among a national cross section of 1,305 adults, released March 6, 1986; September 4–7, 1986, among a national cross section of 1,255 adults, released September 15, 1986.

THE STAGGERING BURDEN ON THE AMERICAN CONSUMER IN SUSTAINING GOOD ECONOMIC TIMES

■ THE PIVOTAL ROLE OF THE CONSUMER

During the 1970s and 1980s most Americans have enjoyed some of the best and some of the worst of times. At times during this period, both inflation and unemployment have soared over the 10% mark. There have been three recessions —in 1975, 1980, and late 1981–83. But there has also been record growth of the economy—uninterruptedly so during the period between 1984 and 1986.

By all odds, the key to the growth and prosperity the U.S. has enjoyed has been the behavior of American consumers. Purchases of products and services by the public account for two thirds of the nation's economic activity. Since 1980, in constant 1972 dollars, such buying has increased 26% faster than the overall growth of the economy.

There is little doubt that the country would have been in far deeper trouble during the 1980s had it not been for consumer buying. The sale of American goods abroad has declined, but domestic demand has more than made up for this shortfall.

So what consumers are thinking, how much confidence they have in the economy, what kind of value they think they can get for their money in the marketplace all obviously can make the critical difference between recession and prosperity, between economic stagnation and healthy growth.

■ THE SIGNS ARE STILL OPTIMISTIC FOR 1987

A key to consumer spending is how optimistic or pessimistic people are about the economy. When people think bad times are ahead, they spend less. When they are convinced that good times are in the offing, they spend far more. For example, in the winter of 1980 there was a sharp falloff in consumer confidence, and a recession quickly followed later that year. The same thing happened a year later, and in the fall of 1981 there was another recession. In October 1986 there was a moderate decline in confidence, which if it deepened might have signaled another recession. But as 1986 ended, confidence in the economy among the consuming public rose five points.

Although unemployment has remained at roughly the 7% mark nationwide, people are nonetheless optimistic about finding work. And, despite the fact that the farm and energy belts covering major parts of the Midwest and the Southwest have been suffering from recession conditions, most people remain optimistic about business conditions where they live. In turn, this underlying optimism has produced a remarkable and unbroken inclination on the part of the consuming public to go out and buy at a level that likely will sustain relatively modest but steady growth of the economy through most of 1987.

■ A WARNING SIGN: VALUE FOR THE MONEY IS HARD TO COME BY

Although inflation has slowed dramatically since the 1970s, the American people learned much during that extended period of high prices. Most of all, they became convinced that buying on price alone was not enough. The key to smart buying, most have come to believe, is to make sure you get good value for the money.

When the American people are asked to rate most of the major products and services they shop for, in five out of eight categories, more people believe they get poor value for their money.

Here is the lineup of just where people think they get better and worse value for the money:

☐ In the financial and legal area, consumers are most inclined to think they are getting ripped off. Only 7% rate their credit-card charges as good value for the money, while 46% say they are poor value. The general impression is that the rate of interest charged on credit cards is excessive. And now that the new tax reform law will not allow the interest on such charges to be deducted from taxes, the public's howls can be expected to increase. People are even more indignant about lawyer's fees, and they are also unhappy about the value they get from bank service charges. Consumers are sending a clear warning signal to the purveyors of such services.

☐ Also high on the consumers' list of poor value for the money is health and personal care. No more than 5% feel they get good value from hospital charges, while a much higher 58% say they receive poor value for their money at hospitals. Much the same negative feeling exists about health and life insurance, and doctors' and dentists' fees. However, the prevailing impression is that personal care products give better value for the money. And the one positive note in the health area is in prescription drugs, where 34% feel they get good value, compared with no more than 22% who say that the value for the money is poor.

☐ Another source of annoyance is transportation. People feel they tend to get ripped off in the purchase of used cars, auto repairs, and auto insurance. By a small margin, they tend to see airfares as reasonable. Foreign-made cars are believed to give better value for the money than American-made autos.

☐ In the home service area, there is also some evidence of consumer discontent. People are particularly upset at what they feel is poor value for the money in appliance repairs.

□ A whole other group of miscellaneous items that are important to people yield a harvest of real discontent. Movie prices are a sore point, with over five times as many people saying they get poor value for their money at movie houses as those who are satisfied. The same is the case with cable television charges, college tuition, children's toys, and the cost of U.S. postage.

□ Finally, there are four areas, all essential to daily life, which come up golden on giving real value for the money. One is food. Poultry is thought to be the best buy for the money in food, followed by fruits and vegetables, meat, and fish. Restaurant meals are also believed to be a good buy for the money, by a narrower margin. The one exception in the food area is fast foods, where people tend to think they get ripped off more than they get good value.

□ In the apparel area, consumers tend to believe they get good buys in both men's and women's clothing, as well as in the purchase of shoes.

□ In home furnishings, people are inclined to think they get good value for their money. This is particularly the case with appliances these days, but also with carpets and, by a lesser margin, with furniture generally.

□ Finally, in the area of telephone service, both local and long distance, people feel they get their money's worth from this essential service.

But overall, on 2 out of every 3 items tested, the consuming public is inclined to think it gets poor value for the money.

■ CONSUMERS ARE THANKFUL FOR PAUL VOLCKER OF THE FED

The American people are well aware that policies at the federal level have been in effect during most of the 1980s that have distinctly helped the economy. To a degree, the Reagan administration has benefited from this public satisfaction.

But close to nine in every ten people are familiar with the

policies that have been followed by the Federal Reserve Board, under the stewardship of Chairman Paul Volcker. A 65%–21% majority nationwide believes that Volcker chose the right policy by tightening money during periods when inflation was running high and of easing money and by lowering interest rates during periods when the economy seemed to be heading for another recession.

A 56%–39% majority is inclined to give Volcker chief credit for keeping inflation down. He is particularly admired for not yielding to easy money policies, which would have revived the growth of inflation. He is also credited with helping to get the U.S. dollar down abroad to help make American products more competitive in world markets. The only area in which he is criticized is in his efforts to keep Third World countries from defaulting on their debts to American banks.

When asked to give him an overall rating, a 56%–37% majority comes up positive on Chairman Volcker. This is high tribute, indeed, for an appointed official, and it is clear evidence of the unique role he and the Fed have played throughout this period.

OBSERVATION

It is evident that the American consumer's buoyant optimism has played an important role in bringing the country out of three recessions over the past decade and is largely responsible for maintaining consumer demand and providing for economic growth in 1987. The signs are positive that steady, if not spectacular, growth will continue for at least another year.

However, in the widespread unhappiness among consumers about the value they receive from many products, there is also a sharp warning to American business not to raise prices again to sustain profits, and also to maintain the quality of the merchandise and services being offered in the marketplace. If public disenchantment with value for the money were to grow, consumer demand could decrease, which in turn could bring about another recession.

At the leadership level, Chairman Paul Volcker of the Federal Reserve in effect has been the partner of the consuming public. Often Volcker has made the American people take stiff medicine for their ills, by tightening the money supply, keeping interest rates up, and not allowing inflation to grow in wage or price increases. The people obviously appreciate these efforts. A sizable 61%–24% majority would favor President Reagan reappointing Volcker to another term as chairman of the Fed when his term expires in August 1987. Few expect that Volcker will accept a third term or that Reagan will offer it to him.

But the popularity of Volcker is a significant indication that after suffering from double-digit unemployment and inflation, the American people are experienced and sophisticated enough to know that tough medicine may often be the only cure for the economic ills in the latter part of the twentieth century.

"The Value of the Dolls," from *Across the Board*, December 1985, copyrighted by the Conference Board.

"Consumer Attitudes and Buying Plans," conducted by NFO Research, Inc., for the Consumer Research Center of the Conference Board, released December 1986.

The Harris Survey, conducted by Louis Harris and Associates, April 19–21, 1986, among a national cross section of 1,252 adults, released May 26, 1986.

U.S. Bureau of Economic Analysis, *The National Income and Product Accounts of the United States, 1929–76*, and *Survey of Current Business*, July issues, as reported in the U.S. Bureau of the Census, *Statistical Abstract of the United States: 1986* (Washington, D.C., 1985), Table 719: GNP in Current and Constant (1972) Dollars: 1970–1984, p. 432.

THE FADING IMPACT OF GRAMM-RUDMAN

■ THE EASY WORLD OF LEGISLATING FISCAL RESPONSIBILITY

In the mid-1980s a phenomenon occurred that would have caused professional politicians of the past to roll over in their graves: the public really began to care about deficit spending.

When asked what major issues affecting their lives they think the federal government should do something about, right up there with the basic concerns about keeping the economy prosperous and finding ways to avoid war and to achieve peace is *cutting the federal deficit.* The old assumption in politics was that people liked the goodies that federal spending brought. It was too much to ask that they really worry about the consequences of deficit spending. Republicans and other conservative types objected to profligate spending not out of political expediency, but instead as a matter of high moral principle.

But along with respected economic leaders, such as Federal Reserve Chairman Paul Volcker, the American people began to worry deeply about federal deficits running in excess of $200 billion a year. Such huge deficits had the effect of causing a collision between private and public borrowing, which in turn could create a return to inflation and record-high interest rates. One of the reasons for the high value of the dollar abroad, which had crippled the sale of American products in the world, was these deficits. This also meant that high interest rates in the U.S. would attract foreign capital into this country. That produced a situation in which the U.S. debt was being financed by foreign investors.

By 1985 and 1986, nearly every responsible person had become convinced that the federal deficit was an evil that had to be attacked. Even political liberals had long since admitted that federal spending had gotten out of control and had to be trimmed back. But the question was: What can be done to effectively control the deficit?

So in 1985, Senator Phil Gramm of Texas came up with what he claimed was a fail-safe solution. Above all else, he reasoned, don't leave it up to the Congress to bring the budget into balance. There must be some automatic mechanism that would *require* that the budget be balanced. He joined with Republican Senator Warren Rudman of New Hampshire and Democratic Senator Ernest Hollings of South Carolina in proposing a bill that would set a ceiling of $172 billion on the federal budget deficit and that would cut the deficit by $36 billion a year until it reached zero in 1991. When Congress failed to meet these targets, automatic across-the-board cuts would be made in all federal programs.

■ THE PUBLIC'S REACTION TO GRAMM-RUDMAN: ARE YOU KIDDING?

Right after Gramm-Rudman was passed, the American people expressed the following skeptical views of what was likely to happen:

□ By 64% to 32%, a majority simply did not believe that "the scheduled cuts would really be made in spending year by year as the new law called for."

□ By an even higher 83% to 15%, a majority was convinced that the federal deficit would not be reduced to zero by 1991.

□ By 70% to 25%, a big majority concluded that "when the Congress and the president can't agree on the cuts to be made, then it is inevitable that a new tax increase will be passed to cut the federal deficit."

The public concluded that the cuts in spending and increases in taxes needed to balance the budget would be made not through some "device" but only when the will is found to make the necessary tough decisions.

In fact, Gramm-Rudman had many of its teeth pulled by a U.S. Supreme Court decision that declared one of its key provisions unconstitutional because it mandated what should be an executive branch decision to a semiautonomous part of government, the comptroller general's office. Under the provisions of the law, this interpretation throws the decision back to the Congress, in effect nullifying the automatic across-the-board cuts. As opponents of Gramm-Rudman claimed, a computer cannot be substituted for conscious human decision-making by the president in cooperation with the Congress.

The impracticality of Gramm-Rudman was immediately apparent when in 1986 some of the cuts that would have to be made under its provisions were tested with the public. A 54%–43% majority was willing to go along with drastic cuts in defense spending. But by margins ranging from 2 to 1 to 5 to 1, big majorities of the public opposed cutting funds to clean up toxic-waste dumps, federal aid for education, loans to college students, price supports and credit for farmers, research funding for science and health, and federal health programs for women and children.

■ THE ULTIMATE ANSWER TO GRAMM-RUDMAN

Just as nearly every responsible person had become convinced that federal deficits were not good, so, too, the conviction was nearly universal that budget cuts had to be accompanied by tax increases to achieve a balanced budget. Only 26% said that the budget could be balanced by spending cuts alone, and only 4% through tax hikes alone. A sizable 62% majority said that the budget could be balanced only by a combination of spending cuts and tax increases. Significantly, a 79%–19% majority of the people said they would be willing to raise their own taxes, "if the burden was equally shared by all."

Tax increases might be easier to come by with the public than most politicians are willing to admit:

□ A 67% to 28% majority would favor a tax on products imported from abroad.

□ By 55% to 37%, a majority would favor an oil imports fee.

□ By 48% to 47%, a plurality would support a national sales tax.

□ Only a narrow 53% to 44% majority would oppose a 30-cent-a-gallon tax on gasoline if the entire tax revenues were dedicated to reducing the deficit.

□ The one tax that absolutely would not go down would be a 10% surcharge on federal income taxes, opposed by 69% to 26%.

OBSERVATION

The lesson of Gramm-Rudman, much as with proposals for a constitutional amendment requiring a balanced federal budget, is that deficits simply cannot be legislated out of existence. They are people-made, and only people will be able to hew out the hard decisions necessary to eliminate them.

The public knew immediately upon its passage that Gramm-Rudman likely would not work, as did most politicians who voted for it. The exercise was essentially a sham to provide candidates running for reelection with an easy out.

Whether or not the federal system would finally muster the courage to bring federal deficits under control was still an open matter as 1987 dawned. President Reagan, who is adamant about opposing all tax increases, still maintains that the answer is cuts in spending. Democrats are divided on whether to risk voter wrath by raising taxes, as conventional wisdom has it, or just to blame incumbent Republicans for the big deficits.

The ultimate irony of 1986, however, was that conservative economists had reached the conclusion that it was desirable to have some stimulation of the economy from federal spending, so it was no great disaster if Gramm-Rudman did not really work.

The Harris Survey, conducted by Louis Harris and Associates, December 27, 1984–January 2, 1985, among a national cross section of 1,255 adults, released January 31, 1985; January 3–7, 1986, among a national cross section of 1,254 adults, released January 27, 1986; April 5–8, 1986, among a national cross section of 1,254 adults, released April 21, 1986.

TAX REFORM: IT MIGHT NOT BE PERFECT, BUT IT'S AN IDEA WHOSE TIME HAS COME

■ THE EROSION OF FAITH IN PROGRESSIVE TAXATION

For many years the official approach to taxation in the country was best summed up by Senator Russell Long's classic bit of doggerel, written when he virtually single-handedly ran the Senate Finance Committee:

> Don't tax you, don't tax me
> Tax that fella behind the tree.

By the middle of the 1980s, however, yet another, even deeper conviction was dawning on the American people. Increasing numbers felt that the basic tax principle of "tax according to ability to pay," which had been adopted in the Sixteenth Amendment to the Constitution back in 1913, had become a mockery. Thus, by 1984, a 57%–33% majority of the public believed that what had been touted for years as a progressive tax system—whereby people paid higher rates as their income went up—was fundamentally unfair and even unsound. A 56%–43% majority also bought the conservative claim that "the present tax system discourages people from wanting to make more money, because the more you make, the more you have to pay in taxes."

But the real rap on the tax system was summed up in the 85%–13% majority who agreed with the criticism that "the basic thing wrong with the current system is that the rich get away with paying too little and the average person gets stuck paying too much." Common reasoning was summed up in the statement that while "most lower- and middle-income people now pay what they owe in federal taxes through payroll deductions, most higher-income people get out of paying much of their taxes by having tax accountants and lawyers who show them how to use loopholes in the tax law for tax shelters and other devices." A nearly unanimous 86%–7% majority agreed with that assessment.

Thus, by 1985, there was a clamor for change in the tax system, spurred by populist sentiment among the more privileged. On the one hand, Americans felt that the old system stifled initiative and punished risk-taking. On the other hand, they felt a deep sense of inequity that the rich and big business were paying little tax, while those who had their taxes withheld were paying through the nose.

The trouble was that too many people were inclined, as Russell Long had shrewdly put it, to "tax that fella behind the tree," and to leave all the benefits for themselves untouched. Most of the business community felt this way and employed lobbyists who were convinced they could kill tax reform because Russell Long's old ironclad rule would finally prevail. In the end Senator Long himself was one of those who helped pass the final version of tax reform.

■ THE MUDDIED WATERS OF TAX REFORM

Because the thrust for tax reform was coming from two opposite ends of the spectrum—those who wanted to cut the taxes of the privileged to increase initiative and those who felt the privileged were getting away with murder—some common ground had to be reached. The conservatives proposed a "flat tax" of 14%, which would have allowed everyone to pay the same rate no matter how big their income. This failed by almost 2 to 1 when tested with the American people. On the other hand, the old system of taxing according to ability to pay was also criticized, by 3 to 2 majorities as well, as in fact being inequitable in the way it actually worked. At that point, Senator Bill Bradley of New Jersey and Congressman Richard Gephardt of Missouri, two moderate Democrats who had drafted the first serious tax reform measure, relabeled their bill "a fair tax." What they meant was that there would have to be at least two tax rates: a lower rate of about 15% for middle- and lower-income people and another rate of about 27% for those in upper-middle- and higher-income brackets. This would still drastically cut the rate the rich would pay, but at least there would remain some semblance of the progressive principle of ability to pay.

The first tests of this "fair tax" approach showed a 62%–25% majority who said they would prefer it to the current system. But there was still a long way to go. From the outset, the key to tax reform was not to convert it into either a tax hike or a tax reduction in the aggregate. It had to be revenue-neutral, or else it would be subject to the tugging and pulling of those whose taxes should be raised and of those whose taxes should be lowered. In fact, this turned out to be the process in the end.

But the strange combination that came together to pass the final tax reform measure—Chicago Congressman Dan Rostenkowski, chairman of the House Ways and Means Committee, and President Ronald Reagan—was aided enormously by the wise and persistent guidance of Senator Bill Bradley. They agreed to keep the measure revenue-neutral. Otherwise, it would have certainly come a cropper. The public favored neutrality by over 2 to 1.

The next major hurdle was to decide which loopholes should be eliminated. Nearly eight in ten never would agree to the elimination of deductions of interest paid on mortgages. Though undoubtedly the biggest loophole in the land, this was the sacred cow that had to be preserved. Also preserved were deductions of payments on medical expenses, deductions for payment of state and local income taxes, and deductions for charitable contributions, and a relatively few others.

The balancing act that faced Rostenkowski in shepherding a revenue-neutral and respectable tax reform bill through Ways and Means and then the House of Representatives was how to yield enough to keep the bill alive, but, at the same time, not to yield so indiscriminately that the final measure would become a travesty, the fate of tax bills from time immemorial.

Down to the wire, the public manifested much confusion and even skepticism about just what a tax reform bill would contain. After all, the long-standing suspicion was that most tax bills ended up helping special interests that had lobbying clout. Thus, when pressed, the public was inclined to think the final version of tax reform would help the rich and big business. Only a minority thought it would help middle-income families and two-earner households. Most important, only 47% thought it would help them and their family. Most also thought it would not have a major influence on the economy, nor on tax simplification. But a substantial 41% were plainly worried that it would increase their own tax burden.

■ HOW ROSTENKOWSKI MOVED TO ALLEVIATE TAXPAYERS' WORST FEARS

In the end, Chairman Rostenkowski adroitly avoided making tax reform a grab bag for special interests, kept it revenue-neutral and still closed literally hundreds of loopholes. He accomplished all this courageously by discontinuing tax deductions on Individual Retirement Accounts (IRA) and the marriage deduction, by converting the capital gains tax into the same rate as all income, and by eliminating deductions of most interest paid on credit card and other charge accounts.

But the central elements that ensured public support for the tax reform measure lie elsewhere. The final bill virtually eliminated all federal income taxes paid by anyone who fell into the poverty or near-poverty category. No one with an income below $12,500 would pay any tax. This provision added a great deal to the growing sense that tax reform was not simply lowering maximum taxes on rich people and companies, but also showing compassion toward the least fortunate, some of whom actually paid taxes.

But easily the most important provision of the House tax reform bill centered on increasing corporate taxes while lowering individual taxes by a roughly equal amount. An estimated $140 billion over a 5-year period will be taken off the federal taxes of individuals and added to the taxes of corporations. This single bottom line never received less than 2 to 1 backing from the American people. As was shown in detailed and repeated questioning, without doubt the key that always galvanized public support for tax reform was the mention of this massive transfer of the tax burden from individuals to corporations. The public was willing to allow the maximum tax that business would pay drop to 33%, but in the aggregate, corporations are still going to pay more taxes. It was a time when the American people and their representatives in Congress were convinced that as long as taxes generally were not being raised, they were willing to go along with tax simplification, a closing of loopholes (including some popular with the public, but mainly those enjoyed by the wealthy), and a measure that lowered the basic rates paid by individuals and corporations.

By the time the voting took place, a better than 3 to 1 majority finally gave its support to the compromise tax reform bill coming out of Congress.

OBSERVATION

Thus, what congressional leaders and the president called tax reform really carried the day by conveying to the public that corporate America was going to have to pay more and that individuals would pay less. Disillusioned by what they had grown to believe was the distortion of the intent of taxing according to ability to pay—the original premise of progressive taxation—the public was willing to substitute a new system that would stick it to those corporations that used the loopholes to avoid or defer the payment of taxes, even though it would also mean far fewer loopholes and deductions for ordinary taxpayers.

There is no doubt the final bill would never have passed both houses of Congress and signed into law unless there had been a strange and unusual coalition of liberal Democrats, headed by House Speaker "Tip" O'Neill, and conservative Republicans who followed their president's urgings to vote for it. It is ironic that Ronald Reagan took the populist cause and stuck it to major segments of business and equally ironic that moderate and liberal Democrats were willing to accept vastly lowered taxes for high-income people.

In short, while no one really knows whether or not the tax reform measure will help or hurt the economy, nonetheless it was a remarkable bill that took much away from the privileged. It also said loud and clear that in the future much of the investment decisions will be left up to individuals, far more than in the past, and to those who will act for them as financial institutions they trust. In the future the federal government will be using taxation as a means to redistribute the wealth far less, but the working poor will also find relief from paying taxes as they had to before.

Of course, before long, the high-paid lobbyists for special interest business groups, especially those from industries whose former tax breaks were wiped out, will be back again to eat away at the reforms. At the other end of the spectrum, newly elected House Speaker Jim Wright wants to put off the tax cuts that the reform measure gave to the wealthy. But the chances that tax reform will be repealed quickly and easily are slim. The public sometimes has a way of opting for the greater good, and this is one case where that is precisely what happened.

The Harris Survey, conducted by Louis Harris and Associates, November 26–29, 1984, among a national cross section of 1,255 adults, released December 17, 1984; August 5–11, 1986, among a national cross section of 1,248 adults, released August 18, 1986.

The Gallup Poll, conducted by the Gallup Organization, September 3–17, 1986, among a national cross section of 978 adults, released September 28, 1986.

Business Week/Harris Poll, conducted by Louis Harris and Associates, July 12–15, 1985, among a national cross section of 1,252 adults, released July 29, 1985.

SOME TOUGH ANSWERS ON HOW AMERICA CAN REGAIN A COMPETITIVE EDGE IN THE WORLD

■ **IS THE U.S. OVER THE HILL ECONOMICALLY?**

When a cross section of top American businessmen was asked to choose between the U.S., Japan, and Western Europe on which is best on key economic attributes, the results were startling:

□ On which produces the best-quality products and services, the Japanese win with 58%, the U.S. is a distant second at 21%, and Western Europe gets only 7%.

□ On which has the highest rate of increase in productivity, again Japan wins hands down with 75%, followed by the U.S. at 11%, then Western Europe at 6%.

When the American people were asked the same questions, three in every four went along with the business leaders' judgment on productivity, but disagreed on which nation turns out the best-quality products, saying that accolade belongs to the U.S. by 54% to 34%.

But there is little doubt that traditional American confidence in the nation's economic prowess and capacity to outcompete the rest of the world has been badly shaken. For example, when asked why they think the U.S. is exporting so little to Japan, the public answered by 56% to 35% that this deficiency was due far less to restrictive Japanese import policies than to the fact that American goods "are not competitive with Japanese products."

The painful consequences of the decline of America's competitiveness are not hard to find. From 1960 to 1976 the biggest trade deficit the U.S. ever faced was $9.5 billion in 1976. Since 1977 the annual trade deficit grew from $31.1 billion to $67.1 billion in 1983 to $112.5 billion in 1984 to $124.4 billion in 1985. This means that foreign manufacturers are now selling roughly 50% more in this country than American producers are exporting abroad. To be sure, there might be all sorts of explanations for this bad turn of events, such as the high value of the dollar abroad and the much lower value of other currencies in this country—which makes American products more expensive abroad and foreign merchandise cheaper in the U.S. But the bottom line is that by the middle of the 1980s it was painfully evident that the products of the vaunted free enterprise system in America had become far less competitive abroad and the appeal of foreign goods in the U.S. had risen sharply. This meant that American products and services were finding it much more difficult to compete abroad. The ultimate ignominy was the additional fact that American-made products were having a hard time competing with foreign goods and services in the U.S.

■ FACING UP TO TOUGH CHOICES

By the mid-1980s, close to nine in every ten Americans expressed serious concern over competition from Japan. But in addition, a spate of reasonably good products began to appear in the marketplace from countries such as Korea, Taiwan, Singapore, Mexico, Brazil, and other countries. While wage standards in Japan had finally just about caught up with those in the U.S., imports from these other nations brought Americans face-to-face with some mean and ugly choices.

In some countries in Asia and Latin America, wage rates for assembly line workers who turn out cars and other major products run as low as $2 an hour. By 68% to 29%, a sizable majority of the public and a higher 86%–13% majority of top businessmen reject the proposition that "the only way American firms can compete with foreign competition is to lower wages, which might cause a decline in the standard of living." In the proud postindustrial society of the U.S., late in the twentieth century, the notion of cutting wages and then living standards obviously is an unacceptably painful alternative.

Perhaps more surprising is the solid 55%–37% majority of the American people and an overwhelming 94% to 4% of top business leaders who also reject the notion that "the only way American firms can compete is to have tariff barriers established, which might cause prices to rise at home." The simplistic trade barrier answer is not acceptable to the American people, no matter how much some politicians seem to think the country wants it and it makes good politics to advocate it. Instead, the public's instincts lead them in quite another direction. When given a choice between straight-out restrictions on products from other countries coming into the U.S. or reciprocal arrangements under which American goods are allowed into countries and those nations' products in turn are allowed into the U.S., a 73%–23% majority opt against trade restrictions and for reciprocity. Similarly, when faced with a choice of finding ways of making America competitive or erecting tariff and trade barriers to keep foreign competition out, a 69%–25% majority firmly rejects trade barriers and opts for the U.S. finding ways of becoming competitive again.

■ STEPS TO MAKE AMERICA COMPETITIVE AGAIN

Rather than trying to meet competition by driving down American wage rates and living standards, sizable numbers of people are prepared to try some radical corrective measures.

One approach is to automate many of the low-skill jobs, as

is being done in Japan. The way to beat $2-an-hour assembly line labor is to automate plants so they do not need human beings in the $2-an-hour slots. Americans would favor this by close to 3 to 1. However, if that is done, then they also recognize that new jobs will obviously require a much higher level of skills. Indeed, by a big 81% to 16%, a lopsided majority of business executives is convinced that if American companies compete by exporting low-skill jobs, then new high-skill jobs will have to be created to maintain the standard of living.

Thus, eight in ten people in the country conclude that it will take a highly skilled labor force to meet economic competition from abroad. And that will mean a total overhaul of how workers are trained in this country. Indeed, 81% say that how well the labor force is educated can now make a major difference in the capacity of the country to maintain its status as a leading economic power. Only through better education, they believe, will the country find a way to turn around productivity over the long haul. That better education must consist of massive infusions in the schools of math, science, and technological comprehension, an ability to think through tough problems, a capacity to write and reason well, to learn how to figure out what one doesn't know and then to learn how to find it, while at the same time understanding a complex society and how to be a good citizen in it. Basically, people conclude, today's schools must be overhauled drastically to be capable of producing a new and far more sophisticated labor force. Significantly, two out of every three people in the U.S. feel confident that this can be done.

■ LOVE THOSE JAPANESE PRODUCTS BUT HATE THAT COMPETITION

By 60% to 20%, a majority of the American people feel that competition from Japan does American industry more harm than good. There is obvious resentment against the Japanese making inroads into American markets and making it harder to sell U.S. products.

Yet those same Americans are precisely the people who create the biggest and most profitable market for Japanese products—right here in this country. A substantial 67% of the consumers report having purchased a major product that was manufactured in Japan, up from 58% who made such a buy in 1971. Over those 15 years, the number of Americans who bought Japanese cameras went up from 26% to 51%; the number who bought TV sets from Japan, up from 9% to 51%; automobiles, up from 2% to 34%; motorcycles, up from 4% to 18%. Among those purchasing Japanese-made products, the number buying clothing is currently at 33%, video tape recorders (identified as Japanese) at 30%, and computers at 6%. On the average, over eight in ten Americans are highly positive about Japanese products they have purchased. When asked what they like most about Japanese products, 51% say they are inexpensive, but almost as many, 48%, say they are high quality.

In the end, then, the most powerful argument working against this country erecting trade barriers to the Japanese is that the American people themselves like Japanese products and insist on their right to buy them.

Nonetheless, Americans feel just as strongly that it is high time that both the U.S. and Japan take real steps to reduce the over $40 billion annual trade deficit that exists with Japan each year:

□ 86% say American business must change its strategy to find ways to crack the Japanese market with American products.
□ 81% believe the government of Japan must be forced to allow U.S. products into that country, "not just to say it can be done and then keep it from happening through red tape," which has been the experience of many American manufacturers in Japan.

□ A 58%–37% majority would "restrict the number of products from Japan that can be sold in the United States."

□ A slightly higher majority would favor allowing a limited number of products from Japan into this country. But if the Japanese companies want to sell additional amounts of the same products here, they must open plants in the U.S. employing American labor to make those products. This in fact is what is happening in the automobile industry, where it is estimated that by the early 1990s the Japanese might well be selling as much as 40% of all cars sold in this country, but with a majority of those autos produced in the U.S. by American labor.

OBSERVATION

A substantial 88% of the American people are disturbed that America is finding it painfully difficult to compete economically in the world's markets. There is widespread recognition that in a number of traditional manufacturing areas it is virtually impossible for the United States to compete without drastically reducing wages and living standards—an unacceptable solution. Also not viable, say strong majorities, is adoption of protectionism.

Instead, Americans opt for a whole set of other alternatives, few of which have been really tested or tried. These range from having foreign manufacturers open plants here that would employ American labor to being much tougher in forcing other countries to strictly abide by reciprocal trade agreements, and to retaining the work force so that productivity here will be higher than anywhere else and the products and services generated will be superior to those of any other country.

If these solutions sound radical and untried, the truth is that they are. But if they are ignored the desperate alternatives are economic decline or protectionism—keeping out foreign competition. Rapidly evaporating is the illusion that American management and labor are so efficient and so creative today that foreign competition will finally fold one day and steal away. This issue of making America competitive again will haunt the politics, the concerns, and the conscience of America as few problems will for the rest of the 1980s and into the 1990s.

The revival of excellence for a nation comes neither rapidly nor easily.

A Survey of the Reaction of the American People and Top Business Executives to the Report on Public Education by the Task Force on Teaching as a Profession of the Carnegie Forum on Education and the Economy, conducted by Louis Harris and Associates for the Carnegie Forum on the Economy and Education, June 30–July 25, 1986, among a national cross section of 1,513 adults and 202 top line executives from the *Business Week* 1,000 top corporation list, released August 1986.

Americans' Attitudes Toward Japan and the Japanese People, conducted by Louis Harris and Associates for *Asahi Shimbun,* October 13–28, 1986, among a national cross section of 1,602 adults, released 1986.

U.S. Department of Commerce, *Survey of Current Business,* June 1986 and December 1986.

THE SAD TALE OF THE FALL FROM GRACE OF YET ANOTHER PRESIDENT

■ SOMETHING OLD BUT ALSO SOMETHING NEW

When he was elected to the White House at age 69, Ronald Wilson Reagan was the oldest president-elect in the history of the republic. Fittingly, he espoused what he maintained were old values of conservatism and vowed to restore unabashed and old-time patriotism. He talked about standing tall for America and bringing back pride to a nation that had been demeaned in recent years by the lost war in Vietnam and then humiliated by the long Iranian hostage siege under President Carter.

In his own "aw shucks" way, Ronald Reagan was as old-fashioned as Mom's blueberry pie, a genuine nice guy, a throwback to what used to be great about the past. The American people were ready for all this and they loved it. He achieved poll ratings from his fellow citizens that were unmatched in modern times.

But in many ways Ronald Reagan is also a more modern president than any of his recent predecessors. He is made for the television era. He is a master communicator. He knows how to look good, how to talk well, how to flash a twinkle in the eye, how to tell a good yarn, how to devastate an opponent or uplift a nation with a single, superbly timed one-liner. A classic case was his "There you go again" rejoinder to Jimmy Carter in the pivotal 1980 presidential debate.

Ronald Reagan may be old-fashioned, like the homilies he

pays tribute to, but he is also a totally modern man in terms of his capacity to communicate. Few can rival him in his artistic mastery of television. When he makes a speech, a sizable number of the American people lean forward to listen, while almost all his opponents elicit no such response. To paraphrase what Marshall McLuhan said a generation earlier about TV, in Ronald Reagan's case the user of the medium almost became the message. Early in 1981 a 62%–34% majority said that "he is the first president in a long time who makes interesting speeches that give you an 'up' feeling." His 1984 speech at the Normandy beaches in commemoration of those who died in the World War II invasion of Europe brought tears to the eyes of most who viewed it.

This power of communication was a key to his success in the White House. A big 80%–18% majority felt his ability to take his case to the public over the head of Congress gave him the upper hand in dealing with the legislative branch, as only FDR had before him. Even after suffering major damage as a result of the Iranian arms debacle, a 55%–41% majority still admire and deeply respect his power to communicate.

■ A POWERHOUSE AT THE POLLS

Ronald Reagan was able to inspire, perhaps more than anything else, confidence in his leadership ability. He looked like a leader, sounded like a leader, and, thus, most concluded, surely he must be a leader. By Election Day, 1984, a massive 71%–26% majority felt that "he has an attractive, forceful personality, and is a real leader." In 1983 a sizable 61% to 36% felt that he had "the leadership qualities and personality that a president should have." Back in 1981, after his inaugural, an 80%–16% majority said he had "the most attractive personality of any president in a long time."

Indeed, right after he took office, a record high 77%–17% majority gave him a positive rating on "inspiring confidence in the White House." In the midst of the 1981–82 recession, this rating slipped to a low of 39%. But then it rose into the high 40% range in 1983, and in 1984 it soared back to 61% positive. After the election in 1985, it remained in that stratospheric range, and within days before the November 4, 1986, election, it rose to 66%–30% positive.

Yet another key overall measure is the job rating. On this measure, a president is rated by the public on the *job* he has been doing, in contrast with the confidence rating, which is more of a gut reaction. In his first year in office, Reagan hit a near-record 67% positive on his overall job rating. This slumped to a low of 38% in the middle of the recession early in 1983. But he rose to the mid-50s range in 1983 and went up to 62% during his reelection campaign of 1984. In 1985 it climbed to an all-time high of 71%–29% positive. In 1986 the Reagan overall rating stood at 66%–33% positive just before Election Day, 1986. This put him between 16 to 31 points higher than the average for presidents since Kennedy.

The more sensitive measure over the years has been the confidence rating. When this drops, almost always his overall job rating will also drop a month or two later.

But no matter how he stands in January of 1989, when he leaves the White House, Ronald Reagan will go down in history as a phenomenon among presidents in his capacity to generate a massive emotional outpouring of affection and regard from his fellow citizens.

■ THE INCREDIBLE TEFLON EFFECT

The Reagan performance is all the more remarkable because on a whole roster of major issues, the public gave him negative ratings, long before the Iranian arms episode surfaced. For example, in the area of defense, one of his strengths, he had been rated 64%–32% negative rating on giving the taxpayers good value for their dollar on defense spending. On his support for a constitutional amendment to ban abortion, he was given a 54%–40% negative rating.

On the way he has handled affirmative action for women and minorities, he had a 58%–36% negative rating. On his handling of the issue of pressuring the government of South Africa to end apartheid, his rating was 64% to 27% negative. His appointments to the U.S. Supreme Court were 49% to 41% negative. On his cutting the rate of unemployment, which has hovered around the 7% mark all during his two terms, his rating was 60% to 37% negative. On protecting the environment, he was 61% to 33% negative. On his handling of farm problems, he was accorded a 68%–27% negative rating. On his proposed cuts in student loan programs, he came up 70% to 27% negative. On handling the federal deficit, he was 62% to 34% negative. On handling the situation in Central America, 61% to 29% negative. And, on handling nuclear arms reduction negotiations with the Russians, 55% to 42% negative.

Even in the area of reaction to him personally, he has been widely criticized by the public. For example, President Reagan has had a penchant for making off-the-cuff remarks that he would later regret. Once in a radio studio, before one of his regular Saturday broadcasts, he made a remark about sending bombers to Russia. Two out of three people criticized him for that. A 62%–35% majority has been critical of his close aides, such as Attorney General Edwin Meese, former Deputy Chief of Staff Michael Deaver, and former Political Director Lyn Nofziger, who have been the subject of official special investigations. A 56%–38% majority worries that he still might want to cut Social Security, which he has pledged not to do. A majority has been concerned that he will get the country into war unnecessarily.

Yet, somehow, none of these criticisms, disagreements, or doubts seemed to make any difference to the vast majority of the public. They rolled right off him, and the love affair with Ronald Reagan continued as before. This phenomenon became known as the Teflon effect. Somehow he had a coating that would not allow any of the criticisms to penetrate or dent his overall confidence and job ratings.

It must also be pointed out that throughout his time in office, with the exception of the year and a half during the recession in late 1981 and 1982, he has also enjoyed basically positive ratings on the way he has handled the economy —a bedrock and basic issue for any president.

■ DRAMATIC DISCLOSURES OF THE IRANIAN ARMS DEAL PENETRATE THE TEFLON COATING

By far the most disastrous decision for Ronald Reagan was his agreeing to sell arms to Iran. Fully 81% of the American people have felt that the Ayatollah Khomeini and his government are enemies of the United States. A major reason for Reagan's victory over Jimmy Carter in 1980 could be attributed to the frustration of the country over the failure to get the American hostages out of Teheran. No matter how compelling the reason to open up relations with so-called moderates in the Iranian government or the desire to free the Americans hostages in Lebanon, any president would run an enormous risk of deep public criticism for sending arms to the government of the despised Ayatollah.

For Ronald Reagan, the disclosure of his actions was a shock that the American people would not soon recover from, nor forgive him for what he did. A 71%–21% majority said they felt upset "that after all the tough talk from President Reagan that he would never make deals with the Ayatollah Khomeini of Iran and other terrorist leaders, he ended up secretly making a deal with, and shipping arms to, Iran."

Almost as troublesome as the basic fact that such arms had been shipped to Iran was the explanation that the President and his White House staff gave as to why the United States conducted negotiations with Iran. At a press conference shortly after the disclosures, the president, himself, claimed the arms had been shipped as a gesture to improve relations with moderates in the Iranian government who might succeed the aging Ayatollah. He steadfastly denied that the deal was made to get the hostages out. A 66%–22% majority simply did not believe that explanation. To a solid 68%–21%, a majority of the public was convinced that an arms-for-hostages deal was attempted, and did not work. Belatedly, in early March, the president finally admitted that the deal was supposed to be arms for hostages—and that it failed.

But the net impact on what people now thought of President Reagan was decisive. A big 82% to 12% condemned him for making the decision to send arms to the Iranians in the first place. By 70% to 25%, another sizable majority was critical of how the president handled the investigation into the whole affair. An even higher 76%–16% majority was negative about the way the president let the White House staff handle aid to the contras in Nicaragua, who purportedly received some of the profits from the sale of arms to Iran.

These sledgehammer blows took their toll. Reagan's ability to inspire confidence in the White House dropped from 66% to 43% positive within three weeks of the first disclosure of the Iranian arms deal. Then it went back up to 48% positive a week later. But by late February 1987 his confidence rating had plummeted to 35% positive, a drop of 31 points. The traditionally lagging indicator, his overall job rating, dropped, but not by nearly as much. It went down from 66% to 51% positive after the Tower Commission report.

However, other indicators were more telltale. On his overall handling of foreign policy, the president dropped from 53% positive just before the initial bombshell to only 32% positive. On his handling relations with Russia, down within a year from 64% to 40% positive. On his handling the situation in Central America, down from 54% to 25% positive. On his handling the federal deficit, down from 36% to 24% positive. Finally, on the key issue of handling the economy, he dropped from 68% to 43% positive.

Clearly, confidence in Ronald Reagan's ability to govern was shaken across the board.

OBSERVATION

By any measure, the disclosures over the Iranian arms deal and its aftermath shook the American people's confidence in President Reagan—to the point that it seemed doubtful he could regain the levels of faith the people had in him before the affair was uncovered. By a margin of 78% to 18%, the prevailing judgment was that "when he was secretly sending arms to the Ayatollah Khomeini in Iran, while at the same time condemning terrorism, he lost the respect of many people and badly hurt his effectiveness as a leader at home and abroad."

Once weakened by this central and overwhelming criticism, other negatives about the president took deeper hold. For example, a 66%–27% majority now felt that he had broken campaign promises to balance the federal budget "when his own budgets have produced record federal deficits." Now a 59%–35% majority disagreed with his position that "the federal deficit can be cut without raising taxes." A sizable 62%–33% majority believes that "he has encouraged the rich and big business to be more greedy, while neglecting to help the hungry, the homeless, and the poor in this country."

His political legacy was reflected in the disastrous showing of Vice President George Bush against Democratic front-runner Gary Hart. Bush was running behind Hart by 16 points, 53% to 37%, in January 1987, as compared with the much smaller 8 points, 50% to 42%, in November 1986, when the Iranian arms debacle began to surface.

A serious question that remained was just how effective a wounded Ronald Reagan could be during his remaining two years in office.

But he did have these favorable ratings going for him:

☐ In terms of the job he had done in office, roughly half the public was willing to say, on balance, he had done a good job.
☐ By 54% to 41%, a majority still credited him with having done an effective job of bringing down inflation and making the economy healthy again.
☐ By 57% to 40%, on balance, a majority also held the view that Ronald Reagan was "an attractive, forceful personality, and is a real leader."
☐ A 55% to 41% majority thought he was still capable of giving them an "up" feeling when he made a speech.

The remnants of the base Ronald Reagan had built remained in this residual positive feeling. But there was one essential and critical difference between now and the past. Before this episode, with the exception of the recession of late 1981, the specific criticisms of the president had mounted but overall confidence in his capacity to lead had never wavered. Now it seemed unlikely he could turn on the charm and successfully deflect adverse criticisms.

He was able to make a comeback from the decline he suffered during the recession by presiding over the recovery of the economy and the return to good times. Now, once again, he needed not reassuring or inspirational words that would re-create the old Teflon coating but some dramatic development that would prove his worth as a president.

The obvious development to carry such weight was a major breakthrough in talks with the Soviets on nuclear arms reduction. But if all the Reagan theories about how to deal with the Russians were right, the central question was how a much weakened President Reagan could persuade the Soviets to make concessions at the bargaining table. The Russians might be tempted to assume that a weakened president would be more likely to strike a deal.

With the respected and politically skilled Howard Baker as his chief of staff, it will be possible to have a kind of national unity government until 1989. This will enable Reagan to remain in the White House and the government to function; joint policies with the Democratic Congress can be agreed upon, and perhaps arms deals with the Russians can be made.

More probable was the prospect that Ronald Reagan would serve out his remaining time with the people permanently saddened that he had let them down. At the same time, despite a certain loss of faith, the personal fondness for the man who uplifted them so many times would likely remain.

———————————

The Harris Survey, conducted by Louis Harris and Associates, January 22–25, 1981, among a national cross section of 1,250 adults, released February 12, 1981; April 29–30, 1981, among a national cross section of 1,255 adults, released May 4, 1981; May 6–10, 1981, among a national cross section of 1,250, released June 8, 1981; October 28–November 3, 1981, among a national cross section of 1,249 adults, released November 26, 1981; March 12–16, 1982, among a national cross section of 1,249 adults, released March 25, 1982; July 9–14, 1982, among a national cross section of 1,250 adults, released August 2, 1982; August 5–10, 1982, among a national cross section of 1,254 adults, released August 16, 1982; January 2–5, 1983, among a national cross section of 1,254 adults, released January 13, 1983; August 18–22, 1983, among a national cross section of 1,257 adults, released September 5, 1983; March 1–3, 1984, among 1,227 voters, released March 12, 1984; July 20–24, 1984, among 1,264 voters, released August 20, 1984; October 12–14, 1984, among 1,393 likely voters, released October 19, 1984; December 27, 1984–January 2, 1985, among a national cross section of 1,255 adults, released January 21, 1985; March 2–5, 1985, among a national cross section of 1,256 adults, released March 25, 1985; November 22–24, 1985, among a national cross section of 1,258 adults, released December

19, 1985; January 3–7, 1986, among a national cross section of 1,254 adults, released February 10, 1986; April 19–22, 1986, among a national cross section of 1,250 adults, released May 12, 1986; August 5–11, 1986, among a national cross section of 1,248 adults, released August 25, 1986; October 13–14, 1986, among a national cross section of 1,253 adults, released October 20, 1986; October 29–November 1, 1986, among 1,207 voters; November 21–24, 1986, among a national cross section of 1,252 adults, released December 1, 1986; November 26–December 2, 1986, among a national cross section of 1,250 adults, released December 5, 1986; January 9–13, 1987, among a national cross section of 1,249 adults, released January 16, 19, 1987; January 9–18, 1987, among 1,782 likely voters, released February 16, 1987; February 20–24, 1987, among a national cross section of 1,250 adults, unreleased.

Business Week/Harris Poll, conducted by Louis Harris and Associates for *Business Week,* October 22–23, 1984, among 1,296 voters, released November 5, 1984.

THE PREMATURE AND UNEXPECTED END OF AN ERA

■ THE TURNING POINT IN LATE 1986

As 1986 ended, it was evident that the U.S. was going through yet another of those turbulent and even tragic moments when doubts surround the highest office of the land and the political outlook drastically deteriorates. Two years ahead of schedule, the U.S. suddenly faced the prospect of entering the post-Reagan era.

In rapid succession, the political picture was radically changed, beginning with the strange summit at Reykjavik, and then the decisive defeat of the Republicans in their bid to keep control of the U.S. Senate, and finally the shock of the revelations that the U.S. had been involved in dealings with Iran for 18 months, capped by secret arms shipments to a regime that over eight in ten Americans view as the enemy. A substantial 71%–21% majority of the American people was deeply upset "that after all the tough talk from President Reagan that he would never make deals with the Ayatollah Khomeini of Iran and terrorist leaders, he ended up secretly making a deal with, and shipping arms to, Iran."

The result clearly was serious. Basic confidence in the capacity of yet another president to govern has been shaken. The full impact of what has happened will not be evident for a year or two; but without doubt the power and the options of the Reagan White House will never be the same again. It is unlikely that anyone will want the president to leave office, and the overriding reaction is one of shocked sadness rather than indignation. From now until January of 1989, it will be a time of lowered expectations and lessened faith. Much as if there had been an untimely death in the family, there will not be much heart in pointing accusing fingers and seeking out culprits. Instead, it will be a time to try to plot the future and look ahead to attacking unfinished business, absorbing what remains from what has passed, rejecting what was clearly wrong, testing the waters for new leadership and new courses to take. Much will rest on the shoulders of Howard Baker and a new White House staff; they will have to know just what initiatives to introduce and what compromises to make in order to arrive at policies concerning the budget, national security, and foreign policy matters.

■ RONALD REAGAN WILL STILL LEAVE A SIGNIFICANT MARK

The suggestion has been made, and indeed a case can be made, that by fall 1986 Ronald Reagan had accomplished most of his objectives. The six years that this president has occupied the White House have been marked by some major and sweeping changes that will not be easily swept aside.

The public is firmly convinced that aided and abetted by the policies of Chairman Paul Volcker and the Federal Reserve Board, the Reagan administration was able to lead the country out of the deep recession of the 1980s and to preside over one of the longest recoveries the country has ever experienced. The hallmark of this period has been the proven capacity to reduce the fires of inflation, on the one hand, and to sustain gradual and steady growth, on the other.

Oddly enough, this economic success has been accomplished not through an abdication of governmental power, but precisely as a result of a specific kind of intervention. The instruments have been control of money supply, tough tightening when inflationary forces appeared to be gathering momentum, and a slackening and easing of that policy when a recession once more seemed imminent. Rightly, in the minds of most Americans, a brilliant job of managing the economy has been done. While White House policymakers might not have initiated the long recovery, they intelligently did little to undo or to deter the Federal Reserve's policies from having maximum impact.

Previous Democratic tinkering with inflation, including price controls, jawboning, presidential pressure, and other devices had been notably unsuccessful in attacking the virus of inflation. The Reagan policy of essentially trusting the private sector to respond in a relatively free market mode, within the constraints and guidance of Federal Reserve policy, worked remarkably well. In the future, even if the Democrats take over complete control of the federal government in 1988, it is highly unlikely that they will go back to the pre-Reagan nostrums on how to handle inflation and economic growth.

In the Reagan years there has been a distinct easing in the regulatory restrictions over business. The period has been marked by substantial capital expansion and growth, major efforts by much of American business to become more lean and hungry, steps to cut back on wage scales that were out of line with productivity, and, until recently, an attempt to turn around the rate of productivity increase in the U.S. after a long period of decline. Obviously, business has done well in the Reagan years. Whether or not business in turn will rise to the challenge of fulfilling the potential of becoming competitive again in the world remains to be seen.

■ LESS POSITIVE LEGACIES OF THE REAGAN ERA

But all has not been a positive economic experience under the Reagan stewardship. Indeed, it is amazing and even incredible that the economy has been able to survive and do as well as it has in spite of the fact that the same Reagan administration that allowed Volcker's magic to work has also had a dismal record in controlling federal spending and the federal deficit. The Reagan years will long be remembered as a time when federal debt levels were raised to an aggregated total greater than that of all the previous years of the country's history combined. The public is not firmly convinced that the main culprit has been what even pro-defense advocates admit has been nothing less than profligate spending on national defense. Together, President Reagan and Secretary of Defense Caspar Weinberger went on a weapons-spending spree in the name of the vaunted national security of the country. Together, they have not only increased the debt burden but laid the groundwork for real troubles later on.

There will come a time when future generations will likely have to pay for such fiscal irresponsibility. Given the president's refusal to raise taxes to help balance the budget, and despite pious provisions of Gramm-Rudman, which is rapidly fading in impact, it would be a mistake to assume that the hemorrhaging of federal spending will come to an early end. One fact is understood by the public: if federal spending is brought under control, it will not be essentially the result of measures the Reagan administration has initiated. Instead, it will be done in spite of the persistent refusal of this administration to bite the bullet on the spending issue.

There are other pieces of unfinished business in the economic area that obviously need tending to. One concerns the record negative balance of payments the U.S. faces. It is remarkable that as this trade deficit has hit heights never before dreamed of, there has not been more backlash to take steps to restrict imports or to build tariff barriers to keep competitive and lower-priced products out. Yet, by margins of 2 to 1 or better, the American people reject the notion of going the protectionist route. There is *real* pressure in textile, shoe, steel, microchip, and other industries to take restrictive measures. But the desire for such action is distinctly not the prevailing mood of the country. The problem of the trade deficit is serious; the dependence of the U.S. on foreign capital to underwrite the national debt is a high risk; the export of jobs in basic industry is damaging. The worry over just how competitive American industry really is in the world is a problem that close to eight in ten people in the nation and over nine in ten business and other leadership types think is very serious.

But the prevailing mood on meeting competition from abroad is one of restraint and levelheadedness. The basic instinct of the people and their leaders is not to blame others abroad for the plight the U.S. is in, but rather to examine their own discipline, their own institutions, their own system, and their own capabilities before blaming others. Thus, virtually no one buys the notion of quick fixes on making America more competitive in the world.

Both the public and the leadership are convinced that the U.S. must make radical changes in the status of its labor force. It must train a whole new generation to be superior in math and science and in problem-solving. And that means a radically changed and improved education system. Americans are well aware that Japanese students outscore American high school students in math, science, and other key subjects. They want to educate a work force that is so much better educated and so much more creative and capable of solving problems that this country will once more be able to out-produce the rest of the world. The people will settle for nothing less than a vast overhaul of industrial values in terms of new industries to emerge and new productivity levels to be achieved.

There is yet another economic area that has changed during the Reagan years, and it is precisely the opposite of what Reagan partisans had keenly hoped would happen. This matter, which will become urgent business in the post-Reagan era, centers on issues dealing with environmental, work, and product safety. In their rush to deregulate business, the Reagan people have often made no distinction between government regulation of areas that are strictly economic and those that involve human health and safety. As a consequence, two things have happened.

First, the American people have become frightened about the consequences to themselves and their families of toxic-waste dumps that have not been cleaned up, drinking water that might be contaminated, products and working conditions that are unsafe, and the failure of industries to take preventive measures on health. Second, industry has become cynical about getting away with allowing relatively high risks in the health, safety, and environmental areas because of the laxity of federal oversight. This kind of mind-set is likely to cost business dearly in the period ahead. A substantial 70% of the public is critical of business for not respecting the law, and 69% are critical of business for not properly respecting health, safety, and environmental laws. In the next two years, the drumbeat to make business the target of crackdowns for violations of safety standards can be expected to accelerate. The protection provided by the Reagan administration against tough enforcement standards is likely to be rapidly neutralized and then eliminated by the time 1988 arrives.

■ IS THE ECONOMIC ISSUE SLIPPING AWAY FROM THE REPUBLICANS?

The shape of the politics of the post-Reagan era was formed more in 1986 than most were aware. The central fact is that the hold of the conservative Republicans was broken, and it is not likely to be regained again for a long time to come. From now on, it is likely that the deficit issue will be working for the Democrats rather than for the Republicans. The GOP can no longer expect to automatically have more credibility on spending cuts because the defense establishment is now viewed as the central villain. Nor will Republicans be able to sit back and contentedly proclaim that people have never had it so good for so long in the protracted recovery.

Indeed, in thirty out of fifty states in the country, there is a rapidly growing conviction that they are being left out of the recovery. The troubles on a state and regional basis along the farm belt, the energy belt, and the Sunbelt all threaten to erode the general impression that times are good in the country and will remain that way. The economic issue is beginning to turn against the Republicans. By February 1987 the Democrats were trusted more than the Republicans on cutting federal spending—by 47% to 41%, a total reversal from a GOP lead of 57% to 32% in 1985. On handling the federal deficit, the Democrats lead by 41% to 38%, a complete change from the Republican 52%–37% edge on this issue in 1985. In addition, any sign of a return of inflation, which could occur through business trying to make up for slow growth in sales by raising prices immediately, would be taken as a further sign that Republican policies no longer work. If the Republican edge on inflation disappears, the economic issue will be totally lost to them, and the gains of the 1980s will then be wiped out.

■ THE SHIFT IN FOCUS AWAY FROM MILITARY ARMS AS THE CURRENCY OF POWER

On foreign policy, Republican strength has been rooted in their 1980 claim that they could rebuild the country's military power, which in turn would make the Soviets finally come to terms on agreements to reduce nuclear weapons. This philosophy was expressed many times by President Reagan as "peace through strength." Indeed, by a thumping 59% to 31%, the Republicans consistently hold the edge over the Democrats on which party can do a better job of building up the defense of the country.

But by 1986 the Republicans were losing their edge on the defense and national security issue. A big 3 to 1 majority felt that spending on defense was out of control. Only 13% now support increasing defense spending, compared with 71%

who gave support in 1980. Waste in the Pentagon, defense contractors involved in fraud and greed at taxpayer expense, reports of major suppliers not paying any federal income taxes, systems that didn't work, all have sapped the defense establishment of its former reputation as a sacred cow. Not only have people finally reached the point where they are convinced that the U.S. has more than closed any gap that existed with the Soviet Union in terms of actual defense capability, but there is a distinct sense that defense outlays have reached a level of overkill.

Another serious cloud that now will hover over the defense issue involves the key issue of using military arms as the currency of power. The Iranian arms episode pointed up dramatically the degree to which the Reagan administration had become accustomed to using military sales or aid as a primary leverage in relations with other countries. Somehow, in the case of Iran, the assumption was that whether the objective was to open up new bridgeheads with more moderate elements in the Teheran government or to obtain the release of hostages, shipments of arms would do the trick. Over and over again, the evidence was mounting that the standard Reagan way to court favor with any foreign power, friendly, neutral, or even hostile, was to work out an arms deal.

Reagan's approach is not popular with the American people, who feel that it can have dire consequences for the world. In fact, a clear 56%–37% majority of the public is opposed in general to the U.S. sending military aid to other countries. The set of public opinion on this issue is significant and is scarcely understood by either the administration or the Congress:

□ While a 62%–29% majority acknowledges that such military aid probably helps the national security of recipient countries, a 47%–45% plurality does not think it "helps our own national security."

□ A surprising 47%–45% plurality of the public does not think such U.S. military aid helps prevent the spread of communism.

□ A big 80%–16% majority worries that American arms shipments to other countries "gets us too involved in other countries' affairs."

□ Another overwhelming 80%–14% majority is convinced that such military aid harms U.S. relations with countries other than the recipient country. Most feel this works in two ways. First, they worry about other nations feeling that the U.S. has let them down when more arms are sent or sold to a rival nation; shipment of arms to Pakistan and subsequent deep concern by India is an example of this. But people also are disturbed that once a nation has been the recipient of American military aid, it builds up an insatiable appetite for more and more, until whole regions become veritable powder kegs threatening the peace of the world.

□ Finally, a 65%–23% majority worries that military aid "lets dictatorships use their military power against their own people." This prospect probably appalls the American people more than any other aspect of U.S. arms shipments. In the Philippines and Haiti, just to cite two cases, American public opinion was delighted to see the overthrow of repressive dictatorships that had been heavily supported by American arms and other assistance.

The Iranian arms affair has already highlighted the seamy underground dealings that characterize the use of military weapons shipments as the currency of power. By the time the investigations of the House and Senate have been concluded by September 1987, the chances are great that the American people will have soured even more on the use of military aid as a major component of foreign policy. And because such shipments of arms have been so central during the Reagan years, it is entirely likely that the public disdain will hurt the Republicans far more than the Democrats.

The public's wariness of military strength as the basis of foreign policy means that in political terms the key to achieving success in foreign policy in the future will far more likely be the easing of tensions that can escalate into war as well as efforts to obtain sound and equitable agreements that can build the chances for peace.

Without question, the crucial goal is how to find the way to come to some significant and honorable agreements with the Soviet Union. Yet six years have now passed, and the Reagan administration has little tangible to show in this area. A significant arms control agreement could go a long way toward reestablishing the credibility of and confidence in the wounded Reagan administration and the president himself. It could also give the Republicans an issue base as they approach the 1988 presidential election. But it likely will have to cover more than reduction of intermediate nuclear missiles.

However, close to a 2 to 1 majority is convinced that no significant accord will be reached, despite some optimism that has been generated by the White House on the basis of the ongoing Geneva talks between the two nations.

If there is no breakthrough on arms control with the Soviets, the Republicans will face the very real prospect of losing their big edge on the economic issues while having a foreign policy with no appeal. Surely, it will be difficult for the GOP to rally public opinion behind issues such as aiding the contras to keep the communist threat out of this hemisphere or maintaining an antiterrorist stance in the wake of the Iranian arms debacle or keeping the Atlantic alliance together after the deep distrust that has been sown by the Iranian episode.

In addition, contributing to the woes of the Republicans will be the apparent comeback of certain issues of compassion, such as helping the poor, giving women a better break, and helping to improve the lot of children. All of these show signs of moving far more front and center than they have been during the Reagan years. And all of them are far more likely to help the Democrats rather than the Republicans.

Indeed, in late polling just as this book was about to go to press, the Democrats were showing a massive lead for the 1988 elections, with Bush losing to Gary Hart by 16 points and Bob Dole also losing by an almost identical 15 points. Of course, such polling must be taken with a grain of salt because it was conducted at the floodtide of negative public reaction to the Iranian arms affair. Similar polling in 1974, at the height of the Watergate debacle, showed Republicans losing in 1976 by almost as wide margins. However, President Ford came within two points of getting elected as a Republican in 1976.

But there is little doubt that as the 1988 election comes into view the odds are going to make the Democrats the favorite to win back the White House and to keep control of both houses of the Congress. If that happens, it will have been a full decade since the Democrats had such control of the federal establishment. But a key question that is properly being asked is, Are the Democrats ready to assume the mantle of national leadership again?

■ THE DEMOCRATIC DILEMMA: HOW TO CHANGE WITHOUT LOSING THEIR IDENTITY

During the Reagan years, Democrats of all stripes have been searching their political souls for answers to a number of questions. Chief among them is what happened to shut them out of power at the White House for 16 out of the last 20 years.

But in 1986 the Democrats suddenly had a windfall of monumental proportions. After 6 long years in the minority, they won back control of the U.S. Senate by a healthy 55–45 majority. With the Iranian arms debacle, Republicans have been thrown on the defensive more than at any time since Watergate in the mid-1970s. The chances are that if and when President Reagan tries to support their position, the public will be far more skeptical and reluctant to accept what the man in the White House says as an article of faith. For the first time in 12 years, the Democrats will go into a presidential campaign as the favorites to win.

Yet, when comedians and pundits alike joke about how the Democrats are entirely capable of what Democrat Leon Henderson once accused the Republicans of back in the 1940s of "snatching defeat from the jaws of victory," many Democratic leaders and rank-and-file members express fears that the doubters among them might be right.

The public itself has some doubts about the Democrats:

☐ By 62% to 32%, a majority of the country agrees with the criticism that "the Democrats' big problem is that they haven't had many new economic ideas since the New Deal, which took place close to forty years ago."

☐ An even bigger 71%–27% majority also agrees with the charge that "in recent years, the Democrats have come up with inept and poor candidates for president, such as Jimmy Carter and Walter Mondale." It is true that the Democrats haven't won a presidential election since 1964 except for 1976, when Gerald Ford was defeated probably because of Watergate and the pardon of Richard Nixon.

☐ A much smaller 50%–45% plurality also goes along with the charge that "the trouble with the Democrats is that they are too inclined to take up the cause of special interest groups like the unions, women's activist groups, civil rights groups, and others." In fact, further probing on this charge reveals that unions may well have taken all the other groups over the side with them when they were lumped together. For exam-

ple, by 57% to 39%, the American people do not think that
"women's groups trying to move too fast for equal rights for
women" have had too much influence over the Democratic
party. An even bigger 62% to 34% feel that "black activists
such as Jesse Jackson" also have not had an undue influence
over the Democrats. Similarly, a 69% to 22% majority does
not think that "Jewish activists who lobby too much for
Israel" have too much influence over the Democrats. The sole
exception is the labor unions. By 50% to 43%, a plurality does
feel that "labor unions seeking special legislation for their
members" have too much influence over the Democrats.

As for ideology, among a cross section of those who call
themselves Democrats—42% of all voters, compared with
33% who say they are Republicans and 20% who identify
themselves as independents—26% wish their party would be
more conservative, 18% more moderate, and 14% more liberal. But the biggest single group by far is the 36% who want
the Democratic party to remain what it has been.

The Democrats have both the luxury of having a base that
still is the largest in American politics but also the problem
of taking a risk of eroding that base if they move in directions
that are radically different from what they have stood for in
the past. They have to take care not to cast aside lightly their
traditional mantle. Sizable majorities of the public are convinced that before this most recent era the Democrats produced outstanding presidents, such as Roosevelt, Truman,
and Kennedy. Three in every four give them credit for having
compassion for the least privileged. A majority feels positive
about the Democrats when they challenge sacred cows of the
business and defense establishments.

The major cross the Democrats bear, however, is the sense
that they have not come up with much that is new in the
economic area. There is some irony here. By and large, the

credit given Ronald Reagan and the Republicans comes from the success of the policies pursued by Chairman Paul Volcker of the Federal Reserve, a Democrat who was appointed first by a Democratic president, Jimmy Carter. And the basic idea for tax reform, for which President Reagan has won plaudits, came from Senator Bill Bradley, a New Jersey Democrat, aided by his Democratic colleague in the House, Congressman Richard Gephardt of Missouri.

The great debate raging in the Democratic party today is whether to actively take a stance that would separate the party from its old New Deal policy of trying to help the less privileged, and, by implication, to use government to redistribute some of the wealth by taking from the rich and giving it to the poor. The charge is made by more conservative elements that Democrats can't win elections anymore by appealing to an underclass that is now only a minority of the electorate. The countercharge is made by more liberal elements that if the Democrats think they can win by being more conservative than the Republicans, they will find voters flocking to the original conservatives, the GOP, and not to a pale imitation called Democrats.

In fact, this debate on both sides probably misses the point, and if it persists, the Democrats could lose their golden chance in 1988. The Democrats *can* gain real economic credibility—

☐ If they are willing to take the gamble of provoking voter wrath and come up with a plan to end budget deficits. Just as Richard Nixon was able to open up communist China to the West, when a Democrat might have been impeached for attempting it, so the Democrats behind a figure such as Congressman William Gray, chairman of the House Budget Committee, a black from Philadelphia, could well get away with steps to cut spending and raise taxes. And they could earn the respect of the voters in the process. A 2 to 1 majority say they would deeply respect politicians or the political party that had the courage to do it.

☐ If they are willing to reject pleas that they pander to protectionist sentiment and are willing to come up with a tough program to make the country economically competitive again.

☐ If they are willing to go all out to allow government once again to help the homeless and the hungry and those in need, but at the same time to come up with a plan to bring those on welfare into the mainstream of the work force and to make the argument that the country cannot afford to have large numbers of uneducated, unproductive indigent who are a drain on the national resources.

☐ If they are willing to act as tough monitors of business excesses and at the same time to allow business the freedom to operate with minimal constraints where it is doing a reasonably effective job of growing and creating new industries and enterprise.

In short, it is entirely possible for Democrats to win back the bread-and-butter issue, if they show some economic literacy.

■ AS FOR THE REPUBLICANS, THEY HAVE AN IDENTITY PROBLEM NOW, TOO

All is not lost for the Republicans in 1988 by any means, despite the warnings by respected GOP prophets, such as Kevin Phillips, who believes basic turnovers by party take place every 20 years, *and* 1988 will make 20 years of basic Republican rule at the presidential level.

For one thing, as long as the Democrats do not fill the vacuum on the economy, the Republicans can still lay claim to having presided over the sharp decline of inflation and one of the longest recoveries. This claim is believed by no less than a 55%–33% majority of the electorate. The Republicans can also take credit for having rebuilt the defenses of the country, although this is dicier terrain, because they will then have to defend the way defense spending has been handled. And that in turn opens up the whole federal deficit problem, which by 1988 may well make the Republicans be known as the party of the last big-time spenders.

The real question for the Republicans in 1988 is whether the party will continue down the path that proved so successful for Ronald Reagan in 1980 and 1984, with all-out endorsements of conservative ideology, including most of the planks of the old Moral Majority on abortion, sex education, anti-gay rights, and many other social nostrums put forth by the evangelical preachers. They must also decide if they want to continue to endorse some of the claims of supply-siders, especially those who say that federal spending is not the issue, and that all that needs to be done is to expand the economy so that the federal establishment will have enough added revenues to keep many of the old programs in place. The Republicans must decide if they want to continue to pursue an essentially hard line on defense spending and foreign policy that in effect says that the Russians will come to terms only when forced to do so by U.S. military superiority. And the Republicans must decide if in the South and selected Sunbelt and even Northern states and communities they want to at least implicitly use the race issue as a rallying point among the white majority.

One effect of the Iranian arms debacle is that it is likely to reduce the hold that the New Right and neoconservatives have had upon Republican activists in 1988. The early failure of either the Reverend Pat Robertson or Congressman Jack Kemp to put together an essentially right-of-center candidacy suggests the distinct possibility that the Republican party in 1988 will shed much of its bedrock conservative hue and opt once again for a more moderate candidate, such as Senator

Bob Dole or Governor Thomas Kean. Dole is gaining rapidly in the early polls, and it is not unlikely that rank-and-file Republicans will soon express a preference for such a moderate choice in 1988.

President Reagan's appointment of former Senator Howard Baker to replace Donald Regan as chief of staff spelled the end of the conservative Republican revolution. Conservatives, such as Richard Viguerie, bitterly acknowledged this. Regan let "Reagan be Reagan," and the consequences after two years in early 1987 were a disaster. Howard Baker will provide a moderating buffer against ultraconservative actions the president might be tempted to take. He will also initiate, under the Reagan system of granting the chief of staff "prime minister" status, more moderate positions on domestic affairs and more openings for agreement with the Soviets in arms talks. Above all, Baker will avoid some of the confrontations with the Democratic Congress that would cause a total paralysis of the federal establishment under a weakened president.

■ A NEW ORDER IN THE MAKING?

No matter what happens in 1988 and whatever the fate of the Republican or Democratic parties, for most of the citizens of the U.S., the issues and the questions they seek to answer will remain, especially since so many do not go to the polls on Election Day. Barely a majority of 53% of those eligible to vote cast their ballots in presidential elections, and no more than just over one in three come out to vote in the off-year elections for Congress and the governorships. Obviously, most Americans do not live and die by what happens politically.

The fate and direction of the economy—whether or not the long run of relatively good economic times will continue—is certainly a pivotal matter. The chances are high that whoever succeeds Paul Volcker at the Fed will not radically depart from Volcker's approach. Of course, it is possible that Volcker himself will continue at the Federal Reserve Board, if he bows to the will of Congress and the business community.

The quest and deep desire for finding some common ground with the Soviet Union to reduce nuclear weaponry and to ease tensions between the superpowers will continue, no matter what party is at the helm.

The growing demand that public safety and health matters be tended to will not diminish and in all likelihood there will be a marked change in these areas, no matter the political balance that prevails.

Similarly, the conscience of the country appears to be turning toward caring far more for those who are suffering from malnutrition, homelessness, and poverty. No matter who wins in 1988, there will probably be more help for the less fortunate.

And no matter who succeeds Ronald Reagan, the need to make the country competitive again in the world will become perhaps the nation's top priority at home and abroad. And, on this score, it is unlikely that rank appeals to chauvinism and protectionism will carry the day. Instead, tough appeals for self-sacrifice, discipline, and truly radical departures from past practices will be heeded far more than empty demogogic pleas.

In a word, by early 1987 it was evident that an era of passive acceptance was ending and a new order was emerging, somewhat unexpectedly, but it would be a change that the people would be willing to accept and even welcome.

In addition to surveys reported in Section III: *The Harris Survey,* conducted by Louis Harris and Associates, December 27, 1984–January 2, 1985, among a national cross section of 1,255 adults, released January 28, 1985; April 1–3, 1985, among a national cross section of 1,254 adults, released May 2, 1985; April 5–8, 1986, among a national cross section of 1,254 adults, released May 5, 1986; September 4–7, 1986, among a national cross section of 1,255 adults, released September 29, 1986.

Business Week/Harris Poll, conducted by Louis Harris and Associates for *Business Week,* October 13–14, 1986, among a national cross section of 1,253 adults, released October 15, 1986.

The Gallup Poll, conducted by the Gallup Organization, March 7–10, 1986, among a national cross section of 1,004 adults, released April 13, 1986.

MAJOR EVENTS OF 1986: HOW THE AMERICAN PEOPLE REACTED

JANUARY 1986

THE EVENT	HOW THE PUBLIC REACTED
Jan. 7—President Reagan announces sanctions against Libya for the bombings in the Rome and Vienna airports.	By 59% to 33%, a majority favors defending U.S. planes and ships that are attacked, but *not* going to war with Libya over the attacks. By 83% to 7%, they view Libya as an enemy nation. (*Harris Survey*, 1,255 adults, conducted Jan. 1986)
Jan. 15—Gramm-Rudman budget control law is certified by the Congressional Budget Office.	83% is skeptical that the new law will reduce the federal budget to zero by 1991; between 69% and 82% of the public object to cuts in health, student loans, and environmental protection under the new law. (*Harris Survey*, 1,254 adults, conducted Jan. 1986)
Jan. 16—Geneva arms reduction talks with Soviets reopen; Gorbachev proposes a worldwide ban on nuclear weapons by the year 2000.	A 74%–22% majority reacts favorably to the Soviet proposal. (ABC/ *Washington Post*, 1,504 adults, Feb. 1986) 65% worry that the Gorbachev proposal is a piece of propaganda. (*New York Times/CBS News*, 1,581 adults, conducted Jan. 1986)

THE EVENT	HOW THE PUBLIC REACTED
Jan. 23—Oil prices plunge to 6-year lows to below $20 per barrel; oversupply is blamed by OPEC.	Only a 48%–23% plurality welcomes oil price decline, (*Business Week/Harris Poll*, 1,877 adults, conducted Apr. 1986)
Jan. 28—Space shuttle *Challenger* explodes right after takeoff, killing the entire crew, as millions watch on television.	92% express personal upset; 63% say it's like losing a member of family; a 56%–43% majority say they would not go up in space if selected to join a crew. (*Harris Survey*, 1,255 adults, conducted Feb. 1986)

FEBRUARY 1986

THE EVENT	HOW THE PUBLIC REACTED
Feb. 5—Reagan submits record $994 billion budget for fiscal year 1987; substantial increase in defense and crippling cuts in domestic programs to meet Gramm-Rudman targets.	The public sharply disagrees with Reagan on the budget: 59% want to cut defense, 51% oppose cutting social programs, 88% oppose cutting entitlement programs. (*Gallup Poll*, 1,570 adults, conducted Jan. 1986)
Feb. 7–25—Philippines elections are held amid allegations of fraud; U.S. House Committee votes a halt in direct aid; Marcos flees to the U.S., Corazon Aquino becomes president.	85% of Americans think Aquino would have won an honest election; majorities are convinced she will help the poor, form a progressive democracy, fight corruption and communists, be a reliable U.S. ally. (*Harris Survey*, 1,305 adults, conducted Feb. 1986)
Feb. 9—Probe shows NASA was warned on rocket safety.	The public is skeptical that the full story on the *Challenger* disaster will ever come out; doubts that those responsible will be rooted out; still, by 62% to 35%, says the space program is worth spending billions on. (*Harris Survey*, 1,255 adults, conducted Sept. 1986)

THE EVENT	HOW THE PUBLIC REACTED
Feb. 17—Johnson & Johnson announces the end of all nonprescription medicine in capsules, 9 days after a Tylenol-caused death in New York State.	91% praise Johnson & Johnson for the way it handled the latest Tylenol poisoning case; 62% favor taking all capsuled medicines off shelves. (*Harris Survey*, 1,305 adults, conducted Mar. 1986)
Feb. 19—Federal Reserve Chairman Paul Volcker announces the dollar "has fallen far enough"; fears too sharp a decrease will fuel inflation; says confidence in the dollar is needed to finance trade and budget deficits.	A 52%–41% majority backs Volcker on trying to get the value of the dollar down abroad; 65%–21% majority gives high marks to Volcker's money control policies. (*Harris Survey*, 1,252 adults, conducted Apr. 1986)

MARCH 1986

THE EVENT	HOW THE PUBLIC REACTED
Mar. 4—Former UN Secretary General Kurt Waldheim is accused by World Jewish Congress of having a Nazi past; Waldheim runs for Austrian presidency.	Over 2 to 1 believe the charges against Waldheim; but most think the charges were raised to affect the election outcome; 51% to 34% want him kept out of the U.S. (*Harris Survey*, 1,250 adults, conducted June 1986)
Mar. 13–15—The USSR proposes an indefinite continuation of the moratorium on nuclear weapons testing if the U.S. complies. The U.S. says the Soviets are not leveling about the test ban proposal.	An 83%–14% majority favors a compromise to limit the size of nuclear tests. (*Harris Survey*, 1,255 adults, conducted Sept. 1986)
Mar. 27—The Senate narrowly approves Reagan's request for $100 million in aid to the contras in Nicaragua; the House rejects aid to the contras.	A 62%–25% majority opposes aid to the contras; by 62% to 32%, a majority of Americans worried about U.S. involvement in war in Nicaragua. (*New York Times/CBS News*, 1,601 adults, conducted Apr. 1986)

THE EVENT	HOW THE PUBLIC REACTED
Mar. 31—Former White House aide Michael Deaver is charged with illegal lobbying/consulting with foreign countries.	By 45% to 34%, a plurality thinks Deaver was wrong to handle foreign clients right after leaving the White House; by 2 to 1, thinks he should have avoided such clients; only 37% believe that the charge is an attempt to embarrass President and Mrs. Reagan. (*Harris Survey*, 1,243 adults, conducted May 1986)

APRIL 1986

THE EVENT	HOW THE PUBLIC REACTED
Apr. 8—U.S. conducts two underground nuclear tests, underscoring lack of interest in the Soviet moratorium.	By 56% to 35%, a majority believes the U.S. should join the Soviets in banning nuclear tests. (*Gallup Poll*, 1,552 adults, conducted Apr. 1986)
Apr. 9—The full Senate rejects Reagan's proposal to eliminate key domestic social programs.	87% oppose cuts in Medicare; 54% oppose cuts in aid to public transportation; 56% approve space program freeze; 62% oppose end of federal revenue sharing. (*Harris Survey*, 1,253 adults, conducted July 1986)
Apr. 10— Halley's Comet comes closest to Earth—39 million miles away.	While 92% are aware of Halley's Comet, only 6% (nearly 10 million people) view it. (*Gallup Poll*, 1,570 adults, conducted Jan. 1986)

THE EVENT	HOW THE PUBLIC REACTED
Apr. 14—After Arab terrorists seized TWA plane in Athens, U.S. jet planes bomb Libya in a retaliation raid.	Although 72% rally behind the president in the bombing, majorities would have preferred an Allied boycott of Libya, moderate Arab moves against Libya, and even encouragement of Egypt to take over Libya militarily; worry about war between U.S. and Libya. (*Harris Survey*, 1,252 adults, conducted Apr. 1986)
Apr. 28—The USSR discloses a nuclear accident at Chernobyl that experts say may have occurred up to four days earlier.	Support for nuclear power plants drops from 71% in 1976 to 49% in 1986; 73% would oppose nuclear plants near their homes, up from 45% ten years earlier. (*Gallup Poll*, 1,004 adults, conducted June 1986)

MAY 1986

THE EVENT	HOW THE PUBLIC REACTED
May 2—The Reagan administration warns the news media about leaking classified information; CIA Director William Casey threatens to prosecute the *Washington Post* if the paper prints classified story.	By a narrow 44% to 42%, the public thinks that printing leaks serves the public interest; by 49% to 39%, thinks when government criticizes the press for printing leaks, the government is covering up problems. (Gallup/Times Mirror, 891 adults, conducted July 1986)
May 22—House passes trade legislation designed to force Reagan to retaliate with protectionist measures if U.S. goods are restricted abroad. Reagan denounces the bill.	Americans are resentful over trade barriers placed on the U.S. But a 55%–37% majority rejects devising tariff barriers in the U.S. Reciprocal trade arrangements are preferred by 73% to 23%. (Harris/Carnegie Forum, 1,513 adults, conducted July 1986)

THE EVENT	HOW THE PUBLIC REACTED
May 25—Hands Across America takes place—5 million people form a human chain, from New York City to Long Beach, Calif., to urge funds for the homeless and hungry.	89% see hunger as a serious problem; the number who think it is "very serious" is up 19 points in 2 years. (*Harris Survey*, 1,250 adults, conducted Nov. 1986)

JUNE 1986

THE EVENT	HOW THE PUBLIC REACTED
June 4–5—Two Americans are found guilty of spying: Jonathan Pollard for Israel and Ronald Pelton for the Soviet Union.	Americans want a tough crackdown on spying: 62% favor a mandatory death penalty for anyone caught spying; 63% believe in firing government managers who have spies working for them. (*Harris Survey*, 1,254 adults, conducted Jan. 1986)
June 5—Yuppie Wall Street broker Dennis Levine pleads guilty to earning $12.6 million from insider trading.	63% think insider trading is common on Wall Street; 82% think most Americans would make insider trades if they had the chance; 53% say they themselves would make such illegal transactions. (*Business Week/Harris Poll*, 1,248 adults, conducted Aug. 1986)
June 11—The U.S. Supreme Court reaffirms women's right to abortion.	A 50%–47% plurality favors the 1973 Supreme Court decision legalizing abortion; 55% to 37% oppose a constitutional amendment banning abortion. (Harris/Planned Parenthood, 2,510 adults, conducted Sept. 1985)

THE EVENT	HOW THE PUBLIC REACTED
June 12—The U.S. Public Health Service estimates that deaths from AIDS will increase tenfold by 1991.	A 73% majority is convinced that an AIDS epidemic is likely; 70% want a greater government effort to treat and cure AIDS. (Newsweek Poll, 756 adults, conducted Nov. 1986)
June 17—President Reagan names Justice William Rehnquist to be Chief Justice of the U.S. Supreme Court.	A 58%–30% majority opposes Rehnquist's confirmation because of charges that he once signed a restrictive housing convenant and was involved in harassment of black voters. (*Harris Survey*, 1,248 adults, conducted Aug. 1986)
June 19—Basketball star Len Bias is found dead from cocaine overdose.	By 73%, the nation backs mandatory random testing of pro athletes for cocaine. (*NBC News/Wall Street Journal*, 1,600 adults, July 1986)
June 25—The House of Representatives passes $100 million aid for contras in Nicaragua.	By 60%, a majority still opposes aid to the contras. (*Harris Survey*, 1,207 adults, conducted October 1986)

JULY 1986

THE EVENT	HOW THE PUBLIC REACTED
July 2—The U.S. Supreme Court reaffirms the affirmative action decision.	By 75% to 21%, a majority favors affirmative action for women and minorities; 82% say that after years of discrimination, they should be given special training and advice. (*Harris Survey*, 1,255 adults, conducted Sept. 1985)
July 4—The U.S. celebrates the 100th anniversary of the Statue of Liberty.	By 49% to 43%, a plurality feels the celebration was made too commercial. (*Harris Survey*, 1,250 adults, conducted June 1986)

THE EVENT	HOW THE PUBLIC REACTED
July 9—The Attorney General's Commission on Pornography releases its report, which urges the removal of pornographic material from store shelves.	By 69% to 29%, the public is opposed to a ban on nudity magazines; by 54% to 43%, opposed to a ban on theaters showing X-rated films; by 62% to 36%, opposed to a ban on the sale or rental of X-rated cassettes for home viewing. (*Gallup Poll*, 1,539 adults, conducted Aug. 1986)
July 22—Mexico and the International Monetary Fund sign an agreement waiving past requirements on Mexico's sizable loans.	61% of Americans are worried about how Mexico will repay its $98 billion debt, but 93% think it's important to have a friendly neighbor to the south. (*Harris Survey*, 1,253 adults, conducted July 1986)

AUGUST 1986

THE EVENT	HOW THE PUBLIC REACTED
Aug. 6—William Schroeder, second artificial heart recipient, dies.	Americans got to know Schroeder on TV; 66% think his case shows the time is near when a failing heart is no longer fatal, but 60% also feel his case had too much media hype. (*Harris Survey*, 1,255 adults, conducted Jan. 1985)
Aug. 15—The House and the Senate pass defense authorization bills at levels 10% below what the president requested—a major setback for the Reagan defense program.	Backing for increases in defense spending dropped from 71% in 1980 to 13% in 1986; waste, greed, and overkill have combined to convince the public that defense spending is out of control. (*Harris Survey*, 1,253 adults, July 1986; *Gallup Poll*, 1,004 adults, conducted March 1986)

THE EVENT	HOW THE PUBLIC REACTED
Aug. 18—Roman Catholic priest Charles Curran is barred from teaching theology at Catholic University because his teachings on sexual morality vary from the official Vatican stand.	Catholics disagree with the decision by 45% to 32%. A 57% majority feels the Catholic Church's official position on sexual morality should be changed. (*Gallup Poll*, 978 Catholics, conducted Sept. 1986)
Aug. 23–30—Soviet UN employee Gennadi Zakharov's arrest in New York on a spy charge is followed by Soviet arrest of U.S. news reporter Nicholas Daniloff in Moscow. After major protests by the U.S. government and journalists, Daniloff and Zakharov are released.	76% are convinced that Zakharov is guilty of spying, but only 32% think Daniloff is guilty. By 49% to 41%, a plurality favors a direct swap to get Daniloff back. A 56% majority opposes putting off the summit if Daniloff is not released. (*Harris Survey*, 2,057 adults, conducted Sept. 1986)

SEPTEMBER 1986

THE EVENT	HOW THE PUBLIC REACTED
Sept. 11—The Dow Jones Index falls a record 87 points in one week, a 6.6% drop; record was 12.8% on Oct. 28, 1929.	Despite the drop, only 16% of stockholders expect the market to drop further, while a much higher 46% correctly predict its rise; 74% are confident the stock market will not crash in the next two years. (*Business Week/Harris Poll*, 1,255 adults, conducted Sept. 1986)
Sept. 15—President Reagan signs an executive order requiring drug testing for federal employees in sensitive posts.	A 72%–25% majority favors drug tests for key federal employees, although only 44% back such tests for all workers. (*New York Times/ CBS News Poll*, 1,210 adults, Sept. 1986; Newsweek Poll, 758 adults, conducted July, 1986)

THE EVENT	HOW THE PUBLIC REACTED
Sept. 22—Japanese Premier Yasuhiro Nakasone offends minority groups when he reportedly said the presence of minority groups lowers the level of intellect in the U.S.	By 49% to 42%, a plurality does not think the Nakasone remark was offensive, although a 60%–39% majority of blacks and a 86%–13% majority of Hispanics think it was. (Harris/Asahi Shimbun, 1,602 adults, conducted Oct. 1986)
Sept. 25–27—The House and the Senate pass a tax reform bill by wide margins.	By 77% to 17%, a majority backs the final bill, mainly because of the $140 billion shift in taxes from individuals to business; otherwise, the public is skeptical that the bill will help the middle class. (*Harris Survey*, 1,248 adults, conducted Aug. 1986)

OCTOBER 1986

THE EVENT	HOW THE PUBLIC REACTED
Oct. 2—Congress overrides Reagan's veto of economic sanctions against South Africa—a major foreign policy defeat.	A 54%–32% majority favors the congressional override of the veto. (*Business Week/Harris Poll*, 1,253 adults, conducted Oct. 1986)
Oct. 5—American soldier of fortune Eugene Hasenfus is captured when a helicopter carrying arms for the contras is shot down in Nicaragua; he said he worked for the CIA and then denied it; was convicted and then was released before Christmas.	By 58% to 19%, Americans are convinced that Hasenfus was working for the CIA; 47% believe Nicaragua has a good case against him. (*Harris Survey*, 1,207 adults, conducted Oct. 1986)

THE EVENT	HOW THE PUBLIC REACTED
Oct. 11–12—Gorbachev and Reagan meet in Reykjavik, Iceland; both sides claim making sweeping offers of major nuclear arms reductions; the summit is hung up over Reagan's refusal to yield on the Strategic Defense Initiative.	A 54%–40% majority sees the summit as a success; a month later a 52%–41% majority see it as a failure. (*Harris Survey*, 1,253 adults and 1,207 voters, conducted Oct. 1986)
Oct. 17—The immigration bill finally passes the Senate, after a decade-long effort.	Americans basically are not generous about admitting more immigrants into the country. Only 7% want more immigrants, 35% the same number, 49% fewer; by 44% to 34%, they think recent immigrants cause more problems than make contributions. (*New York Times/CBS News Poll*, 1,618 adults, conducted June 1986)
Oct. 17—Congress passes legislation outlawing mandatory retirement.	By 3 to 1, the public has favored allowing people to work as long as they can hold down a job. (Harris/ National Council on the Aging, 3,427 elderly adults, conducted 1981)
Oct. 17—The president signs a $9 billion toxic-waste Superfund bill.	A 67%–29% majority supports the Superfund cleanup. (*Harris Survey*, 1,254 adults, conducted Apr. 1986)
Oct. 18—The 99th Congress adjourns; Tip O'Neill retires after 10 years as Speaker of the House.	A 57%–31% majority says Speaker O'Neill will be remembered as one of the best House Speakers; 72% view him as warm and compassionate. (*Harris Survey*, 1,207 voters, conducted Nov. 1986)

NOVEMBER 1986

THE EVENT	HOW THE PUBLIC REACTED
Nov. 4—Democrats regain control of the U.S. Senate by 55–45 margin and continue dominant control of the House; GOP gains 8 governorships.	For the first time in the 1980s, GOP loses its decisive edge on economic issues; chances for a new Republican majority fade. (*Harris Survey*, 3,895 voters, conducted Oct.–Nov. 1986)
Nov. 3–14—Reports out of Beirut of U.S. arms deals with Iran are finally confirmed by the president, but he stoutly denies an arms-for-hostages deal; the White House reveals that some of the money from the Iranian arms deal went to the Contras in Nicaragua.	The president's confidence rating drops 21 points in one week, and continues to drop another 14 points by January; by 81% to 12%, the public condemns the Iranian arms deal; 68% think it was an arms-for-hostages deal; 69% think the denial is a cover-up; Reagan credibility is badly damaged. (*Harris Survey*, 1,252 adults, conducted Nov. 1986; 1,249 adults, conducted Jan. 1987)
Nov. 6—Reagan pocket-vetoes the clean water bill on the grounds that $18 billion is too much to spend.	By 3 to 1, the public favors the Clean Water Act. (*Harris Survey*, 1,249 adults, conducted Dec. 1986)
Nov. 14—The Securities and Exchange Commission announces that arbitrageur Ivan Boesky will pay $100 million in fines and from insider-trading profits; Boesky is barred from securities trading for life.	A 67% majority believes insider trading is common on Wall Street; 66% feel insider trading should be illegal, up from 52% in August. (*Business Week/Harris Poll*, 1,252 adults, conducted Nov. 1986)

THE EVENT	HOW THE PUBLIC REACTED
Nov. 29—The U.S. officially abrogates living up to the SALT II Treaty by making operational the 131st B-52 bomber armed with a nuclear-tipped cruise missile.	By a 3–2 margin, a majority wants the U.S. to continue to abide by the provisions of the SALT II agreement. (*Harris Survey*, 1,250 adults, conducted June 1986)

DECEMBER 1986

THE EVENT	HOW THE PUBLIC REACTED
Dec. 1–16—The Iranian arms affair dominates the news; National Security Council Adviser John Poindexter resigns; Lt. Col. Oliver North is fired from his NSC post. North and Poindexter plead the Fifth Amendment; independent counsel is named to probe the entire affair; special House and Senate probes are planned for 1987; the Senate Intelligence Committee report strongly suggests that an arms-for-hostage deal was the basis for arms shipments; the president rejects Republican pleas that he dismiss Chief of Staff Donald Regan.	8 in 10 people feel the president made a serious error in sending arms to Iran; the government of Ayatollah Khomeini is viewed by 81% as an enemy of the U.S. A 71%–21% majority feels let down by the president, who promised he would never do business with the Khomeini regime; the entire affair will drag on until the fall of 1987. A plurality wants Donald Regan dismissed. (*Harris Survey*, 1,250 adults, conducted Nov. 1986; 1,249 adults, conducted Jan. 1987)
Dec. 8—Secretary of State George Shultz reveals he was uninformed by the White House about secret communications with the U.S. ambassador to Lebanon seeking the ambassador's cooperation in the Iranian arms deals.	A 77%–14% majority believes the president made a mistake in ignoring Shultz and Weinberger's opposition to the Iranian arms deal; by 64% to 28%, a majority thinks Shultz would be justified in resigning. (*Harris Survey*, 1,252 adults, conducted Nov. 1986)

THE EVENT	HOW THE PUBLIC REACTED
Dec. 31—For 1986, the gross national product rises to 2.5% weakest since the 1982 recession; personal income rises 3%; personal savings drops 1.2%; but consumer spending rises by a significant 2%; for Dec. 1986, unemployment is down to 6.7%, consumer prices are up only 1.1% since Dec. 1985—all in all, a year of modest economic growth.	Consumer optimism about the national economy remains high, as does their feeling about the economy where they live; spurred by the desire to get last sales-tax deductions on big-ticket items, December spending was at record levels; consumer spending intentions remain moderately high; continued good times continue to depend in major way on sustained consumer demand. (Conference Board, *Consumer Attitudes and Buying Plans,* 5,000 households, conducted Dec. 1986)

ABOUT THE AUTHOR

LOUIS HARRIS, dean of America's public opinion analysts, is known for his innovative polling. His surveys played a major role in the 1960 presidential election of John F. Kennedy. His polls on race in the late 1960's, on aging, the arts, and women's rights in the 1970's, and on the rise of Ronald Reagan, health, children and education in the 1980's are all recognized as landmark efforts. Harris's surveys and counsel have been long sought out by leaders of both parties in the U.S. government, heads of state abroad, corporations and foundations, and the news media. He is well known for his incisive analyses of his polls—regardless of their implications for the establishment. He has said many times to his colleagues, "Don't be so open-minded that your brains fall out."